A BLACK INTELLECTUAL'S ODYSSEY

Martin Kilson, 1969

A BLACK INTELLECTUAL'S ODYSSEY

FROM A PENNSYLVANIA MILLTOWN TO THE IVY LEAGUE

MARTIN KILSON

With a foreword by Cornel West

And an afterword by Stefano Harney and Fred Moten

DUKE UNIVERSITY PRESS · DURHAM AND LONDON · 2021

Printed in the United States of America on acid-free paper ∞
Designed by Matthew Tauch
Typeset in Arno Pro Regular and ITC Franklin Gothic Std
by Westchester Publishing Services

Library of Congress Cataloging-in-Publication Data
Names: Kilson, Martin, author. | West, Cornel, writer of foreword. |
Harney, Stefano, [date] writer of afterword. | Moten, Fred, writer of
afterword.
Title: A Black intellectual's odyssey : from a Pennsylvania milltown
to the Ivy League / Martin Kilson ; with a foreword by Cornel West ;
and an afterword by Stefano Harney and Fred Moten.
Description: Durham : Duke University Press, 2021. | Includes
bibliographical references and index.
Identifiers: LCCN 2020046921 (print)
LCCN 2020046922 (ebook)
ISBN 9781478013297 (hardcover)
ISBN 9781478021513 (ebook)
Subjects: LCSH: Kilson, Martin. | African American political
scientists—Biography. | African American educators—Biography. |
African American college teachers—Biography. | African Americans—
Intellectual life—20th century.
Classification: LCC JC274.5.K55 A3 2021 (print) |
LCC JC274.5.K55 (ebook) | DDC 320.092 [B]—dc23
LC record available at https://lccn.loc.gov/2020046921
LC ebook record available at https://lccn.loc.gov/2020046922

Cover art: Photograph of Martin Kilson, 1969.

FOR MARION

and

JENNIFER, PETER, AND HANNAH

and

JACOB, RHIANA, MAYA, CAILA, ZURI, AND CIARAN

CONTENTS

The One and Only Martin Kilson

CORNEL WEST

This historic memoir provides a rich and riveting glimpse into the life of an unprecedented figure in the American academy, modern scholarship, and Black intellectual history. Like his great predecessor W. E. B. Du Bois, Martin Kilson tells his story within the contexts of communities and institutions, families and civic associations, persons and social movements. From the heartfelt dedication to his intellectual companion and loving wife, Marion, his marvelous and mature children, and his blessed grandchildren and great-grandchild, to his analytical reflections on Barack Obama's history-making election, Kilson takes us on a fascinating journey from a small northern company town in Pennsylvania to the heights of Harvard University. His style is quintessentially Kilsonesque.

Kilson's thick descriptions of the complex ways in which social structures shaped his lived experiences and those of his friends and family give us a vital sense of his mid-twentieth-century upbringing in Ambler. From his free Negro roots, Black church foundations, and lower-middle-class sensibilities, Kilson brings us into his ever-changing world, which enabled his own maturation yet fell short of any collective liberation (especially of poor people). His "we" consciousness—a "we" that is democratic in content and cosmopolitan in character as he matures—is aided by multicultural solidarities (on the Mattison school playground and as part of the Ambler Tigers athletic team) and abetted by multiracial alliances (under the auspices of "WASP acceptability" and "liberal civic activism"). He is deeply shaped by the "helping-hand ethos" of the best of Black culture and forever harsh on the "status climbing" of the worst of middle-class culture.

Needless to say, Kilson never loses sight of white paternalism—in its benevolent or dictatorial forms—nor the open-mindedness of the best of white fellow citizens. In short, Kilson is a consummate humanist in his shaping and in how he shapes others. Yet this sentence of modesty echoes throughout his memoir: "But enough about me."

An authentic intellectual humility and curiosity drive this text. He dares to embark on adventures and uncharted territories—in mind, heart, soul, and body. But he does not flaunt his courage nor applaud his brilliance. The painful divorce of his devoted parents is handled with gentle care. And the joy of his beloved mother, Louisa, wedded to his incredible success is briefly mentioned and then poignantly left to linger on the page. The prophetic words of his father, the Reverend Martin Luther Kilson Sr., loom large: "Young Martin is going to be somebody someday!" Though said about the young Martin who sits on his shoeshine box, to the chagrin of his father's church congregants, the sense of self-respect and self-confidence of father and son is deep.

Kilson's treatment of his pivotal years at Lincoln University is classic and resonates with the best novel of Black college life, *Sundial* (1986) by L. C. Morse (my dear brother and fellow Princeton PhD, who also attended Howard University and the London School of Economics). Kilson's letter of defiance and disappointment in the relative lack of intellectual awakening and political consciousness—primarily due to fraternity-centered frivolous hedonism and cruel hazing—remains on the door of the library for months. Yet the grand example of President Horace Mann Bond (who is abruptly fired with no advance notice in 1957) is a counterweight. And Kilson candidly acknowledges that many of these same fraternity men matured and became serious professionals and citizens. We should add that many of Kilson's heroes were Alpha Phi Alpha men, such as W. E. B. Du Bois, Paul Robeson, Martin Luther King Jr., John Hope Franklin, and Thurgood Marshall. Kilson's stellar record and brilliant achievements at Lincoln— first in his class and acceptance to Harvard—launch him even further into the upper echelons of American society.

It is revealing that Kilson spends more time on his small-town formation than on his Harvard education. He is aware of his history-making breakthroughs in graduate school and on the faculty. But he downplays his PhD and monumental professorship at Harvard. Such firsts are meaningful to him, but what is more significant to him is how he uses his success and preserves his personal integrity and tenacity. Kilson exemplifies the wise insights of his fellow Harvardian William James, who noted in his 1903 lecture "The True Harvard" that integrity is found not in the status-climbing of clever people who worship popular idols or pursue vulgar ends but rather in those who find joy in *Veritas*-seeking and independent thinking to better our world. Kilson was never a naive utopian thinker, yet he also never lost his zeal for truth and justice. He never ever sold his soul for a mess of Harvard pottage.

Kilson's integrity and tenacity in the life of the mind are what struck me most deeply when I met him my freshman year at Harvard in the fall of 1970. I enrolled in his legendary Social Science 132 course on Black politics; spent countless hours in his office at Apley Court, 16 Holyoke Street; reveled with his precious family in Lexington, Massachusetts, and Dublin, New Hampshire; learned to eat Chinese food and enjoyed their home cooking; and, most importantly, was enriched by a love from him and them that was and is sublime and supreme. Kilson taught me by example for nearly fifty years what it is to be a serious intellectual with one's own voice, style, and temperament. My own odyssey is unimaginable without his odyssey—just as we both are flawed yet fighting figures who find joy in our commitment to Black honor and American democracy. This means keeping alive the best of the great traditions of grand peoples, of everyday peoples of varying excellences, who with imagination, intelligence, and courage try to leave the world a little better than we found it. He did!

Martin Luther Kilson Jr. was sui generis. We shall never see the likes of him again!

PREFACE

The idea of writing an autobiographical account of my life—starting with my growing-up years and taking me all the way to where I find myself now, in a position to look back on it all—occurred to me quite soon after I retired from my teaching and research obligations at Harvard University in 2003. I quickly realized I didn't want to focus only on the strictly personal features of my background; I wanted to relate something much greater, in fact, than my own life. To achieve this, I decided to examine the societal agencies through which I evolved as a Black citizen in an oppressive, oligarchical, white-supremacist twentieth-century nation-state society; I endeavored to use the context of my memoir to relate the broader history that was unique to the small African American community in the Northeast that was my home during the 1930s and 1940s.

Thus, in the following pages, I have also written a biography, essentially, of the two Black communities nestled in eastern Pennsylvania most familiar to me: the factory town of Ambler in which I spent my childhood and the neighboring rural village town of Penllyn, both of which arose in the nineteenth century and progressed in special ways in the twentieth. While portraying facets of the social, civic, cultural, educational, and political patterns of these communities, I have simultaneously related my metamorphosis out of those patterns—which was largely dependent on my leaving them. In the pages spanning my childhood years in the 1930s until 1949, the year I entered college, the reader receives a twin portrait of the personal and institutional parameters of my memoir. The remainder of the book relates the tale of my professional maturation, from my undergraduate years at Lincoln University, a Black college, to my years at Harvard University, first as a graduate student and then as a professor.

As I write this preface, a basic observation comes to mind, one that defines the sort of African American community in which I grew up and which laid the groundwork for my outlook and my education: that African Americans such as my ancestors, who lived in the post–Civil War and Reconstruction-era American society outside the South, were fortunate to have had access to some degree of "democratic space" during the first half of the twentieth century, space that their southern brethren were deprived of. For them and for me during my youth, this meant freedom from the cruelest, most pernicious features of American racism that restricted the social life of Black people in the South during the Jim Crow era, a deadly and devastating period that spanned nearly three-quarters of a century, from the late 1800s to the 1950s. For that 40 percent of Black folks who resided in the North and elsewhere across the country by 1950, racism was by no means absent, but they enjoyed—or, I should say, we enjoyed—a small measure of opportunity to participate in American society that was almost totally denied southern Blacks because of the systematic implementation and execution of racist practices and white-supremacist ideas. I was fortunate to be born into a family and in a place that allowed me to pursue a path on which so many other African Americans of my generation, and even of today's generation, have sadly never set foot.

Call this memoir idiosyncratic, original, or what you will; my hope is that readers will find within these pages a useful tale of one African American intellectual's odyssey from the racist margins of twentieth-century America to a rich and vital participatory presence in that same nation.

ACKNOWLEDGMENTS

Since Martin Kilson's death in the spring of 2019, many helping hands have assisted in transforming his manuscript into the book you hold. Although Martin had the opportunity to review many of Julie Wolf's editorial suggestions, she completed her work on the manuscript during the summer of 2019, always taking care to retain Martin's voice. Cornel West with his introduction and Stefano Harney and Fred Moten with their afterword made distinctive contributions to their former professor's story. In addition, Fred and Stefano introduced the manuscript to Elizabeth Ault at Duke University Press. After the press's acceptance of the manuscript for publication, I have had the privilege of working with many of its staff members, especially Elizabeth Ault during the acquisitions process and Ellen Goldlust during the production process. I am so grateful to each of these individuals for their essential roles in the creation of *A Black Intellectual's Odyssey*. I know how much Martin Kilson wanted his story to be published and how very pleased he would have been with this volume.

MARION D. DE B. KILSON
SPRING 2021

Rev. Martin Luther Kilson Sr. and Louisa Laws Kilson with their children, 1933. Martin Kilson is standing on the lowest step.

Growing Up in a Northern Black Community, 1930s–1940s

I was born in East Rutherford, New Jersey, on February 14, 1931, but the childhood home of my memory is Ambler, Pennsylvania, a small factory town in Montgomery County. Ambler gained its incorporated status as a borough in 1881. In that same year, Ambler's first major industry was organized, the Keasbey & Mattison Company—originally a chemical factory and later an asbestos-textile factory built along the railway line at the town's southern end. Ambler built its first public elementary school in 1883. During most of the nineteenth century, white families of English and German origin (Quakers, Presbyterians, and Lutherans) dominated in the rural area.

Ambler was bordered by farms—the Buckley farm on the southwest, the Marple farm on the north, the Wentz brothers' farm on the east. While most of Ambler's residents found employment in the asbestos-textile factory, during the summer a good number labored part time slaughtering pigs and picking vegetable crops (tomatoes, string beans, lettuce, corn, potatoes). The majority of these farm laborers weren't Ambler residents, but some nearly two hundred African American migrant workers from Virginia, who labored primarily for the Wentz brothers. When the factory struggled economically during the 1930s, some of Ambler's local African American workers kept food on their families' tables as crop pickers alongside the migrant workers. Vegetable crops from the Wentz brothers' large fields were shipped down the Delaware River from Lambertville, New Jersey, to Camden, New Jersey, home to the Campbell Soup Company, one of the country's largest canning facilities. There was another segment of the African American working population not accounted for in the factories or farms: domestic workers. Though they were primarily female, serving as maids, launderers, house cleaners, and seamstresses, men also found gainful employment in this sector, as chauffeurs, gardeners, handymen, and caterers.

The foregoing might be viewed as the sociological baseline of my small, northeastern African American community. My ancestral roots there predate this modern social system by decades.

....

I have long known that my family's history is tightly interwoven into the fabric of my hometown. But to understand the history of Ambler, one must first know something about its neighbor to the northwest, the small farming village of Penllyn. In the antebellum years, Penllyn functioned as a carriage depot along the Underground Railroad, a subterranean route along which thousands of Negro slaves—aided by white (often Quaker) abolitionists—were smuggled out of southern slave states to freedom and refuge in the North.[1] It was partly in this way, during the Reconstruction period and into the 1890s, that Penllyn, only one hundred miles north of Maryland, gained its original, core Black population (about one hundred souls by 1900).[2] Subsequently, there would be two other primary sources for Penllyn's growing Black population. The first of the new arrivals were migrant laborers hailing mainly from Westmoreland County, Virginia, who entered Penllyn during the summer months to work on white-owned farms. In some cases, when winter settled in, migrant laborers and their families chose to stay in Penllyn rather than return to Virginia.

A number of my maternal ancestors had their roots among those migrant families. My great-grandfather Luther Clayton—a very fair-skinned African American who married a dark-skinned lady, my great-grandmother Bessie—settled in Penllyn in the 1880s as a farm laborer and later worked as a carpenter. Luther and Bessie's daughter Cora Clayton married my grandfather William Laws in the 1890s. William Laws was a housebuilder for Black families in Penllyn and Ambler as well as a leading figure in Penllyn's Bethlehem Baptist Church, which was erected in wood in 1887 and which William Laws helped rebuild in 1907, this time with a stone edifice. Their only child—my mother, Louisa Laws—was born in Penllyn in 1901.

The Laws branch of my family had been in Penllyn for nearly two decades before Great-Grandfather Luther Clayton arrived. Black artisan families who left Philadelphia during the decade after the Civil War to settle in towns outside Philadelphia County made up the second core group to bolster the Black population of such towns and cities as Allentown and

Reading, in Berks County, and Norristown, Flourtown, Fort Washington, Spring House, North Wales, and of course Ambler and Penllyn, in Montgomery County. My great-grandfather Jacob Laws was among these artisans.

Born in 1844 to free Negro parents in a free Negro community in Kent County, Delaware, Jacob Laws migrated to Philadelphia as a teenager, following thousands of other free Negroes from Delaware who had laid the foundation for a network of African Methodist churches during the early 1800s. Two are of particular importance: the African Methodist Episcopal Church (AME), initially launched in 1796 in Philadelphia by the Reverend Richard Allen and fashioned into an institutionalized church denomination, separate from the white Methodist churches, in 1812, and the African Union Methodist Protestant Church (AUMP), which was founded by the Reverend Peter Spencer in Kent County, Delaware, an area with a sizable free Negro population, and which expanded to Pennsylvania during the 1830s. Out of these African Methodist churches evolved a core sector of the modern African American social system.[3]

Soon after migrating to Philadelphia, Jacob Laws married Angelika Thomas, herself a free Negro migrant from Delaware, who had been born in Worcester County, Maryland. In March 1864, following his marriage, my great-grandfather heard Frederick Douglass speak at the Lombard Street AME Church in Philadelphia. Inspired by President Abraham Lincoln's January 1863 Emancipation Proclamation, which promulgated freedom for Negro slaves as a goal of the Civil War, the great Black abolitionist leader was traveling throughout the North to rally and recruit free men of color to enlist in the Union Army. Jacob Laws responded to Douglass's message by joining up, becoming one of 180,000 or so courageous African American men who left their homes to strike a blow for Negro freedom and contribute toward the fashioning of an American republic not built on slave labor. As a private in the Twenty-Fourth Infantry Regiment of the US Colored Troops, Jacob Laws trained for war at Camp William Penn, ten miles outside Philadelphia, in the village of La Mott.

After the war, in the summer of 1865, Jacob Laws returned to Philadelphia, and in 1870, he and several other Negro Civil War veterans left the city to settle in small towns outside Philadelphia County, including Penllyn in Lower Gwynedd Township. Once settled, Jacob Laws and his veteran compatriots organized the first church for Penllyn's small Black community, an AUMP built in the neighboring village of Spring House. Fifteen years later, in 1885, my great-grandfather and his circle of veterans migrated from Lower Gwynedd Township to Ambler, and their church migrated with them. "[Moving] their house of worship on wheels from Penllyn where it was located [in 1870] to Ambler, in a section later [called] Poplar Street," they reestablished their Emanuel AUMP.[4]

In addition to building and establishing the churches that would continue to sustain the African American populations of Ambler and Penllyn, these veterans contributed greatly to their new home, bringing with them a variety of artisan skills, among them catering, gardening, carpentry, and bricklaying. Many of this circle were literate; my great-grandfather could read but not write. Some of their descendants still resided on North Street when I was growing up, and two of these soldiers lived into the 1940s. To think that I have memories of heroes who served in the US Colored Troops is truly amazing.

I still remember many of their names: Arthur Burnett, Jefferson Carr, John Colbourne, Daniel W. Dowling, Robert Moore, Jacob Ford, John Taylor. Should my memory fail me, these names and others wouldn't be lost, because a solid historical record exists in the headstones of Ambler's Rose Valley Cemetery. Established in the 1880s to serve the African American communities in Ambler, Penllyn, and the neighboring towns and located at the northeast corner of Ambler on northern Butler Avenue, the cemetery is one of the oldest functioning Negro burial grounds in the area surrounding Philadelphia County.[5] The history that Rose Valley preserves is almost entirely male. Among the names of all the veterans of the Civil War, the Spanish American War, World Wars I and II, the Korean War, and the Vietnam War, only one woman's name appears: Hazel F. Luby.

While it honors the service of these heroes, the cemetery is also a reminder of an ugly, inescapable aspect of this country's history. Marking each veteran's headstone is an official American Legion Brass Star with a small American flag, placed there by the Black American veterans' post, Daniel W. Dowling Post 769.[6] The post was organized in 1946, when African American veterans, returning home after vanquishing Nazi and fascist governments in Germany, Italy, and Japan, were denied membership in Ambler's all-white McCann American Legion Post, located in the upper-middle-class Lindenwold Avenue neighborhood. To be excluded from such posts, whether in the South, where segregation was legalized and enforced, or outside of it, where segregation was not the law but often the default, was an insult to America's Black veterans, whose ancestors had served bravely in every major war since the beginning of this nation's history, including the American Revolution.[7] Among those petitioning the

Pennsylvania state headquarters of the American Legion for permission to organize their own post was my older brother, William Laws Kilson, who had a business career after World War II.

Black Churches as Social Anchors

Starting in the late nineteenth century, three churches became the foundation stones of the fledgling African American communities in Penllyn and Ambler: Emanuel AUMP, Bethlehem Baptist, and Zion Baptist, founded in North Ambler in the late 1880s.

In 1907—some twenty-two years after being moved to Poplar Street near the town's commercial district—the board of trustees of Emanuel AUMP authorized several members to obtain a property deed at the corner of North Street and Woodland Avenue in North Ambler. There, the congregation constructed a new church: a fieldstone edifice with stucco covering, bordered by a stone, stucco-covered parsonage that housed the pastor's family. During the 1930s and 1940s, when my father, the Reverend Martin Luther Kilson Sr., pastored Emanuel Church, this was our home.

On my father's side, I descend from free Negroes and from men who devoted themselves to the church. During the late eighteenth century, my paternal ancestors—free Negro citizens—lived in Kent County on Maryland's Eastern Shore, where their names appeared in US census records, proof of their free status. There, in August 1808, my paternal great-great-grandfather Isaac Lee was born. Literate at a time when few Blacks were, Isaac Lee was a boot maker and farmer. He married Hannah Emory, a Methodist clergyman's daughter, and organized the St. Paul AME Church in Kent County in the 1840s. More than two decades later, after the Civil War, Isaac Lee's son-in-law, the Reverend Joseph Martin—my great-grandfather—would pastor that church.

Clergymen figured prominently on many branches of both sides of my family tree, and both my father and his older brother, Delbert, followed in their ancestors' pastoral footsteps. My father earned his high school certificate through a correspondence course (he probably would not have been able to get a more traditional high school education in the rural Maryland community in which he grew up) and subsequently attended an AUMP Bible seminary in Wilmington, Delaware. Ordained to the ministry in 1922, he pastored three AUMP churches in New Jersey (Port Jervis, East Rutherford, and Camden-Merchantville) before the denomination appointed him assistant pastor of Emanuel Church in Ambler in 1928. The memory of my mother's grandfather Jacob Laws, who had an authoritative presence among several AUMP bishops, influenced my father's appointment. My father's brother, my uncle Delbert, pastored a Colored Methodist Episcopal Church in the shipbuilding city of Chester from the 1940s through the 1960s.

From a sociological perspective, it was fortunate for me that my father's church was in the northern section of Ambler. Most of the town's four hundred or so African Americans at the time lived in South and West Ambler in homes originally built in the 1890s and early twentieth century by Keasbey & Mattison for its white workers—mainly Italian, Irish, and Polish. By the 1930s, the factory's Black workers lived in those homes as well. Our African American neighborhood in North Ambler was unusual for its home ownership and for its proximity to upper-middle-class white homes.

The two-block African American neighborhood of North Street and Woodland Avenue that bordered Emanuel Church originated in building lots that were made available through two upper-middle-class white families, the Mattisons and the Knights. Richard Mattison owned the asbestos-textile factory, and Harold Knight was a lawyer and real estate agent of the Quaker faith who arranged in the early 1890s the sale of the lots and the provision of mortgages to a group of Black families with the Mattisons' Ambler Building and Loans Company. A number of the Black families affiliated with Emanuel Church had connections to the Mattisons, the Knights, and other well-to-do white families , through their employment as domestic servants and artisans.[8]

The African American neighborhood along North Street and Woodland Avenue in North Ambler was a unique enclave within the context of Ambler, directly bordering as it did upper-middle-class white neighborhoods. In the 1930s and 1940s, white families exiting their homes to their garages looked upon the backyards of African American homes. Indeed, on North Street, where I lived, the backyards of African Americans were separated from upper-middle-class white homes along Bethlehem Pike by an unpaved alleyway, which white families traversed in their automobiles to reach their garages. The unusual set-up drew attention. Visitors to Emanuel Church from Philadelphia-area African Methodist churches would often ask my mother, "How come Negroes live so near the white folks, Sister Kilson?" My mother's reply: "Because the white folks want their Negro help nearby."

Churches, Social Class, and Cultural Patterns

In 1940, the great African American sociologist and Fisk University professor Charles S. Johnson wrote that the "Negro church was much more than a place of religious worship; it was a broad social institution for the Negro."[9] Johnson articulates precisely the crucial role performed by Ambler and Penllyn's turn-of-the-century Black churches, which functioned at the core of these developing communities during the late nineteenth century and through the first half of the twentieth. Of the Bethlehem Baptist Church in Penllyn, Gloria Stewart Jones writes that it "served as the focal point of the black community and people came from Gwynedd and adjacent townships to worship there. . . . Between 1885 and the 1980s, the church was essential to the growth and stability of the community. . . . At one time, out of necessity, every social and cultural event that occurred in the [Penllyn] village was associated with the church. Businesses were developed through the church. Art, music, and history were cultivated in the church."[10]

According to Jones, Bethlehem Baptist's role in the social growth and stability of Penllyn's Black community spanned nearly a century. Zion Baptist and Emanuel AUMP functioned similarly for Ambler's much larger African American population during the same period. African American families who were involved in a variety of business activities usually played important roles in the leadership and operation of these churches. Among the members of Emanuel Church, Harry Lane operated a disposal business, George Williams was a caterer, Linda Rust and Gladys Newman ran home-based laundry businesses, Henry Ashton operated a shoe repair shop in Ambler's commercial district, and John Bailey ran a grocery store. There was similar overlap between business ownership and church leadership at Zion Baptist: Frank Thompson ran a gardening business, John Hopson did carpentry repair work, and Eugene Smithy operated a house-painting business. James Dean operated one of the community's two home-based barbershops, and the head of the Ayres family managed and sold real estate for the Black community. Many of these individuals were the nearby "help" to whom my mother had referred in speaking to church visitors.

Between World Wars I and II, Ambler's Black community was home to several well-to-do families. The first to achieve upper-middle-class status was Robert Brown's family, who lived in the North Street–Woodland Avenue neighborhood. Robert Brown, an individual of brown-skinned hue who was originally from Virginia, had attended high school and settled in Ambler in the 1890s. A carpenter by trade, he launched a formal home-building business by World War I, first for African American clients in Penllyn and then in Ambler. I recall the children in his neighborhood running admiringly alongside the two Robert Brown Home Builder trucks when they appeared on their rounds.

In the 1890s, Robert Brown married into one of the neighborhood's few solid middle-class African American families, becoming the husband of the fair-skinned daughter of the Civil War veteran Daniel W. Dowling, an administrative clerk in the Ambler Borough Roads Department and Ambler's only African American male citizen to hold a middle-class job at the time. Two of the couple's daughters were among the first African American youth to graduate from Ambler High School: Evelyn in 1920 and Marion in 1926; both became teachers. A son and fellow Ambler High graduate, Carlton, attended Drexel Institute of Technology in Philadelphia and became a civil engineer. After World War I, Robert Brown was among several founders of a business and civic organization known as the Guidance League, which invested in small-scale businesses in the African American communities of Ambler and Penllyn. Others involved in the league were the Baileys, the Lanes, the Ayreses, the Lawses, the Thompsons, the Williamses, the Burrells, and the Gordons—community-minded families who tended to be active in church life as well.

The Dicksons were the second African American family in Ambler to achieve upper-middle-class status. A handsome, dark-brown-skinned man with a courtly bearing, Mr. General Dickson operated a construction business that made his one of Ambler's wealthiest African American families. He was the only Black contractor licensed to build sidewalk pavement in Ambler from the 1920s to the 1940s. I recall sidewalk skating in the 1930s and 1940s and seeing business markers on pavements bearing the General Dickson Company imprint, and I still have a photograph of one. As were many of the upper-middle-class Black families in Ambler and Penllyn, the Dicksons were important members at Zion Baptist Church.

Also in Ambler's Black upper middle class was the light-skinned family of Dr. Foster Smith, Ambler's only African American dentist. He trained at the Harvard Dental School in the 1920s, one of only two Black students in the class. The Smith family home, the only African American home in Ambler located in an upper-middle-class white neighborhood, was a stately stone Victorian on the main commercial street, thanks to a liberal white doctor who broke with convention to sell it to him. Despite their home's proximity to white people, the Smith family's circles were still Black. In his practice, Dr. Smith tended to African American patients, and the family's social life revolved around other well-to-do African American families— but instead of staying in Ambler, they traveled some twenty-five miles for their society, in Philadelphia. There were simply no other Black people of their status level in our town, and they felt the need to go elsewhere. They thereby avoided social ties with Ambler's Black social institutions, including the community's Black churches.

At the head of another of Ambler's upper-middle-class African American families was Dr. Esquire Hawkins, Ambler's sole black physician. Dr. Hawkins had attended two Black institutions of higher education: Talladega College in Alabama and Howard University in Washington, DC. A handsome, dark-skinned man of regal bearing, he delivered medical care to the Ambler-Penllyn Black communities and also saw Italian American patients. Although they were white, Italian Americans, who had come to Ambler largely to build both the owners' mansions and the workers' housing, were poorly regarded in the non-Black community, occupying a low status among their Catholic brethren. Neighbors of the Dicksons, the Hawkinses lived in a brick Victorian home in West Ambler and were important members of the Bethlehem Baptist Church in Penllyn. As a child in the mid-1930s, I recall seeing Dr. Hawkins visit patients on North Street and Woodland Avenue in North Ambler. He walked swiftly and erect, always with a smile on his face. On occasion he stopped at the Emanuel Church parsonage to say hello to my parents. Gloria Stewart Jones writes affectionately about Dr. Hawkins during the last several years of his life:

> A few years before he died, Lillian and June Stewart co-chaired a committee that organized a dinner to honor Dr. Hawkins and his service to the community. The celebration was held in Edwards Hall at the Bethlehem Baptist church. Fellow professionals [Black doctors from Norristown] and patients from the Penllyn-Ambler community and beyond gathered to honor him. He was deeply moved by this gesture and was unaware that the community held him in such high regard. He died just a few years after, and Alexander Cruz, MD took over his practice and was dedicated to his patients in the same way as Dr. Hawkins.[11]

The social pattern among African American families in Ambler who were successful professionally and active socially in the churches was mirrored in Penllyn. During the 1890s in Penllyn and into the first two decades of the twentieth century, my maternal grandfather, William Laws, was a carpenter and house builder who functioned as a deacon under the Reverend Cesar Edwards, Bethlehem Baptist Church's founding pastor. The centennial history of Bethlehem Baptist contains several references to my grandfather's role in the church's development, including at the point when the initial groundwork was being laid for the construction of the church's new stone edifice in 1908.[12] The master of ceremonies for the laying of the cornerstone was carpenter and house builder Robert Brown.

In her history of Penllyn, Gloria Stewart Jones mentions several such relationships between business families and Bethlehem Baptist Church. One example was the Bronson family, which operated Penllyn Village's ice cream parlor, "serving the community for at least three decades," Jones writes. There were others who overlapped the benefits from their business activities to assist the affairs of Bethlehem Baptist Church:

> Before the era of the supermarkets, corner stores . . . were a necessity for the residents and [such] small stores were operated by Bob Johnson, George Johnson and Al Johnson . . . at various times. Not everyone owned a car and "Ice boxes" not electric refrigerators were the mainstay. Howard Gordon's store supplied the staples and necessary items such as coal oil for stoves, kerosene for heaters, bread, and other staples. "Miss Daisy" Gordon . . . pumped coal oil, that customers bought to fuel their cooking ranges, into containers filled from a tank in the rear of her store.[13]

The Perry family followed the same pattern. Walter Perry operated a milk distribution business in Philadelphia but attended Bethlehem Baptist Church in Penllyn. His sister, Helen Perry Moore, a 1920 graduate of Ambler High School, was the Penllyn-Ambler Black community's second schoolteacher and the first African American principal of Penllyn Elementary School, beginning in the late 1930s. She played an important role in the affairs of Bethlehem Baptist Church for over half a century.

For the families who lived and worked in Ambler and Penllyn, whether their businesses were "mom-and-pop" style or more formally established, those who ran them entertained an organic connection to their African American communities. A central feature of that bond involved important contributions to Black churches. This dynamic was fundamental to the interplay of African American community social patterns and African American churches in my hometown. As I peer back today across the two-thirds of a century since I left Ambler for college in 1949, the ties between Black families, churches, and youth figure prominently in my mind's eye. I remember the visceral feeling I had when I entered the campus of Lincoln

University for the first time, far from home, and my eyes fell upon a familiar sight in an unfamiliar place. I was surprised and moved to see a brick AUMP church standing next to the campus gateway along the Old Baltimore Pike, some sixty miles from Philadelphia. It had been erected in the 1830s. I recall saying to another freshman walking with me through the university's gateway: "My great-grandfather organized an AUMP church in my hometown in 1885, and my father pastored that church." The connection was strong and meaningful. Throughout my adult years, those organic bonds spawned perpetual life memories that prevail to this day.

A Helping-Hand Ethos and Black Social Life, 1920s–1960s

What was especially important about the involvement of business-owning families in African American churches was that members such as Harry Lane, who ran a disposal business, and George H. Williams, who operated a real estate business, helped to establish a helping-hand ethos in their communities in the early twentieth century. I'm referring to the idea of extending the social benefits that one enjoys (owing to education, business success, inherited wealth, or just plain luck) to assist in the social advancement of others.

During my growing-up years, a broad swath of life in the Ambler-Penllyn Black communities was saturated with evidence of helping-hand endeavors, and individuals closely associated with the towns' several churches were at the forefront.

Black-Church Dinners

During the years of the Great Depression—1929 to 1939—which covered about half of my childhood, I vividly recall Ambler-Penllyn's many helping-hand efforts within our Black community, including the church dinners organized by my father's church, for which tickets were sold to members and non-members, including upper-middle-class white families for whom church members worked as domestic servants. These families usually bought extra tickets to support their employees' house of worship.

The dinners were lively, cooperative affairs, with many families contributing both money and food.[1] The basement of Emanuel Church was an attractive and festive spot on these evenings, with crepe-paper hangings, flowers contributed by the white-owned Ambler florist shop, and four rented long tables and chairs, not to mention handsomely dressed waiters and waitresses, all of whom were parishioners. From the church kitchen, with its large cast-iron stove and ovens, emerged luscious dishes and appetizing bursts of good smells. Some of the proceeds were used to provide financial assistance to the poorest families who couldn't meet their rent payments or buy their children's school clothing.

My Father and the Helping-Hand Ethos

My father, the Reverend Martin Luther Kilson Sr., a rather handsome, brown-skinned gentleman of medium height, was a very resourceful Methodist clergyman, raising about one hundred Rhode Island Red chickens in the backyard of Emanuel Church's parsonage. He built the chicken house and raised the hens from the time they were little yellow chicks purchased through a mail-order catalog from Montgomery Ward department store in Chicago. My younger brother Richard, my older brother William, and I contributed to my father's enterprise, taking on the unpleasant chore of cleaning calcified chicken dung from the chicken house floor, scrubbing it clean, and spreading fresh lime all around. During the worst years of the Great Depression, my father often gave chickens or dozens of eggs to poor families in the church.

In these matters, my father differed markedly from the clergy who pastored Ambler-Penllyn's two Baptist churches. Those ministers were more solidly middle class than my father was. Neither the Reverend Fuller Holden of Ambler's Zion Baptist, whose parsonage was two houses removed from the Emanuel parsonage on North Street, nor the Reverend Guy McGee Sr. of Penllyn's Bethlehem Baptist had to perform "food-enhancing tasks" for their families, such as raising chickens or digging up part of the backyard for a vegetable garden. Whereas the Reverend Holden had one child and the Reverend McGee had four, my parents had seven. At three hundred or so congregants, drawing from such nearby towns as North Wales and Lansdale, their churches were larger and more well-off than ours, with its smaller congregation of about 125.

A mark of the greater affluence of Zion and Bethlehem Baptist, as I recall from my viewpoint as a five-year-old, was that those churches assisted their pastor's yearly purchase of new automobiles—Buicks, I think. Our church could afford only to provide my father a rather beat-up secondhand

Plymouth when I was in second grade, around 1938, and it was still on the road when America entered World War II. Furthermore, my father's Plymouth was used in very different ways than were the Buicks of Rev. Holden and Rev. McGee. On Saturdays in summer during the Depression years, Pop transported a half-dozen working-class men from Emanuel Church to work as crop pickers on the Wentz brothers' vegetable fields. The pickers placed tomatoes in bushel-sized baskets and lined the baskets along the roadway beside the tomato fields, where their haul was ultimately counted by a farm foreman and listed in his account book. When the workday ended around six o'clock, the foreman gave the pickers tally sheets to be redeemed at an office shack at the entry gate, where a bookkeeper paid ten cents per bushel basket. In the fall Pop would load up a different group, transporting another half-dozen men to the Marple Farm, located on the boundary of Ambler and Penllyn, to slaughter pigs during early Friday evenings and on Saturdays. On these trips, my father, dressed in work clothes and an old straw hat, rolled up his sleeves and joined in the picking and slaughtering. Such dirt-under-your-nails farm work came naturally to him. Born in 1899, he had spent his early twentieth-century boyhood on his father's and grandfather's farm in Kent County, Maryland, milking cows and doing all the rest.

I recall many times as a young boy squeezing in between church members in the back seat of my father's Plymouth and tagging along on a hot summer's Saturday to the Wentz brothers' farm. I joined in the crop picking, especially of the tomatoes and string beans, and, like the main crop pickers—usually African Americans—I enjoyed the lunch break when we were free to eat as many tomatoes as we liked, sprinkling them with salt from salt shakers the seasoned pros carried in their pockets. My father relished that tomato lunch break as much as the others did. There's not a purer scent from Mother Nature, one sweeter or more pleasant, than that emanating from the tomatoes gathered by the hands of tomato pickers. Those were wondrous days!

Boy Scout Troops and Other Church Civic Uplift

The helping-hand ethos of our local church was complemented by more formalized civic uplift functions that greatly strengthened the social life of Ambler and Penllyn's Black communities. To this end, in 1939, the Emanuel Church organized a Boy Scout troop for the Black youth of Ambler.

Millard Scott, a worker in the Keasbey & Mattison factory and a leader in the North Ambler community, was the scoutmaster. During the summer months and into the fall, Boy Scout Troop 32 took occasional weekend camping trips to Dager Woods near Penllyn and to Camp Hill, a Boy Scout campground near Glenside, Pennsylvania. One summer, the troop mustered the resources to attend the official state Boy Scout Camp Delmont, located near the Pocono Mountains.

The Reverend McGee's Bethlehem Baptist Church in Penllyn was also responsive to civic uplift needs and in fact preceded my father's church in the formation of a Boy Scout troop by twenty-five years. Theirs was founded by the housebuilder Robert Brown. Gloria Stewart Jones notes that thirty-five boys from both Penllyn and Ambler participated in the troop.[2] Curiously, Zion Baptist Church's pastor Holden and its board of deacons chose not to provide its community's young boys the opportunity to participate in Boy Scouts.

Summer Playgrounds

Emanuel AUMP also helped construct an official Federal Works Progress Administration community playground for Ambler's Black youth. Launched in the summer of 1936, the playground serving North Ambler's Black community was situated on two acres of land owned by members of both Emanuel and Zion Baptist. An acre divided into several vegetable garden lots formed the playground's border on its south side, while a half-acre wood through which flowed the Wissahickon Creek—a stream that eventually flowed some twenty-five miles to Philadelphia's Fairmount Park—formed the border on its far west. The playground director was the beloved Millard Scott—Mr. Scott, to us kids. He managed the monthly budget with funds from the county WPA headquarters in Norristown and was responsible for providing horseshoes, quakes, sandboxes, badminton sets, volleyballs—whatever items we used on the adjacent ball field.

When it rained, playground events relocated to the second floor of the Odd Fellows Hall in North Ambler. The Hall, as we children called it, was a multistory edifice built by the Black business families who founded the Guidance League, many of whom were also instrumental in developing the playground.

In a sense, the Hall was all things to all people. Standing smack in the center of North Street across from Zion Baptist, it housed the neighborhood's core grocery store, owned by John Bailey—"Old Man Bailey's Store," we kids called it. For old-timers such as John Bailey himself, the store was one of Ambler's "Black Talk" institutions—as were Howard Gordon's butcher shop and grocery store downtown on Main Street, Henry Ashton's shoe store on Lindenwold Avenue, and James Dean's barbershop in West Ambler.

But these places belonged to the adults; the Hall belonged to us, too. It was our refuge on rainy summer days. It had a Ping-Pong table, cards and card tables, checkers, books, and plenty of chairs for sitting around talking, laughing, and, as my mother used to say, "acting the fool." From the time I was five years old, I can recall that Old Man Bailey's Store was a "heartthrob social institution" in the neighborhood. Schoolchildren and older youth were sent down the block before the school day to purchase supplies needed in our busy households—a quart of milk, a dozen eggs, a loaf of Wonder Bread, a bag of flour, a stick of butter. (Pound butter packets were sold a stick at a time in the Depression years, just as cigarettes were sold individually, out of the pack.) During summer months, kids trotted in and out of the store with a dime or a quarter in hand to buy long pretzel sticks, pieces of bubblegum, a bottle of soda pop, a one- or two-dip ice cream cone, or an ice cream bar. If you were lucky enough to have another twenty cents, John Bailey would make you a bologna-and-cheese sandwich—one slice of cheese between two thin pieces of bologna with mayonnaise on top.

The Hall opened around 1920 and is still standing today. I left my North Street–Woodland Avenue neighborhood and my hometown for the first time in September 1949 when I traveled by bus to enroll as a freshman at Lincoln University, some one hundred miles away in southern Chester County. When I'd return home for holidays and summer, it was the sight of the Hall in North Ambler that lighted that special "I'm home" bulb in my soul. My enduring memories of the Hall intertwined with my recollections of those summertime days when the North Street–Woodland Avenue youth at the WPA playground escaped into its bosom, seeking shelter from the blistering sun or from the thunder and rain.

Several other WPA playgrounds served the town's children, and although they were not officially segregated, they were, let's say, neighborhood-focused. The two-block neighborhood of Upper Dublin, which was part Irish American, part Polish American, was located in northeast Ambler across Bethlehem Pike and had a playground at the Catholic Elementary School. A second neighborhood with a similar demographic had a playground spanning three blocks in East Central Ambler (along Argyle Avenue,

Old Ambler Road, and Orange Street). The mainly Italian American neighborhoods in South and West Ambler, covering about three blocks apiece, had their own playgrounds. Outside of North Ambler, there were these three primary geographical sections of Ambler—East Central, South, and West—and each one, although predominantly white, had its own small African American neighborhood.

The WPA playgrounds that I recall most vividly were the one at the Mattison Avenue Elementary School and the South Ambler Playground, which was organized by the Sons of Italy Italian American civic club and located on its two-acre site. (The original Sons of Italy Hall is still standing and today houses an auto repair shop.) Mattison Avenue commenced at the town's commercial center, near the Martin Milk Dairy Company, and extended on a west-to-east axis across one-fourth of Ambler, ending on Bethlehem Pike just across from one of the main twelve-foot-high iron entry gates to the Mattison family estate. Sometimes a group of Black kids from North Ambler would walk or bicycle across town to the Mattison School Playground. Its special attraction was big iron swing frames with maybe fifteen-foot chain links attached, which produced a fantastic thrill when a friend pushed your swing to its highest point—and I mean really high!

During those Depression-era summers, the WPA playgrounds served an incredibly important function, one I recognized only in hindsight: they brought children of different socioeconomic backgrounds together in a freewheeling, open-ended way that five school days a week could never replicate. These socioeconomic lines were drawn not only by race and ethnicity but also by class. Ambler's public schools were probably unusual for a factory town in that the high-status, middle- and upper-middle-class white families often sent their children to the public elementary, middle, and high schools. Even the super-wealthy Mattison family, owners of the main business in town, sent two sons to Ambler's public schools. One of them, Royal Mattison, graduated from Ambler High School in 1931, attended the University of Pennsylvania, and became a civil engineer.[3] Upper-middle-class white families continued to send their children to Ambler High through the 1940s, when my cohort of Black and white working- and lower-middle-class youth were students there, even though private secondary schools such as Germantown Friends, Penn Charter, and Pennsylvania Military Academy were within a thirty-mile radius.

The Mattison School Playground brought together children from a particular "class" neighborhood such as North Ambler with both Black and white children from factory-bordered, working-class neighborhoods in

South Ambler. Not only did kids from all of Ambler's Black neighborhoods play together, but many Italian American children were also in the mix. Most significantly, though, the Mattison School Playground was the only one where middle- and upper-middle-class, white Anglo-Saxon Protestant children—WASPs—interacted with working- and lower-middle-class Italian American, Irish American, Polish American, and African American children. Children of stockbrokers—boys such as Perry and Charles Selheimer and Jack Betts—played alongside children of parents who were often struggling to get by in working-class jobs.

We Black children in North Ambler loved our WPA playground and were there every day except Sunday, when it was officially closed. That didn't stop some of us, though, from wandering over in the afternoon after our church service. A photograph taken in the summer of 1938 by Millard Scott in front of the playground's headquarters ("the shack") shows almost every kid from the North Ambler Black community at that time—not all of us at our best! I'm at the end of the first row with a patch on my forehead. My wound stemmed from a childhood dare involving several of the other boys and me at the playground. It might have been one of the "tough boys"—maybe Paul Thompson—who dared others to compete with him to climb the highest of the wild, sweet black cherry trees with its leathery, paper-thin bark. I stepped forward and accepted his dare, and I climbed highest, winning the challenge and bringing down two pockets full of cherries. As I stepped on the last limb in my descent I fell, cutting my forehead on a stone. To this day I have a small scar from that 1938 fall.

That wasn't my only such youthful dare—not a chance! We had several summer swimming holes around Ambler, one in far West Ambler at the end of Railway Avenue, where the Queenan family had a pig farm. They were the town's only African American farming family, and a family my older sister Vivian would marry into. The rural road bordering their property led to a section of the Wissahickon Creek that was partially dammed, with a fifteen-foot-high bridge above it. One hot summer day a group of us bicycled to the dammed area for a swim, and somebody yelled, "Who will go first off the bridge?" There was a lot of hesitation since the leap was fairly high. Finally I said, "Oh, get out the way. I'll go first."

On another occasion, several kids from the neighborhood bicycled to the northeast corner of Ambler, where the Mattison family estate had one of its several reservoirs. (I think the main one still exists today.) The estate groundskeeper allowed us to swim in the main reservoir located in Upper

Dublin Township during summer months and to ice skate there in the winter. One of the boys in our group yelled, "Let's swim across the reservoir!" It was about forty yards wide. Once again, there was hesitation, and once again, I went first.

As I got older, I sometimes thought about those childhood dares that engaged my buddies and me. What lay behind my responses to them as I passed from puberty to adolescence to my teenage years? Was there something beyond their simply being fun? When I entered Ambler High School in 1944, my circle of friends expanded as I got to know several African American boys from South and West Ambler (Robert Perry, whose parents were caterers, and Stewart Johnson, whose father was a factory worker), and Italian Americans (Leonard Ricci, Danny Donato, and Fred Fedele, whose fathers were factory workers). At the same time, my "dare circle" widened. The dares were no longer boyish pranks but actions that would have consequences for the rest of our lives.

One such high school dare related to the paths we would follow in school and whether we'd break out of the mold in which we were expected to fit. There were three choices of curriculum: college preparatory, commercial, or general arts. From the 1920s through the 1940s, the middle- and upper-middle-class white kids—whom we thought of as WASPs—virtually monopolized the college preparatory curriculum. This wasn't surprising: their parents and grandparents had family income levels that could meet the financial costs of attending college. The commercial curriculum was also dominated by WASPs, but of the lower-middle-class set. The general arts curriculum, which didn't promote college as its predicted outcome, was overwhelmingly populated by African American and Italian American youth. These students' parents, who were primarily working class, would have had to be very thrifty with their meager incomes to send a child to college. This situation exacerbated a social-status division among Ambler High School students, with the children of professionals on one side and the children of workers on the other.[4]

Although this divide was very strong during the 1920s and 1930s, it had already begun to weaken somewhat when my African American and Italian American buddies and I entered the ninth grade in 1944. Dares continued to circulate among our circle, now of an academic nature: Who would take college preparatory courses rather than follow most of the Italian American and African American students into the commercial and general arts curriculum? Our priorities were changing.

Only five of us took the dare: three African Americans, Robert Perry from West Ambler, my North Ambler childhood buddy Lewis Thompson, and me, and two Italian Americans, Danny Donato and Leonard Ricci. Two other Italian American students outside of our circle made the same decision and went a step further on the high school ladder of success. By twelfth grade, Anthony Cuce and Connie Donato, a boy and girl who had chosen the college preparatory curriculum, became the first Italian Americans elected president and vice president, respectively, of an Ambler High School graduating class.

Another high school dare was to sign up for the football team as juniors. That dare didn't interest Robert Perry or Danny Donato, but it attracted me, Stewart Johnson, Lewis Thompson, Leonard Ricci, and Fred Fedele (who wasn't enrolled in the college prep curriculum). At the close of the season, the assistant coach lined the players up along the bench and rattled off who could and could not continue the next season. I fell into the "could not" category, as did Leonard and Fred; Stewart and Lewis were in the "could." Lewis elected instead to sign up for the basketball team, and in his senior year he became its captain, while Stewart made first string on the varsity football team during his junior year. "Return to your books," the coach said to me. "You're a good student, Martin."

I followed the coach's advice. I eventually graduated in the top 1 percent of the Ambler High School Class of 1948 and received a scholarship to Lincoln University, the first college in the United States for African American men, founded in 1854. I enrolled in 1949, and four years later, the year before its centennial, I was class valedictorian. The coach had recognized something in me, and I was proud to live up to his expectations.

Church Picnics

Black churches played an important role in facilitating summertime entertainment for African American youth in the Ambler-Penllyn community. The most prominent was the annual Sunday picnic, a tradition that began in the late 1920s and continued into the early years of World War II.

Organized by Emanuel AUMP, Zion Baptist, and Bethlehem Baptist, the picnic took place in early August. The two North Ambler churches jointly and Bethlehem Baptist singly chartered a fleet of buses to transport church families to a picnic and carnival ground called Menlo Park, located in the rural northern Bucks County town of Chalfont, Pennsylvania.

From the time I was five years old, I remember vividly my mother spending several days preparing food for the picnic. She learned from her paternal grandmother, Angelika Thomas Laws, how to make Southern-style sassafras beer and from a German American family in Ambler how to make old-fashioned American root beer. She'd make maybe forty short bottles of these tasty drinks a week ahead of time, and on the morning of the picnic she'd store them in a large tin tub, packed with lots of chipped ice and covered with a blanket or two. The hard preparation came the day before the picnic, when my mother—aided by my father and older siblings—made several large pails of potato salad and coleslaw, and above all she fried maybe ten chickens gathered from my father's backyard flock. There were, after all, six Kilson children during the 1930s (two young ones, myself and Richard, and four teenagers, Vermadella, William, Vivian, and Bernice; a seventh child, Gwendolyn, was born in 1940), so my mother prepared enough food for our small army.

In her history of Penllyn Village, Gloria Stewart Jones offers an affecting and candid account of one of these great summertime gatherings: "The annual Sunday School picnic held by Bethlehem Baptist Church along with other area black churches at Zeiber's Park in near-by West Point, PA, and later at Menlo Park, in Chalfont, PA, was one of the biggest events of the summer season. *During the years of segregation this was the only day that blacks were allowed to use the park. Segregation was a national bent and not just in the south....* Through the generations, residents, especially the children [in Penllyn-Ambler], looked forward to this outing each year."[5]

The annual Sunday picnic had a special African American cultural aura, defined in part by Black families' preparation of a whole lot of fine picnic food and drinks. Jones characterizes this aura with heartfelt affection:

Families prepared for days prior to the event. My grandmother's home-made root beer was one of our favorites. She began weeks ahead saving old ketchup bottles and other types that were then scoured, sterilized, and then used to bottle the concoction....

The day of the affair each family packed enough of their favorite foods to share with anyone who might stop by their picnic table to chat.... Many dishes were prepared from vegetables grown in their own gardens, and chickens that they had raised themselves. Segregation on the road man-dated that families [cousins] traveling back to the South be provided with enough food for the return trip home, since they would not be served in restaurants along the way.[6]

The nasty context of American racism surrounded the annual Sunday picnic during my growing-up years, but the Black folks I knew did not let that strangle the charm and spiritual renewal of the day.

Jones identifies another feature of the picnic that had a special African American cultural aura about it: the ways that the youth spent our fun time fraternizing. "At the picnic grounds, while older adults chatted with neighbors and relatives from afar," Jones writes, "the young people enjoyed roller-skating and amusement rides at the park. The rowboats were popular with the young and many a romance blossomed on a slow rowboat ride."[7] My buddies and I took rowboat rides, but our real excitement was on roller skates, because our early steps at adolescent boy-girl fraternizing took place on wheels. Besides tossing horseshoes and quakes—I was good at horseshoes—roller skating at the large rink at Menlo Park was my favorite picnic activity, as it was for my brother Richard and my buddies Albert and Julius Cooper, Northern and Paul Thompson, Sonny Williams, and Lewis Thompson. (Lewis and his sister Mary Jane came to the picnic on the Emanuel Church buses even though their parents, Joshua and Nancy Thompson, attended a middle-class church in Philadelphia—something North Street–Woodland Avenue families viewed as "Josh and Nancy looking down their nose at our Negro churches." The picnic was a time for the community to be together, even when parts of it were fractured.)

Northern Thompson was the best roller skater among our buddies, which gave him a little edge at the boy-girl fraternizing game, but others of us were fairly good too, and we circled the rink with determination and confidence that one of the adolescent girls would accept a "hand link-up" and circle it with us.

There was some friendly competition among the buddies as to which adolescent girl to seek out. Between picnic gatherings from 1939 through 1944 (I don't remember going to the picnic after that), I recall staring with my buddies at possible skating partners such as Dorothy Turner, Mary Jane Thompson, Mary Alice Smith, and Anna and Flossie Hopson—all girls from the North Street Ambler neighborhood. Frances Williams and Gracie McGee from the Penllyn community and Annabel Dean from the Central Ambler Orange Street neighborhood also caught our eye.

These girls attracted our attention in school, as well. Gracie and Frances were both friendly toward me, and I liked Frances particularly. Gracie's father pastored Penllyn's Bethlehem Baptist Church, and Frances's father worked in real estate and was also a pig farmer. I was more confident of myself on the rink than on the dance floor, but I nevertheless stepped out in the gymnasium during our school-year lunchtime fun break and moved to the beat of the swing records emanating from the juke box: Glenn Miller, Harry James, Duke Ellington, Jimmy Dorsey, the Ink Spots. Despite the beginnings of a multicultural spirit at Ambler High School in the late 1940s, there was no interracial dancing permitted at this time, and I recall dancing with both Gracie and Frances. Gracie graduated in 1949, a year after I did, and was the first Black student admitted to Beaver College in Philadelphia. Frances graduated in 1950 and attended Cheyney State, a Black college in Pennsylvania. Both of them became schoolteachers.

In the early 1990s I was a keynote speaker at a program at Penllyn's Bethlehem Baptist Church commemorating the Ambler-Penllyn Black communities' first two schoolteachers, Helen Perry Moore, who served as principal of the Penllyn Elementary and Middle School for many years, and Evelyn Brown Wright, principal of North Hills Elementary and Middle School for Black youth in Cheltenham Township, Montgomery County, Pennsylvania. At the close of that ceremony, I encountered Frances Williams and her husband, who was a graduate of my alma mater, Lincoln University. I said to myself, "What a small world."

"Societal Maintenance Tasks"

Throughout my teenage years, I entertained happy thoughts about what might be called the Black church social-healing function. (I obviously didn't use that term when I was a teenager!) The three churches that served the Ambler-Penllyn Black communities from the late nineteenth century onward managed quite well to fashion civic outreach to the broad needs of the mainly working-class families in their congregations. They also endeavored to serve "societal maintenance tasks," which were necessary because of alcoholic and/or spendthrift fathers or angry and undisciplined youth, some of the same problems that plague the wider Black community now.

By sponsoring Boy Scout troops, Bethlehem Baptist in Penllyn and Emanuel AUMP in Ambler performed important functions of civic outreach that helped to implant in working-class Black youth a litany of crucial values and habits relating to self-discipline; respect for elders, teachers, and public order; and civility among youthful peers. I have thought for many years of my adult life that no small part of my own successes in my professional career was connected to these functions.

Yet the Black church wasn't always effective in performing its societal maintenance tasks. I recall those subterranean Negro folk rumors, whispers that made their way along the grapevine with lightning speed, about this or that family's burden with an alcoholic father or a father who gambled away too much of Friday's paycheck from Keasbey & Mattison. Such societal crises often occurred at Ambler's several working-class drinking places with their backroom gambling spots. During the Depression, Ambler had two legal bars, one on Butler Avenue next to the town's only clothing store, Harris Department Store, and the other on the lower east end of Main Street across from St. Joseph's parochial school.

I had a little experience with one of Ambler's bars. I was nine years old and listening to *The Lone Ranger* when I heard an advertisement for Wheaties. For twenty-five cents and several box tops, any child could be the proud owner of a shoeshine box. My friend Northern Thompson and I were bitten by the entrepreneurial bug and sent away for our boxes. Once we had them in hand, we asked our parents if we could go downtown in early evening, between five and eight o'clock—this was summertime— and set up shop and shine shoes in front of the stores. They allowed it, and off we went, planting ourselves in front of one of Ambler's bars. Shoe shining netted us about five dollars in three hours and also gave us an idea of who some of the men were who frittered away their Keasbey & Mattison paychecks inside the bars. My father once mentioned to me that several women in his church told him they "didn't like seeing the preacher's son sitting on a shoeshine box outside a bar." My father dismissed their concerns; he told them that it was all right, because "young Martin is going to be somebody someday." He was right.

Families split up for reasons other than excessive drinking and gambling, but any broken home required repairing from the outside. When the virus of parents' separation or divorce infected a Black family during the 1930s and 1940s, the societal maintenance capability of Black churches was especially challenged. One usually heard about such challenges at Zion Baptist or Emanuel Church through those subterranean folk rumors better known as gossip. Alas, somewhere in the spring of 1941, one such rumor reached me and my younger brother Richard that the virus had infected our family. But before either Richard or I mustered the courage to ask our mother, she told us the jarring news: she and our father were divorcing. Richard and I retired to our bedroom showered in our own tears and went to hug our youngest sister, one-year-old Gwendolyn.

Richard and I felt wounded and set adrift, but happily not for long. My mother's closest friends in the Emanuel AUMP women's auxiliary rallied by her side, loving friends such as Linda Rust, Mary Williams, Hattie Crawley, Annie Lane, and Rose Newman—all members of Ambler's oldest Black families who had ties to the church extending back to the late 1800s. As a quiet and reserved lower-middle-class religious lady, my mother was not demonstrative about her inner feelings, especially in a personal crisis—though she had a marvelous laugh when she wanted to. Thanks to the endless support of these church auxiliary friends—Linda Rust, a launderer, was over at the parsonage daily for several weeks—the trauma visited upon Mother by my father's exit, while troubling to her spirit, didn't diminish her soul. I thank the Lord for that.

Unlike many working- and lower-middle-class African American women who experienced downward mobility for themselves and their children following a divorce, my mother had inherited five houses built by her father, William Laws, and his brother Jacob Laws Jr., two of which were located in the North Street–Woodland Avenue Black community. As painful as it was for my mother, she asked the Roane family to move. They rented the house on the south end of North Street which my mother owned and in which she grew up, but we needed a home. We Kilson children were fortunate. We never suffered the awful pain of having no roof over our heads, of having no place to sleep. With help from Emanuel Church folk, our mother moved all of us from the 2 North Street parsonage to our new home at 27 North Street.

My mother made sure to retrieve around fifty mason jars of vegetables and pears (from the pear trees bordering the parsonage) that were stored in the cellar to transport them to our new home. Canning was a neighborhood affair that commenced in mid-August. In the parsonage, the scent of boiling tomatoes, string beans, carrots, pears, and apples for applesauce and apple butter had been glorious. Fortunately, these unforgettable smells followed us when we moved.

Our new home had a large backyard that was nearly forty feet deep and thirty feet wide, with a quince apple tree that flowered gloriously in the spring and produced small, tart apples that our mother transformed into a tasty jam in the fall. The yard also had a late nineteenth-century cast-iron well pump that my mother had used when she was young and which she kept on the property even after President Roosevelt's administration aided counties and towns in constructing public water systems. My sister

Gwendolyn has lived in the house with her family since the 1960s, and she kept the old well pump intact, painting it red. It stands today as a kind of museum piece, an emblem of an era long past, a remembrance of our mother and our mother's Laws ancestors who helped organize Ambler's African American community in the 1880s.

I can't stress enough how fortunate my siblings and I were. After our parents' divorce, we did not experience crippling discontinuity in our lives. We remained in the social world of an old, cohesive Black community that my mother was born into in 1901 and that my Civil War veteran great-grandfather Jacob Laws and his wife, Angelika Thomas Laws, helped organize in 1885 with the establishment of its African Methodist Church. The "Black community authoritativeness" that shrouded my great-grandparents and their sons continued to shroud our mother. Most important, she received rent from the houses she inherited from her father and uncle, so the now-divorced, lower-middle-class, mild-mannered former Methodist clergyman's spouse could feed her three children still living at home fairly well and house us rent-free.

Even our dinners maintained a certain regularity: a juicy roast chicken with stuffing on Sunday, a carryover from our years in the parsonage when our parents were together (and if extra money was available, my mother would buy a ham once in a while); Sunday leftovers on Monday; navy bean stew with dumplings on Tuesday (marvelous dumplings, too); potato cakes with hot dogs on Wednesday; baked beans with hot dogs on Thursday; codfish cakes with baked beans or string beans that my mother had canned on Friday; and fried Philadelphia scrapple with mashed potatoes and homemade apple sauce on Saturday. Knowing that her kids had a sweet tooth, Mom made delicious basic desserts. Old-fashioned bread pudding and rice pudding were staples, and on Sundays she made fine apple or peach pies from fresh fruit when in season, and from canned fruit when not. Reliable, easy-to-prepare Jell-O was sometimes our dessert several days a week, simply because Mom was too busy to make anything else.

From 1943 to the end of the decade, there were times when my brother Richard, my sister Gwendolyn, and I needed an extra pair of shoes and clothing for school. My mother's friend and next-door neighbor, Gladys Newman, who ran a thriving home-based laundry for well-to-do WASP families, gave my mother three of her clients. When I was in ninth and tenth grade, I recall coming home after school to see my mother sitting at her ironing board, iron in hand, staring down a high pile of washing on the dining room table. That sight inspired me to pull my weight in the family, so I looked for after-school jobs. Those jobs helped me purchase some of my own clothing and shoes and even give several dollars now and then to my brother Richard, who loved high school sports too much to find after-school work. (He got varsity letters in those sports, too.)

I landed a couple of part-time stock-boy jobs in downtown Ambler, at the main drug store and at Ambler's first television store. I also started caddying on weekends, mainly on Saturdays and sometimes following church on Sundays. When I didn't caddy on Saturdays, I occasionally helped a Black dishwasher, Jimmy Allen, at the Howard Johnson's restaurant, which led to work as a busboy, alongside my childhood buddy Lewis Thompson, on Sundays. I was a rather industrious teenager before leaving for college.

Mom never complained openly about the tough task of handling several of Mrs. Newman's clients. Of course she needed the income to supplement the monthly rents she received. But before the divorce, my mother had been one of a small number of wives in the North Street–Woodland Avenue community who neither worked outside their home as domestic servants nor took in laundry to supplement family income. She had been what would be called today a homemaker or a stay-at-home mom for all her married life. During my growing-up years, that was a kind of status marker, denoting a lower-middle-class or middle-class rank in many African American households around the country and in Ambler particularly. There were plenty of homemakers in Ambler's Black communities, ranging from Mrs. Holden, the wife of the Zion Baptist Church minister, to Nancy Thompson, the wife of a chauffeur and truck driver and a member of a church in Philadelphia. Most of the wives and mothers in Ambler who worked outside the home toiled as domestic workers, and there were only two families in which the wife worked as a middle-class employee. Rose Newman, the wife of the chauffeur Andrew Newman, was a nurse in the Butler Avenue office of Ambler's leading white physicians, Dr. Shelley and Dr. Henderson, both of whom saw Black patients. Evelyn Brown Wright, whose husband was a worker and foreman in the Keasbey & Mattison Company, was a schoolteacher.

It dawned on me much later—long after our family life got established in the house that Mom's father and uncle had built and in which her grandparents had lived—that Mom must have inherited a "Spartan gene" from her combined Jacob Laws and Luther Clayton ancestors that kept her emotionally and spiritually steady and sane during the years immediately after her divorce. It soothed my soul when, many years later, Mom told me that my own successful professional career as a college teacher and scholar buoyed her spirit; it was her persistent joy in life. She died in her sixty-eighth year after a heart attack. I've always felt grateful to the Lord that she didn't suffer a long illness.

Neither did my father, who died in his seventy-first year after a ruptured ulcer. The AUMP denomination appointed him to two churches after my parents' divorce. The longer of the two pastorships was in the small town of Hockessin, Delaware, about thirty miles east of Wilmington, home to the headquarters of the mother church, built in 1834. The Hockessin church had been built in the Emancipation era, and my father spent many of his last years as a clergyman mobilizing the funds to replace its old wood edifice with a new brick one. A reconstruction fund for Hockessin's new AUMP church (named Chippey Chapel after the leading late nineteenth-century church leader Edward Chippey) was established before my father died, which pleased him greatly.

3

———

Melting-Pot-Friendly Schools in My Hometown, 1920s–1960s

During the first two decades of the twentieth century, an important divergence in the educational trajectory of African American youth in Ambler and Penllyn occurred, one which revolved around the core racial attitudes of upper-middle-class whites who held leadership positions in the borough of Ambler on the one hand and in Lower Gwynedd Township on the other.

Penllyn's Segregated Schools

Ambler's prominent upper-middle-class white families were affiliated primarily with the Quaker, Presbyterian, Episcopalian, and Lutheran religious denominations. For the most part, these families entertained liberal cultural attitudes toward Black people.[1] By contrast, in Lower Gwynedd Township, where Penllyn Village was located, the same demographic group held conservative views, which translated into an officially segregated public school system. Although some Black children were admitted to Lower Gwynedd's elementary school in Spring House between the 1890s and 1920, starting in 1922, white school administrators imposed full-blown segregation on schools in the township. Gloria Stewart Jones writes, "Penllyn school students did not become segregated until 1923, when amid much controversy a new elementary school was built on Gwynedd Avenue in the village. It was a large, square-shaped two-story brick building. The second floor consisted of a wide hallway with two classrooms on either side with 'cloak rooms' in the rear of each.... Two grade levels were taught in each of four classrooms and the school included grades one through eight. In 1947, the eighth grade was moved to Ambler High School, when the school system was restructured to include a junior high school level."[2]

The segregation of Lower Gwynedd's schools, however, did not immediately translate into professional opportunities for African American educators. Quite the contrary: Jones points out that throughout the 1920s, the teachers and administrators in the segregated system were white. It was not until the 1930s that the Lower Gwynedd Township hired African American teachers at the Penllyn Elementary School or at the all-white Spring House Elementary. As far as Jones's research could determine, the first African American professional to be hired at the Penllyn Elementary School, in 1930, was "Mrs. Tyree, from Philadelphia . . . , the first black to serve as Principal of Penllyn School, followed by Mrs. Yerby." Over the years, other Black hires would follow, among them Natalie Hill Nelson, the daughter of Leslie Pinckney Hill, the late president of Cheyney State Teachers College in Chester County, Pennsylvania, and Ambler's Helen Perry Moore, who began as a teacher and ultimately served for thirteen years as principal of the Penllyn School.[3]

As has almost always been the case when advances toward equality for African Americans take place, the dismantling of school segregation in Lower Gwynedd Township required a combination of civil rights activism by African Americans and adjustment in policy. In response to *Brown v. Board of Education*, the 1954 Supreme Court decision banning public school segregation which helped reshape the education system across the nation, Lower Gwynedd began to desegregate its schools in September 1955, not with "all deliberate speed" but instead quite slowly, integrating some lower grades at Penllyn Elementary into the all-white Spring House Elementary, just four miles away.

Desegregation didn't happen overnight. *Brown* laid down the law but made no suggestions as to how school desegregation could or should be implemented. In Penllyn, the decision was imposed by a civil rights action in Pennsylvania courts initiated by several courageous African American citizens. Thaddeus Smith and his wife led the charge and were assisted by George Robinson, Philip Queenan, and Joseph Stewart, the father of Gloria Stewart Jones. Jones describes the pressure applied by her father and this cohort of activists at the state level:

> They sought the help of a well-respected Black Philadelphia lawyer, the late Raymond Pace Alexander [Harvard Law School graduate, 1923] who was noted for his civil rights activism, and at the time a member of the

Philadelphia City Council. Alexander wrote a letter to the [Penllyn activists] encouraging them in their struggle. He also recommended a young lawyer, the late A. Leon Higginbotham, who, working through lawyer Horace Davenport of Norristown . . . handled the case. This was the first case for the young lawyer, who later became a well-known federal judge. . . . The case was heard in the Montgomery County Court of Common Pleas, and it was determined that, in keeping [Black] students out of Spring House School, the [Lower Gwynedd Township] board was in violation of the Supreme Court decision in *Brown v. Board of Education*.[4]

Ambler's Public Schools

The white upper-middle-class families at the forefront of developing Ambler's public schools from the 1890s into the early twentieth century were likely influenced by liberal attitudes toward Black people, while their counterparts in other townships, in places such as Montgomery County in eastern Pennsylvania, tended to be more conservative. This was the situation in Lower Gwynedd Township, where Penllyn was located, and in Cheltenham Township, where the all-Black North Hills school district was created in the early twentieth century and existed into the early 1960s.

Fortunately for African American youth like me who grew up in Ambler, the principles that defined its public schools were positively democratic, not pseudodemocratic as they were in Lower Gwynedd and Cheltenham Townships. It was, after all, pseudodemocratic principles that enabled racist segregation in the first place. In this regard, the overall character of Ambler's public schools from World War I on stood out by virtue of a "melting-pot–friendly ideology" in its public schools. With this term, I refer to a mindset that rejected the application of ethnically and racially motivated bigotry toward the sizable number of working-class Italian American and African American children who attended Ambler's public schools.

I don't want to overstate the difference between Ambler's schools and others in eastern Pennsylvania. There were certainly contradictions or imperfections in their operation. For example, in terms of integration, what was true for Ambler students was not true for professionals who might have desired a position in the school system. Although Ambler's African American community had produced its first schoolteacher by the late 1920s (Evelyn Brown Wright) and several music teachers by the 1930s (Marion Brown Gaines, Lucille Smith, Dorothy Talley), not one of them was employed in Ambler schools. They could be hired only in all-Black schools in Lower Gwynedd Township, Cheltenham Township (North Hills and Willow Grove), and other segregated districts. My research revealed that even though an African American professional, a lawyer named William G. Smith, was appointed to the Ambler Borough School Board in 1955, the school system didn't hire an African American teacher at any grade level until the late 1960s, when Robert Newman secured a position as a social studies teacher and varsity basketball coach.[5]

I first became aware of the melting-pot–friendly nature of Ambler's schools when I entered ninth grade in 1944. Italian Americans, at about 30 percent, were the largest ethnic group represented in my class, while African American students made up about 15 percent. The Black students came not only from Ambler schools but also from segregated middle schools in Lower Gwynedd and Cheltenham Townships.

From numerous conversations I've had over the years with both my Italian American and African American fellow students, I learned that nearly all remember demeaning experiences in which they were pelted with ethnic epithets and slurs. The Italian Americans were labeled *wop* and *dago*, the African Americans *coon* and *nigger*. These words came from the mouths of other students. Most of the individuals I talked to never identified teachers as perpetrators or conveyors of bigotry.

One possible explanation for the low incidence of bigotry among teachers lies within the "cultural character" of the school staff. A listing of teachers and administrators who worked for the Ambler schools from the World War I era through the 1950s, both at the lower-level grades (the elementary and middle schools) and the upper (Ambler High School), turns up a sizable number of persons of German American descent. Insofar as most were raised in Pennsylvania, they were likely to have been associated with the liberal branch of the Lutheran denomination. Ambler had a Lutheran parish located on the same street as the Forest Avenue Middle School. Other middle-class German Americans in Ambler associated with the Presbyterian Church. Furthermore, as the African American sociologist Horace Mann Bond argues in his brilliant social and intellectual history of my alma mater, *Education for Freedom: A History of Lincoln University*, the German American cultural group in Pennsylvania played a liberal role during the antislavery movement's long struggle to gain the freedom of Negroes in the United States.

My favorite third- and fourth-grade teacher, Miss Schultz, was of German American background, as were Miss Riner, a teacher and the principal of Mattison Avenue Elementary, and Miss Reyneer, Forest Avenue Middle School's principal. The Ambler High School yearbook of 1935 lists the membership of the Ambler Board of Education as including seven men, three of Anglo-American background and four of German American background: George Y. Slyer, William H. Faust, F. C. Weber, and Edwin Faust. Edwin Faust was especially beloved. The Class of 1935 reserved a page of the same yearbook to commemorate his leadership role; he had served as treasurer of the Ambler Borough of Education continuously since 1890. Mr. Faust was from a family that founded a leather tannery factory in North Ambler before the Civil War. In commemorating his exceptional service to public education in Ambler, the text interrelates the rise of Ambler's public schools with that of American public schools in general:

> The year 1890 marks the beginning of the period of rapid advancement of the high school in American education. During the last thirty-five years an average of one *new* high school per day has been established in the United States. Today more than 26,000 public and private high schools serve 6,000,000 young Americans. The year 1890 is not only a red letter day in the history of the American high school but also in the history of the Ambler Public Schools. It was in this year that the Ambler Borough Public Schools was organized. More remarkable still is the fact that Mr. Edwin H. Faust, elected Treasurer in 1890, has served continuously in this capacity from 1890 to 1935, during the entire period of the development of the Ambler schools, from one small grade school to three large, modern, well-equipped buildings, boasting a Junior-Senior High School enrollment of over five hundred pupils. . . . He has handled nearly two and one-half million dollars of school funds.[6]

Administrators and teachers of German American background figured prominently among the staff of Ambler High School from the 1930s through the 1950s, starting with the administrators: the supervising principal from the 1920s through the 1930s was J. M. Fisher, and from the 1940s through the 1950s, E. E. Kerchner took on this position, as well as that of superintendent.[7]

Gloria Jones Stewart relates an interesting and significant event regarding Mr. Fisher: "Virginia Edwards Smith, daughter of Reverend Cesar Edwards, was the first black . . . student from Penllyn to graduate from Ambler High School [in the early 1930s]. She was such an outstanding student that she was selected to be the private secretary to the very liberal [supervising] principal, Mr. J. M. Fisher, a position that a black student had never been offered before. She was inducted into the Wissahickon High School Hall of Fame [successor to Ambler High School] in 1992, and died in 1998 . . . at the age of 101."[8]

The principal's selection of an African American student as secretary in the 1930s offers evidence that melting-pot–friendly ideals occupied a prominent place among Ambler High School's top leaders. In other words, the faculty who imparted their knowledge and intellectual skills to high school students (many of whom were from working-class Italian American and African American families) exhibited a genuine respect for all students, regardless of their background. From the 1920s through the 1950s, the high school's leaders and faculty rejected the ethnic and racial stigmatization of Italian American and African American citizens practiced broadly in white American society.

As the faculty interacted with Italian American and African American students in authentically respectful and "helping hand" ways, these young people were able to develop cultural respect for themselves. They were encouraged to take pride in their own ethnic and racial identities, in their "Italianness" and "Blackness," rather than internalize the negative and self-defeating feelings promoted by the larger society. With support from the public schools in general and the high school teachers in particular, the working-class youth with whom I grew up learned to apply their minds to the serious task of acquiring knowledge and intellectual skills in the same manner that their middle- and upper-middle-class white counterparts did.

Black and Italian American Academic Growth

The participation of working-class Italian American and African American youth in various extracurricular course programs provides a useful gauge by which to measure the students' quest for viable knowledge and intellectual skills at Ambler High School. Although popular sports (football, basketball, field hockey) attracted broad interest, they gained the right degree of inspiration from teachers to participate in activities outside of sports, too.

Over a decade ago I began researching how this goal was realized by Ambler High School's Italian American and African American youth. The main sources for my research were somewhat unorthodox: they were the publications produced by the student body beginning before World War I. A monthly student newspaper called the *Chronoscope* was published until the 1930s, and the early 1920s saw the launch of an annual yearbook, which was written, designed, and compiled by students who also secured advertisements from local commercial and industrial businesses. It was an impressive operation. Printed in Philadelphia, the yearbooks in particular were a treasure trove of firsthand evidence of the achievements of African American and Italian American students alongside their more advantaged white classmates.

As early as the mid-1920s, an African American student, Dorothy Newsom, was a reporter on the *Chronoscope*. During the same decade, Lottie Hunt was a member of the school's French Club. Both of their fathers were factory workers. The 1930s issues of the yearbook also contain ample evidence of the positive influence of the melting-pot–friendly academic regime on Black students. In the yearbook for 1933, just one graduating African American student was a member of the Science Club: Allen Rose, whose father, Warren Rose, was the only African American foreman in an Ambler business, the J. W. Craft Lumber Company. Two years later, that number had increased to three: Jackie Hopson, whose father was a carpenter, Russell Nelson, whose father worked in a chemical factory, and Frederick Smith, whose father was a factory worker.

More than a decade later, the 1942 yearbook showed even more branching out among African American students. Among the ten members of the Photography Club, four were Black. None of the students in the photo were identified, but I recognize one of the African American youth as Hubert McGee, the son of the pastor at Penllyn's Bethlehem Baptist Church who helped me secure a part-time stock boy job previously given only to white individuals. After graduation Hubert attended the Philadelphia College of Pharmacy, the oldest such school in the United States, and in 1944 he became the first African American employed by one of Ambler's pharmacies, the Ambler Drug Store. He closed out his career as the head pharmacist at the Ambler Rite Way Pharmacy. It was here that Hubert, only a few years older than I was, reminded me, "You're the first Negro kid to have this job at this pharmacy, Martin. So do a good job." I performed my tasks (keeping store shelves stacked with products and the soda bar stocked with syrups) after school hours. I held the job from tenth through twelfth grade, so I guess I met Hubert McGee's injunction quite well.

Further exploration of the yearbooks from the 1930s and 1940s revealed that the music programs were accessible to both African American and Italian American students in ways that many other extracurricular activities weren't. No one exemplified the melting-pot–friendly orientation of the music faculty more than Clifford Geary, who directed the school band and orchestra from around 1931 into the 1950s.

Several photographs from the 1935 yearbook show evidence of the early participation by African American youth in extracurricular music. That year's graduating class included nine African American students, one of whom—Thomas Clark, the son of a factory worker—is pictured, listed as having been a member of the band since tenth grade. If one can judge by the yearbooks published between 1930 and 1935, Thomas may well have been the first African American student to perform in the band. In another photograph, of the junior band, four of the twenty members are African American: Melba Clark, Clarence Lucas, and brothers Henry and Joshua Thompson. All were the children of factory workers; the Thompsons' father had a second job as a chauffeur for the Mattison family, the owners of Ambler's primary employer.

When my buddies and I attended Ambler High School from 1944 to 1948, a tradition of participation in the extracurricular music program among African Americans had already been established. Band was a popular choice. In 1946, several children of working-class families joined: Melvin Clark and Virginia Johnson, whose fathers were factory workers; siblings Barbara and Maynard Gant, whose father was a postal worker; and Raymond Lane, whose father owned a disposal business. During the 1948–1949 school year, another five African American students chose to participate: Milton Clark, Barbara Gant, Morris Gant, Russell Lane, and Alicia Stewart. The high school chorus also had a good representation of African American students: Annabel Dean, sisters Flossie and Anna Hopson, Lula Mahoney, Connie Hines, and Dorothy Turner, all daughters of factory workers, and Helen Rose, whose father was a foreman. I recall attending one of the senior chorus's concerts, and their voices were exquisite and engrossing.

Two years later, 1948–1949, one of the six Black students in the band, Alicia Stewart, also performed as a majorette, marching at football games and in public parades, such as the one held on Memorial Day and sponsored by the Ambler Borough's Council. (I vividly recall those parades during the 1930s, when my buddies and I would wrap our bicycle wheels with red, white, and blue crepe paper and trail behind the marching band.) Alicia was the only African American out of the seven majorettes that year and the first Black student ever to occupy a spot on the squad. Her selection demonstrated an unusual level of liberalism in regard to racial patterns in an American public school system. In the South, where legalized segregation prevailed and racism was an onerous fixture in everyday life, such liberalism would never have happened. I would hazard a guess that it didn't happen very often elsewhere in Pennsylvania during the 1940s, either.

Clifford Geary, the music director at Ambler High School, was perhaps the leading practitioner of the melting-pot–friendly ethos. To integrate the music department at all levels—band, chorus, and majorette squad—was a courageously groundbreaking undertaking for the white head of a music department at a white-majority high school in the 1940s. I wish I'd had the chance to ask him why he did it: Was the impetus political or pedagogical? How and why did he develop a color-blind demeanor in a world that wasn't color-blind at all? I don't know what his motivations were, but I know the impact his courageous acts had on me and I'd suspect on the whole student body, both Black and white. I'm sure Mr. Geary's soul is among God's angels.

High School Graduation Patterns, 1919–1940

In general, during the period from World War I through the 1930s, a majority of Ambler's Italian American and African American students dropped out before completing the high school grades, mainly because their working-class families needed the additional income they could contribute from gainful employment—typically as low-pay factory workers especially at Keasbey & Mattison.

To measure the number of students who actually graduated, I looked at yearbook photographs of the senior class and conducted interviews with now-elderly Italian American and African American individuals who attended Ambler High School.

The graduation rate for African Americans expanded slowly between World War I and the 1930s. From conversations with the first African American in Ambler to become a certified teacher in the 1920s, Evelyn Brown Wright, I discovered that from 1916 to 1920, there were only six African American youth at Ambler High School, which had been founded in 1890. Three African American youth—all girls—entered eleventh grade in September 1918: Evelyn Brown, Helen Perry, and my mother, Louisa Laws. Evelyn and Helen graduated in June 1920 and went on to become certified schoolteachers at Temple University and Cheyney State Teachers

College, respectively. My mother had to drop out in 1918 after her father died in the great influenza pandemic of that year. Her mother had died a decade earlier from pneumonia, and she felt responsible for the care of her paternal grandparents, who were in their eighties. Three years after her father's death, my mother met my father at an annual AUMP convention in Wilmington, Delaware; they married a year later. My mother told me many years later that her failure to graduate and become a schoolteacher was one of the greatest disappointments in her life, which she made peace with only when I achieved academic success, graduating from college, earning my PhD, and being appointed the first African American faculty member to teach at Harvard College.

The graduating Class of 1921 included only one African American student, Robert Lee. He attended Howard University, one of the early post–Civil War colleges for Black youth founded by the federal government in the 1870s. Five years later, the graduating class again had a solitary African American student—Marion Brown, the sister of Evelyn Brown and the daughter of homebuilder Robert Brown—as well as two Italian American youth. Marion Brown attended the Taylor Music Conservatory in Philadelphia and became an organ teacher.

The 1930s saw significant growth in Black and Italian American graduation rates. The Class of 1933 graduated five African American youth, four of whom—Nathan Brown, Thomas Henry, Celester Johnson, and Doris Miller—had fathers who were factory workers, and one of whom, Allen Rose, was the son of a lumber company foreman. One year later, six African American students graduated. Salathiel Brown, Etta Smith, and Stanley Watkins were the children of factory workers, while Alton Burrell's father sold real estate, Bertha Queenan's father owned a disposal business, and Mabel Dickson's father was a well-to-do construction contractor. This class reached a record level of graduation for Italian American students, whose profiles resembled those of the African American graduates: Dominic Mallozzi, Paul Marincola, Philip Signore, and cousins Felix and Louis Zollo were sons of factory workers, while the fathers of another set of cousins, Joseph and Rose Romano, operated a grocery store. That year, Rose Romano became the first Italian American to be named Ambler High School's valedictorian. Another member of the Class of 1934, Anthony Signore, would be Ambler High's first Italian American graduate to become a dentist, much as Anthony Civarelli, Class of 1929 and a graduate of Gettysburg College, had become the first Italian American graduate to become a medical doctor.[9]

Ambler High School in the 1930s

While Ambler High School's 1930 yearbook lists not a single African American among the graduating class, by the close of the decade there had been a kind of breakthrough in terms of graduation rates. Eight Black students graduated with the Class of 1935, out of a total of fifty-nine students. In 1939, thirteen African Americans—an unprecedented number—marched in caps and gowns. My sister Vermadella, the eldest of my siblings and the first to graduate from high school, walked proudly among them.

The graduation outcomes for Ambler's Italian American youth by the middle 1930s showed similar patterns. Ambler High School's 1929 yearbook lists two Italian Americans as graduates that year, including future physician Anthony Civarelli. In 1933, the yearbook showed six graduating Italian Americans, as compared to five graduating African Americans. The Class of 1934 included seven Italian American graduates, meaning that the graduation numbers for Italian American youth had reached a kind of tipping point—or so it seemed. For both African American and Italian American youth during the 1930s in Ambler, the high school–level advancement trajectory was entirely unpredictable. For example, the 1935 yearbook lists only two Italian American students in the graduating class, as compared to eight African Americans. Increases in the number of African American and Italian American graduates did not happen in sync or in any sort of predictable trajectory within their own groups.

A glance at Ambler's overall population statistics helps to put these numbers in context. In 1910, the US Census Bureau Report listed Ambler's population at 2,469, of whom 266 were described as "Negro." Twenty years later, according to census figures, Ambler's total population was just under four thousand, with 506 listed as "Negro." The census was less helpful in determining the Italian or Italian American population; although there were categories regarding language spoken at home, country of parents' birth and so forth, an English-speaking Italian American born in the United States would be categorized as white. However, a close reading of the weekly *Ambler Gazette* for the period between the two world wars indicates that by the 1930s, about 25 percent of Ambler's citizens were of Italian descent.[10] Using this admittedly unscientific estimate, the Italian or Italian American population was about double that of the African American population.

Black Youth and Social Mobility, 1920s–1960s

Throughout my adolescent and teenage years, I was aware that a sizable number of my hometown's African American youth had gained a notable level of social mobility beyond our mainly working-class backgrounds.

By "hometown," I mean the twin Black communities of Ambler-Penllyn, whose histories since the 1880s have been closely intertwined. The Black communities of these neighboring towns were consolidated particularly among the high school–age youth from the post–World War I period through the 1960s. Teens who lived in Ambler, like me, who had experienced integration in their lower schools, were joined in high school by Penllyn teens, who were coming out of a segregated school system.

Black Youth Social-Mobility Achievement

Black youth gained several "achievement-oriented influences" from these connected towns that allowed them to make advances in social mobility. The melting-pot–friendly academic practices of Ambler public schools benefited African American students as well as Italian American youth.

Penllyn students, meanwhile, were influenced by a "You can achieve" ethos instilled in them by African American teachers and administrators at all-Black Penllyn Elementary and Middle School. I learned about the impact of that robust ethos from many hours of conversation with Helen Perry Moore, who was the second African American principal at Penllyn Elementary and Middle School, from the 1930s through the 1950s. Mrs. Moore told me that the "You can achieve" ethos that she and other teachers persistently communicated to their students was reinforced by an equally persistent "You must respect yourself" message. My peers who attended Penllyn schools have told me that this lesson, emanating from Mrs. Moore, an attractive lady of regal bearing and authoritative demeanor, resonated deeply and broadly with her students.

A Black-community helping-hand ethos was a third means of enhancing and enabling advances in social mobility among Ambler-Penllyn's youth during this period. Several constituencies within the twin communities practiced this ethos: churches; civic organizations such as the Guidance League and the Odd Fellows; the Zion Baptist Church's Eastern Star women's organization; and, last but not least, the average African American family that lived there.

Starting in the 1930s, the three churches that served the Ambler-Penllyn Black communities joined forces to raise scholarship funds, in part through church dinners, for postsecondary education for academically successful Black youth. While these scholarships never amounted to more than a baseline contribution for a student's continuing education, they perhaps above all represented the Black-community helping-hand ethos. These small but sincere gestures reverberated throughout the societal sinews of Ambler-Penllyn's African American families and stimulated many adults to replicate the helping-hand ethos in their own families, giving the new generation of Black youth opportunities to pursue postsecondary education—opportunities that they themselves never had.

Three families in particular come to mind when I think of the helping-hand ethos as it pertained to African Americans securing postsecondary educational opportunities for their children: the Roses, the Newmans, and the Scotts. At the 1989 induction program for the Hall of Fame of Wissahickon High School, the successor to Ambler High, one of the several African American inductees was Lieutenant Colonel Ruby Rose. She was the sister of Allen Rose, Class of 1933, who was the sole African American member of the school's Science Club. Ruby graduated in 1939, along with my oldest sister, Vermadella, and went on to earn a nursing degree at Philadelphia's Mercy Hospital and School for Nurses. Nursing schools were segregated in Pennsylvania and in all other states in the 1930s, and Mercy Hospital (later called Mercy-Douglass Hospital following a merger with Philadelphia's Douglass Hospital in 1949) was operated by an all–African American medical staff. I recall vividly Lieutenant Colonel Rose's acceptance remarks during the induction, in which she related a poignant tale of the Black-family helping-hand ethos as it existed under her own roof. Her father, Warren Rose, was a foreman at Ambler's Craft Lumber Company.

She told us that he got on the Reading Railway train to Philadelphia every week to deliver her "weekly living allowance from his paycheck." Following her graduation from Mercy Hospital in 1941, the newly credentialed nurse enlisted in the US Women's Army Corps (WACS), joining some 6,500 other African American nurses.[1] Like all of the US armed forces during World War II, the nursing units of the WACS were segregated. Ruby Rose remained an army nurse through three American wars, eventually retiring and returning to our hometown to spend her elderly years.

The Newman family offered a second example of a working-class African American family supporting the postsecondary school education of their children. Albert Newman was a factory worker as well as a chauffeur for the Knights, a well-to-do white family, and his wife, Gladys Green Newman, operated home-based laundry and pastry businesses. Between the two of them, Mr. and Mrs. Newman managed to save enough money to send four of their six children to college during the 1950s and 1960s. Three daughters—Lorna, Ina, and Geraldine—attended Pennsylvania's Cheyney State University, and a son, Robert, attended Temple. Robert became the first African American member of the Ambler High School faculty, hired as a social studies teacher and sports coach in the late 1960s. The sisters became teachers too.

The Scott family, who lived near the Newmans in the North Street–Woodland Avenue community, followed a similar path. Millard Scott was a factory worker and janitor, as well as our beloved WPA playground director in the 1930s and 1940s, and his wife, Evelyn, was a domestic worker. Neither was a high wage earner, but they harnessed their finances and managed to send three of their four children to college during the 1950s and 1960s.

Dashed Family Mobility: The Thompsons

Although a surprising number of African American youth from Ambler found success, it goes without saying that not every family succeeded—even those who seemed destined to. In the late 1930s and the late 1940s, the Thompsons, another African American family living in the North Street–Woodland Avenue community that subscribed to the Black-family helping-hand ethos, sent three of their five children to college. The father, Joshua Thompson, worked as a chauffeur for the Mattison family and as a truck driver in its asbestos-textile factory—a job usually reserved for white workers. The Thompson family's second-oldest son, Joshua Thompson Jr., graduated from Ambler High School in 1941 and spent several years in the US Army, after which he attended Howard University Medical School. While on vacation during his final year of medical school, Joshua Jr. was in a terrible car accident. He was thrown from the vehicle and suffered severe head injuries that made it impossible for him to return to school and complete his training. Two other Thompson children also graduated from Ambler High School: Lewis in my class, the Class of 1948, and Mary Jane in the Class of 1949. Lewis and I matriculated at Lincoln University, and Mary Jane attended a Negro college in North Carolina. Unfortunately, neither Lewis nor Mary Jane completed their degrees. Lewis went on to become a clerk in the city of Philadelphia, and Mary Jane found success as a skilled worker at the major pharmaceutical company Merck in Montgomery County.

That outcome was a terrible disappointment to their mother, Nancy Thompson, who had been a schoolteacher in North Carolina before marrying and moving to Pennsylvania in the 1920s. It was also a tremendous letdown for Mr. Thompson, who was an important civic and political leader in Ambler's African American community and one of only two African Americans on the Montgomery County Republican Party Committee. I know from many conversations with him that he had a deep appreciation for educational achievement among Black folks. When I visited Mr. Thompson a year before he died, he gave me a big hug as we parted and with tears in his eyes said, "Thanks, Martin, for bringing pride and respect to Ambler's Negroes through your professional achievements." I hugged the dear old man back, with tears in my eyes too.

Joshua Thompson's mother was a member of one of Ambler's oldest leading African American families, which was headed by the Civil War veteran Daniel W. Dowling, a member of my great-grandfather Jacob Laws's cohort during the establishment of Ambler's Black community in the late 1800s. His mother's nephew and Daniel Dowling's grandson, Monroe Dowling, was born on the family homestead at the southern end of Woodland Avenue and graduated in 1930 from Lincoln University, where his roommate was Thurgood Marshall, the first African American to sit on the US Supreme Court. Upon graduation, Monroe attended the Harvard Business School and graduated in 1932, among the first African Americans to do so.

During the 1993 spring term, Harvard Business School's African-American Student Union held a conference commemorating Monroe. My wife, Marion, and I attended as his guests, and I thus witnessed the marvelous salutation to Mr. Dowling's career, which I couldn't help but view as a salute to the entire African American community in Ambler, Pennsylvania, where he was born. Monroe spent the first ten years of his childhood in Ambler before moving with his parents to Atlantic City, New Jersey, where his father got a US Post Office job.

I knew the Thompson family quite well, owing to my close childhood and teenage friendship with Lewis. He plays a role in so many of my memories. He used to wait on the front steps of the Emanuel Church parsonage where I lived, just across the street from his Woodland Avenue house, when we were schoolkids, so we could head off together to Mattison Avenue Elementary School and later to the Forest Avenue Middle School.[2] Our route took us to the corner of Green Street and Lindenwold Avenue, where the King & Betz Grocery Store stood. The store's clientele was mainly North Ambler's upper-middle-class WASP families, and whenever its fruits exhibited even a slight sign of spoilage, King & Betz set those pieces in crates outside the store. It was the heart of the Great Depression, and our parents could rarely afford to buy fresh produce, so we kids really appreciated those crates of spoiled fruits, picking out an orange, banana, or handful of grapes for our lunch bags. For a time when I was twelve, my personal fate was tied directly to the King family. Eddie King, their teenage son, who was the local distributor for the *Philadelphia Evening Bulletin*, asked my mother if I could be a paperboy for some North Ambler neighborhoods. I had my own bicycle, and she said I could. Eddie allocated both white and Black neighborhoods to me for my route.

When Lewis and I started junior high school at the end of World War II, in 1945, we were the first Black youth hired on weekends as busboys at a white restaurant in Ambler, the Howard Johnson's on Bethlehem Pike. The head chef, William Foster, a commander in the US Navy during World War II, admonished us, "I know your families are leaders in the Negro community, so do a good job, young boys." Lewis and I also caddied together at the North Hills Country Club in Cheltenham Township, the only white golf course in Montgomery County that allowed Black caddies. Other golf courses in the area, including York Country Club in Upper Dublin Township and the Sandy Run Country Club in the town of Glenside in Cheltenham Township, were entirely off-limits to African Americans who would have liked to work there.

Our caddying paths diverged after just one summer, August 1942. Lewis complained that the sun was too damn hot and that the golf bags were too damn heavy, and he decided not to return to caddying the next year. Lewis was right about the sun and those bags, but I caddied off and on until the summer following my freshman year at Lincoln University. I chastised Lewis: "Forget about the heat and heavy bags, man," I said. "The ten dollars for an eighteen-hole golf round is good money." But nothing could change Lewis's mind. "Caddying isn't for me, Martin," he proclaimed.

Lewis and I had another work-related encounter under the hot summer sun. In 1945, Jack Ledeboer, whose father was a vice president at Keasbey & Mattison, was one of several upper-middle-class white youth who played sandlot pickup baseball games with Black youth in North Ambler. Jack's friend, a farmer's son with whom he attended the private secondary school Germantown Friends School, had asked him whether any of his friends in Ambler could help the Buckley Farm harvest hay in early August. The farm was in the rural neighboring town of Broad Ax, and the pay for three days of work was good—as were the lunches prepared by Mrs. Buckley, who operated the farm since her husband had died. So Lewis, my brother Richard, several other Black youth in North Ambler, and I agreed to help out.

Alas, the work wasn't easy for us teenagers. It involved trailing behind a big hay-baling machine, picking up baled bundles that weighed about sixty pounds each, and tossing those bundles on a truck, where two workers stacked them. From there, we followed the truck to a barn, where two of us lifted bales to a second-story loft where two other teens stacked them. Though we all wore large handkerchiefs over our faces, flying bits of hay were everywhere, and they found their way into our eyes and noses—everything. And man, was that damn old sun hot! After three afternoons helping to harvest hay at the Buckley Farm, Lewis said to me, "Martin, I don't want to do farm work in the damn hot sun ever again." I replied, "Me neither, but I'm still going caddying on the weekend." Lewis laughed and said, "Yeah, go right ahead."

Lewis disappointed his family when he flunked out of Lincoln University. He never achieved the promise that they, or he himself, envisaged for him in his teenage years. There was, however, a "solid redemption element" in my childhood buddy Lewis's soul. Several years before his death, Lewis telephoned me to pick him up for lunch the next time I visited Ambler. When the time came, we lunched at the Turnpike Restaurant in Spring House, reminiscing about old times and catching up on more recent years. Lewis told me that for the first time in his adult years, he felt proud of himself, because his son from his first marriage had graduated from medical school and become a physician. "I paid a big part of his university bills, Martin, and I just *wish* my father and mother had lived to witness this," he said with a proud twinkle in his eyes. "You know how much Mom and Dad grieved over my brother Joshua's mishap that ended his attendance at Howard University's Medical School, Martin." I walked around the table and gave Lewis a shoulder hug as he wiped tears from his eyes. My dear buddy passed away three years later. I traveled to Ambler to attend his funeral, which was at a funeral parlor in Willow Grove, a nearby town in Cheltenham Township. Lewis wasn't a churchgoer, so a church funeral was not for him.

Ambler High School, 1948–1949

When in March 2010 some of my African American high school friends suggested a "homecoming reunion" so we could catch up with those among our peers who were still alive, I thought it was a marvelous idea. The event was scheduled for June 17 at the Spring House Tavern in Lower Gwynedd Township. Alicia Stewart Mahoney (Ambler High School's first Black majorette), Laura Mahoney, and Elsie Johnson Queenan spearheaded the reunion, and they asked me to write some reflections on our youthful schooldays during the 1930s and 1940s.

Before putting anything down on paper, I talked with another high school friend, Helen Rose Baker, about the topics I might address. I've always thought of Helen as a local Ambler intellectual. She kept abreast of local and national politics, and she enrolled in art courses at Gwynedd Mercy College in Upper Gwynedd Township, where she specialized in watercolor painting. She became a prizewinning painter to boot. Helen suggested that I write an academic profile of the Black youth at Ambler High School during the 1940s.

Over the many years since leaving Ambler High School, I've had numerous conversations with Helen and her husband, Richard Baker, whom my wife, Marion, and I usually dropped in on when we visited my hometown. Marion and I made the trek to Ambler several times a year, depending on how many deaths there had been of my old friends or those of my parents and older siblings. We visited for other, more festive occasions, too, such as the annual Memorial Day ceremonies held at Rose Valley Cemetery that were organized by the African American veterans' organization Daniel W. Dowling American Legion Post 769.

I ran with Helen's idea. Initially I thought I'd write maybe ten pages, but by early May, I had produced a nearly forty-page manuscript. I called it

"Growing Up in Black Communities of Ambler-Penllyn, 1930s–1940s" and had forty or so booklets produced by a copy center in Lexington, Massachusetts, my home at the time.

In researching the Ambler High School yearbooks, I discovered that the classes of 1948 and 1949 had the largest number of Black youth ever to graduate from Ambler High School. Before 1948, no more than thirteen African American youth had graduated from any one class. The Class of 1933 was the first to have any significant number of Black graduates, with five. The next-largest group of Black graduates came two years later. The Class of 1935 included eight Black graduates, still primarily of working-class backgrounds. Thomas Clark, Addie Ricks, Adelaide Johnson, Russell Nelson, and Frederick Smith were the children of factory workers. Elsie Gordon's father owned a grocery store and butcher shop, and Jackie Hopson's father was a carpenter; Ralph Burrell's father deviated from the pack a bit, dealing in the more middle-class field of real estate.

Most of the thirteen African American students graduating in 1939 fit a similar parentage profile as those who had come before them: Joseph Ashton, Vivian Campbell, and sisters Jane and Thelma Gant had fathers who were factory workers; Frances Burrell's father dealt in real estate; Frances Hopson was the daughter of a carpenter; Nathaniel Perry's father was a chauffeur and caterer; and Ruby Rose's father was a lumber company foreman. My sister Vermadella, the daughter of a Methodist clergyman, received her diploma with this group. In addition to having the largest number of African American youth in a graduating class to date, the Class of 1939 set a record for the greatest number of Black youth—nine—who selected the college preparatory curriculum (called the Academic and Science Curriculum in the 1930s) instead of the commercial curriculum, which was the more typical choice for African American students.

For my discussion of the academic performance pattern among African American youth in the Ambler High School graduating classes of 1948 and 1949, I have fashioned a table of quantitative data that correlates the number of Black youth with the academic curricula they majored in. These data are shown in table 4.1. Out of a total class size of 129 students, twenty-nine of whom were Black, sixty-two students enrolled in the college preparatory curriculum in 1948, with sixty-seven enrolled in the commercial-general curricula. For the graduating Class of 1948, there were twenty-two African American students—twelve females and ten males—in the commercial-general curricula. Viewed in the context of the total graduating students, the twenty-two African American students constituted 30 percent of all

TABLE 4.1 Attributes of Black Students at Ambler High School, Classes of 1948 and 1949

College Preparatory Curriculum

Class of 1948	Class of 1949
7 Black students	8 Black students
3 females, 4 males	5 females, 3 males

Commercial and General Curricula

Class of 1948	Class of 1949
22 Black students	24 Black students
12 females, 10 males	10 females, 14 males

Source: Ambler High School Yearbooks, 1948 and 1949

Class of 1948 students enrolled in Ambler High School's commercial-general curricula. Among those enrolled in the college preparatory curriculum who planned to pursue postsecondary education, there were seven African Americans.

The ratio of white students to Black students in the total Class of 1949 and in the different curricula remained relatively consistent with the prior year. Out of a class total of 149, thirty-two students were Black. Unlike in the previous year, however, more students overall—eighty-one—enrolled in the college preparatory curriculum, as opposed to sixty-eight who enrolled in the commercial-general curricula. The span between students taking a college preparatory curriculum and the commercial-general curricula had widened considerably. Once again, in the Class of 1949, three times as many African American students—twenty-four (ten females and fourteen males)—enrolled in in the commercial-general curricula as opposed to eight (five female students and three male) in the college-preparatory curriculum. And once again, these students hailed from primarily working-class backgrounds: Barbara and Herman Gant, Dorothy Johnson, Connie Rines, and Milton Clark were children of factory workers; Mary Jane Thompson's father was a chauffeur and factory truck driver; and Martha and Walter Moore were the children of a school-principal mother.

Although those students from the classes of 1948 and 1949 who enrolled in the college-preparatory curriculum were presumed to be heading to college after high school, I never did know how many of the African American students actually did so. From my class (1948), I know that Lewis Thompson attended Lincoln University with me and played on the varsity basketball team there, Helen Rose earned an art degree at Mercy Gwynedd College in Pennsylvania, and Earl Mundell played varsity football at Penn State. The Class of 1949 produced some college graduates who became educators, including Walter Moore and Connie Rines, who went to Cheyney State Teachers' College. Otherwise, I've never been able to keep abreast of the postsecondary education pattern among African American students of those years who studied the college-preparatory curriculum. Yet even with a partial reckoning, the total number of graduating African American students in the classes of 1948 and 1949 who continued their education after high school constituted the largest number of African American students ever to do so.

Higher Education and Career Opportunities

While the youth from middle- and upper-middle-class white families could be certain that Ambler's schools would facilitate real social mobility for them (the wealthy Mattison family, for example, sent two sons to Ambler High School in the 1920s), in the early years of the twentieth century, there could be no such assumption for the average Italian American and African American working-class student. For one thing, as late as the 1930s, a majority of neither Italian American youth nor African American youth remained in secondary school long enough to graduate, which meant that the social and cultural conditions were not favorable enough for most Italian American and African American working-class families to cultivate upward social mobility for their children.

The same weak conditions also kept the majority of working-class Irish American and Polish American youth from continuing into Ambler High School. A perusal of the names under photographs of students in the graduating Class of 1938 (shown in the yearbook from 1937) reveals only six students with Irish surnames and none with Polish surnames, out of a total of seventy-seven graduates. This suggests that class implications weighed more heavily than anything else, even than race, on continuation into high school and, the next step, graduation from it.

There was only one African American youth in the Ambler High School graduating Class of 1926 and two Italian American youth. In the graduating

Class of 1933, there were just six Italian Americans and five African Americans. It took nearly two decades before the number of graduating Italian American and African American youth exceeded the 1933 figures, when the Class of 1949 claimed eighteen Italian American youth and thirty-two African American youth.

In seeking to understand the social-mobility pattern among Ambler High School's Black graduates during the first half of the twentieth century, I went directly to the source and pursued numerous conversations with as many of these graduates as I could over a decade or so, among them early graduates such as Evelyn Brown Wright and Helen Perry Moore, who lived into their nineties, Jane Williams Flowers and the Reverend Guy McGee Jr., who were both in their late eighties as of this writing, Helen Rose Baker, Gloria Stewart Jones, and Walter Moore, all of whom are with us, also in their eighties, as of this writing, and Ina Newman and my sister Gwendolyn Kilson Coleman, both of whom are in their seventies.[3] I was fortunate to speak with Mary Jane Thompson and Jenny Lucas before they passed in their late seventies and with Gracie McGee Taylor, who passed in her sixties. On the basis of these conversations, I developed an understanding of a pattern of "social-mobility job categories" that African American graduates of Ambler High School often pursued during the past half century or so. They can be classified as professional jobs, technical/clerical jobs, and business jobs.

Starting in the late 1920s, several African American graduates of Ambler High School entered the teaching profession. During the 1920s and 1930s, Marion Brown Gaines, Dorothy Talley, and Julia Smith, to name a few, became music teachers. Portia McGee, an early 1940s graduate whose father was the pastor of Penllyn's Bethlehem Baptist Church, was Ambler's first African American student to enroll at the elite Bryn Mawr College, going on to become a schoolteacher. Portia's sister and fellow Ambler High School graduate Gracie McGee was similarly groundbreaking on her path to the teaching profession. Gracie was the first-ever African American student admitted to Beaver College, an elite liberal arts college located on the boundary of Montgomery County and Philadelphia County. (The second Black student to enroll at Beaver College, now Arcadia University, was Anna Deavere Smith, the well-known performer and playwright.)

The number of African American Ambler High School graduates who entered the teaching profession mushroomed throughout the coming decades. Many of these names are familiar, because many of Ambler's African American families found success generation after generation. In the

1940s, Anita, Walter, and Martha Moore, the children of the school principal Helen Perry Moore, became schoolteachers and eventually school administrators. (Another of Helen's children, Joseph Moore, graduated in 1946 and became a civil servant.) During the 1950s, Wanda Brown Lofton, who was from one of Ambler's several African American upper-middle-class families, also became a schoolteacher. Her father, Carlton Brown, was a civil engineer. Throughout that decade and into the next one, several African American students from working-class backgrounds entered the teaching profession as well. Among them were the Newman children—Lorna, Robert, Ina, and Geraldine. There was also Roberta Scott, the daughter of Millard Scott, the church leader and director of the WPA playground in North Ambler during the 1930s and 1940s. Laura Brown, June Gaskins, John Johnson, Buddy Johnson, Marcella Lawrence, Ralph Lowe, Mara Moore, and Shirley Smith Weldon followed suit. Many of this last group attended Morgan State College, one of the early post–Civil War colleges founded in Maryland for African American men.

Several other professions were represented by this sampling of African American high school graduates. Salathiel Brown, Class of 1934, became an industrial chemist—and the husband of my sister Vermadella, Class of 1939, who became a nurse. Jackie Hopson and Henry Carter, both graduates in the 1930s, became professional entertainers, the former a jazz singer, the latter the leader of a jazz band. Among the 1940s graduates, Guy McGee Jr. attended Virginia Union University and became an assistant minister to his father at Bethlehem Baptist Church, while his brother Hubert McGee attended the Philadelphia School of Pharmacy and became a pharmacist. (This was the same Hubert who gave me a job stocking shelves in the pharmacy where he worked.) In the 1950s, Sterling Flowers, the son of a man who owned an automotive dealership, became a lawyer.

Until the late 1940s, in the borough of Ambler and in surrounding townships (Lower Gwynedd Township, Upper Gwynedd Township, Cheltenham Township, and Norristown, the county seat for Montgomery County), most sales and clerical jobs were subject to racial segregation practices and therefore not available to African American high school graduates. A rare exception was the hiring of African American Virginia Edwards to be the principal's secretary at Ambler High School. Such an event had never happened before and wouldn't happen again until after World War II.

Before racial segregation in the sales and clerical fields was dismantled, the Ambler-Penllyn community had seen baby steps toward breaking down these barriers. In the late 1930s, the Harris Department Store hired an African American as a sales clerk: my older brother, William Laws Kilson. My sister Vivian, who graduated during the early 1940s, took a clerical job in the social welfare headquarters in Philadelphia. The following years witnessed the hiring of three African American mail carriers by the Ambler post office: Allen Rose, Leon Hill, and Nathaniel Perry, each of whom was a World War II veteran from lower-middle-class backgrounds. Another Ambler High School graduate and World War II veteran, Eugene Smithey, the son of a housepainter and factory worker, secured a position with the US Postal Service in Philadelphia. Finally, one of my childhood buddies who graduated from Ambler High School in 1949, John Mahoney, became a salesman in an insurance company. The snail's-pace speed with which African American high school graduates were hired in sales and clerical jobs persisted into the early 1960s.

During the twentieth century, about 40 percent of Americans who gained social mobility out of working-class backgrounds into the middle-class sector did so through a variety of what can be called business endeavors. This social-mobility pattern applied quite generally among America's different ethnic and racial groups, especially among African American youth in the Ambler-Penllyn communities during the twentieth century. After World War II, several African American graduates found themselves inspired by entrepreneurial ideas and fashioned business careers for themselves. George Williams Jr., a World War II veteran, entered the real estate business. His father, George Williams Sr., was the only African American white-collar employee in an industrial company in Ambler during the 1930s and 1940s, as well as a leading deacon at Emanuel AUMP. My brother William Laws Kilson, another World War II veteran, also caught the entrepreneurial bug. After the war he worked as a milk salesman for the African American–owned Walter Perry milk distributor in Philadelphia, going on to become a sales manager for the first African American–owned meatpacking firm in America, the Parks Sausage Company, which operated up and down the Atlantic Coast, from North Carolina to Boston. The company became famous for its TV ads showcasing a child enjoying "the pleasingest" Parks Sausage and yelling out, "More Parks Sausages, Mom! More Parks Sausages, please!"

As the years went on, business opportunities for Black people slowly increased, as evinced by the career choices of several African Americans who graduated from Ambler High School during the 1950s and 1960s. Like his brother George, Charles Williams entered the real estate business. Another set of brothers, James and Joseph Cottingham, inspired by their father, Clement Cottingham Sr., who owned an electrical repair business, launched their own such business, and their sister Constance became an industrial mathematician. Still another late-1950s African American graduate, Teddy Hopson, possibly inspired by his jazz-singer uncle Jackie, became a disc jockey in Philadelphia.

Finally, starting in the late 1930s through the 1960s, a fair number of African American graduates of Ambler High School—including women—pursued postsecondary school degrees that enabled them to obtain top-rank professional jobs in academia, nursing, entertainment, and the military. Gloria Stewart Jones, the author of the remarkable history of the Ambler-Penllyn Black communities that has proved indispensable to me in the writing of my own memoir, graduated from nursing school and went into education, becoming a professor of nursing at Gwynedd Mercy College in Pennsylvania. Dolores Robinson, who grew up in a working-class family in Penllyn and graduated from Ambler High in the 1960s, pursued postsecondary studies in communications, which enabled her to gain employment in television in Philadelphia. She later moved to California and established herself as a top-tier professional manager in Hollywood, where her clients included Levar Burton and Wesley Snipes. She is the mother of actress Holly Robinson Peete.

Thus, a few women from graduating classes as early as the 1930s found success in fields that were largely off-limits to Black people of either sex. In general, the male graduates took about a decade longer to establish themselves. I was one of three male graduates from the 1940s through the 1960s to excel in academia. Clement Cottingham graduated in the 1950s and attended Lincoln University a few years after I did, graduating in 1959. He pursued graduate studies at the University of California, Berkeley, and earned his PhD in political science, based on field research he conducted on one of the early independent African states in West Africa, the republic of Senegal. Clement started his teaching career as an assistant professor of political science at Swarthmore College in Pennsylvania and gained a full professorship at Rutgers University. Lawrence Walker, who also graduated from Ambler High School in the 1950s, received a degree from Temple University and joined the US Air Force, achieving the rank of major general and spending his professional life in service.

Mobility

One factor that facilitated a fair amount of social mobility among the African American youth in Ambler and Penllyn was the "cultural governance" of several Black churches during the first sixty years of the twentieth century.

Emanuel AUMP, Zion Baptist, and Bethlehem Baptist were the social anchors for African American working-class citizens in the twin communities. Those churches facilitated a web of social order which in turn spawned an ethos of mutual responsibility among the fathers and mothers in working-class Black families, whereby each parent shouldered family-uplift tasks as best they could. This function was, of course, never perfectly fulfilled in every Black family in Ambler and Penllyn. How could it be? Nevertheless, it was fulfilled enough to enable many Ambler-Penllyn African American youth during the first half of the twentieth century to fashion a sense of "wholesome self-identity."

Accordingly, as Black youth in my hometown and Penllyn progressed through the secondary school system, they were culturally and emotionally stimulated toward self-efficacy, thereby avoiding the self-defeating "I can't succeed" outlook that became widespread among urban poor and working-class African American youth from the 1980s through the remainder of the twentieth century. Eugene Robinson, an African American columnist for the *Washington Post,* has argued that those demoralizing attitudes have contributed to a situation where large numbers of the urban Black working class have become "abandoned citizens."[4]

Finally, the web of social order that the Black churches in Ambler and Penllyn provided their working-class families also inspired a foundation of "wholeness" among Black youth, which eventually allowed students to flourish through Ambler High School's melting-pot–friendly academic environment from the 1920s into the 1960s.

The Kilson Clan

I was the fifth of seven children. My four older siblings graduated from Ambler High School in four consecutive years: Vermadella in 1939, William in 1940, Vivian in 1941, and Bernice in 1942. Vermadella married a fellow Ambler High graduate, Salathiel Brown, with whom she had four daughters. Vermadella became a nurse. One of their daughters became a secretary, one a music teacher, one a department store sales clerk, and one a factory worker.

Next in line was William. After three years in the US Army, he studied business at Philadelphia's Drexel Institute of Technology (now Drexel University) and became a sales manager for the first major African American–owned meatpacking company, Parks Sausage Company. William had two children, a daughter who was a nurse and a son who studied business at the University of Pittsburgh.

Following graduation, Vivian, the third sibling, took a course at a secretarial school in Philadelphia and worked in the city's social welfare administration. She had five children, three daughters and two sons. The oldest, a son, was a linotype setter at one of Philadelphia's major newspapers, the *Evening Bulletin*. The oldest daughter was a secretary, and the other two earned doctorates in education. Vivian's second son earned a degree in architecture at Syracuse University and worked in that profession for a decade, going on to get his MBA at the University of Pennsylvania and finding work in a financial services company. Later a vice president of financial affairs at Temple University Medical Center, he went on to serve first as vice president of financial administration at Dickinson University in Pennsylvania and then as senior vice president and chief operating officer of the nonprofit economic development corporation PIDC in Philadelphia.

My next-oldest sibling, Bernice, was the last Kilson to graduate from Ambler High School before I came along. Following her graduation in 1942, she worked for several years as a gospel singer. Bernice had eight children. From her first marriage, she had a son, Burrell, who was a factory worker and a daughter, Brenda, who was a secretary at Smith Kline and French in Lansdale, Pennsylvania, and in Maryland public schools. Brenda's two children attended Lincoln University and Western Maryland College; one became a schoolteacher, the other a school administrator. Bernice's second marriage was to a DuPont factory worker and produced five children. The oldest son was a noncommissioned officer in the US Marine Corps. The youngest son is a teamster. The oldest daughter did secretarial courses and works as a secretary, while two other daughters are midlevel administrators in food-franchising companies. One of Bernice's daughters, Martina Davis-Hagler, has a daughter—my great-niece Arian Davis—who graduated as a cadet from the US Naval Academy in 2012. I was blessed to attend that marvelous occasion, all the while thinking of Arian's great-great-great-great-grandfather Jacob Laws, who fought as part of the US Colored Troops of the Union Army during the Civil War in order to free the Negro slaves.

My younger brother, Richard, and my younger sister, Gwendolyn, graduated from Ambler High School in the 1950s and 1960s. After two years in the US Air Force, Richard took furniture-making courses and established his own business as a furniture maker. Richard's only child, a son, became a jazz musician. Gwendolyn married after high school and worked in a Phillips Electric factory, becoming an officer in the factory's trade union. She had two sons who graduated from Ambler High School and who, like their mother, became laborers.

Finally, I have three adult children—two daughters and a son. My elder daughter attended the University of New Hampshire and earned a professional degree in education at the Harvard Graduate School of Education; she is an educational consultant and a lecturer in education policy at the Harvard School of Education. My son, an accountant at State Street Bank in Boston, attended the University of Massachusetts Amherst and, like his sister, earned a professional degree in education; his is from Boston College. My younger daughter attended Amherst College and graduated from Harvard Law School; she is a partner in a Boston real estate law firm. I graduated from Lincoln University, earned my PhD at Harvard, and have spent my life as an academic. My children's mother, my wife, Marion Dusser de Barenne Kilson, grew up in a white upper-middle-class family of medical doctors (her father was a professor at Yale Medical School) and attended Radcliffe College, going on to earn her PhD in social anthropology from Harvard University.

Thus, the social-mobility trajectory of my siblings and me might be described as having a fairly good upward pattern. Starting out as we did from a lower-middle-class African Methodist clergyman's household, all seven of us completed high school. Three completed postsecondary studies (nursing, secretarial, and business), but I was the only one to pursue a four-year college degree—the first in my family to do so. Our second-oldest sibling, William, achieved the second-highest mobility pattern after me. Three sisters gained middle-class status for most of their children, while one sister fashioned working-class status for her two sons.

I think that from the 1920s all the way into the first decade of the twenty-first century, the Kilson clan (in its several family subgroups) achieved a fairly good social mobility profile, and I feel confident in saying that the Laws and Kilson clans' similar backstory laid the foundation for the different levels of our success. Our road was paved by who and where we come from. Descending from lines of free Negroes and clergymen on both my parents' sides, we hail from "men of the Bible," as Negro lore characterized my great-grandfather Jacob Laws and his cronies who helped establish Ambler's Black community. My mother often related tales of her grandfather's knowledge of the Bible. Jacob Laws had a keen memory for biblical text, she said, and he delivered the occasional sermon as a lay minister. Above all, he insisted that his two sons, William and Jacob Jr., become fully literate, which they did through the agency of the African Union Methodist Church and public schooling. They went on to become carpenters and church leaders.

Accordingly, my mother was the beneficiary of Jacob Laws's quest for biblical knowledge. She enrolled in public school in the early decades of Ambler's school system. When she entered eleventh grade at Ambler High School in the fall of 1918, however, an awful event occurred: her father's death in the great flu epidemic. She dropped out of high school in 1919 to care for her grandparents and was not able to return. But she had already gained two precious things: a love for learning and a desire to facilitate the social mobility of her children.

My father, an African Methodist clergyman who had completed high school and one year of seminary, and my mother presented a united front in stimulating their children to "finish high school"—a mantra she uttered regularly. All seven of my parents' children did just that. In doing so, five fashioned middle-class lives for themselves and their children, while two remained in the working class. When the Kilson family's social-mobility pattern between the 1930s and early 1970s is compared with that at the national level for African Americans, the third-generation Kilson pattern overall was better than average. And if we use the time frame from the 1970s to the first twelve years of the twenty-first century, I would say that the Kilson family mobility pattern overall compared favorably with the national trend.

Ambler: A Twentieth-Century Company Town

During the 1930s and 1940s, Ambler was a variant of what social historians of nineteenth- and early twentieth-century American society called a company town, in which a single industrial business dominates much of the life cycle of its residents and its operations.

This life-cycle domination was typically broad-gauged. At the least, the town's industry controlled a majority or nearly a majority of employment opportunities, underpinned a major part of economic commerce, underwrote the major bank, and exercised significant influence in the local political process. At the most, the industry exuded a "quasi-autocratic company aura," in which the controlling economic personality—the owner of the dominant business—imposed a kind of dictatorial imprint upon the company town, akin to what late nineteenth- and early twentieth-century mayors did on a much larger scale in industrial cities such as Chicago, Philadelphia, New York, and elsewhere, a pattern that political scientists call boss rule.[1]

Fortunately for the working-class citizens of my hometown, the overall character of company-town dominance in Ambler was of the benevolent rather than the dictatorial type. Of course, this benevolent pattern didn't preclude a variety of economic and political manipulation that favored the upper-middle-class individual and family owners. While the owners certainly enjoyed wealth and privilege that their workers did not, what distinguished the benevolent pattern of company-town life from the dictatorial one was that the owners were invested in the town itself and made philanthropic contributions on behalf of the social advancement of its resident working-class majority.

Such towns were numerous across Pennsylvania, among them Chester, Coatesville, Allentown, Reading, Bethlehem, Hershey, and Pittsburgh. Thanks to Frank D. Quattrone's *Images of America: Ambler*, there is a photographic history of my hometown that illustrates the company-town character it shared with other cities and towns, large and small, of that era. One of the most prominent features of these towns was mansion-type homesteads of the industry owners, and Quattrone's book contains marvelous photographs of the stone mansion that belonged to Dr. Richard Mattison, the primary owner of the Keasbey & Mattison Company, which moved from Philadelphia to Ambler in 1881. Holding a PhD in chemistry from the University of Pennsylvania, Dr. Mattison was always addressed as such by the managerial staff at the company and by citizens in Ambler. The grand home, named Lindenwold, was built in the early 1880s and looked like nothing less than a castle. It was the focal point of the twenty-five-acre Mattison family estate that was located on the east side of Ambler and surrounded by a beautifully sculpted stone wall which had three fifteen-foot-high wrought-iron entry gates. To me, the Mattison family estate was on a par with the better-known Gilded Age mansions built by other wealthy nineteenth- and twentieth-century American capitalists: the Vanderbilts' Biltmore Estate in Asheville, North Carolina, the Harrimans' Arden Estate on the Hudson River in New York, the Roosevelts' Springwood Estate in Hyde Park, New York, and the DuPonts' Longwood Gardens in the southern Pennsylvania mushroom-producing town of Kennett Square.

Like so many others, the Mattison family fell on hard times during the Great Depression, selling the estate in 1936 to the Archdiocese of Philadelphia, which turned it into St. Mary's Orphanage for working-class Irish American children. Fortunately for the children living in North and East Ambler neighborhoods especially, the estate's Roman Catholic administrators permitted us to continue to swim in a lake and quarry reservoir on the property and to bicycle along a paved roadway that encircled the estate. The Mattisons had adorned that roadway with imported stone Shinto religious urns from Japan, which still exist today, as does Lindenwold itself, nestled museum-like along the Bethlehem Pike that connects Ambler and other small Montgomery County towns with Philadelphia County.

A Multiethnic Factory Town, 1880s–1950s

In addition to photographs, Quattrone's book contains historical text that relates key attributes of Keasbey & Mattison's institutionalization of socioeconomic patterns in my hometown. Quattrone traces the company's growth from its origins in Philadelphia to a dominant manufacturer on the world stage: "The partners Henry Keasbey and Richard V. Mattison graduated from Philadelphia College of Pharmacy in 1873 and soon opened a small pharmaceutical laboratory in Philadelphia, producing Bromo-caffeine, milk of magnesia, and similar products. In 1881, seven years before the town [of Ambler] was incorporated, they moved their whole operations to Ambler, where chemical whiz Mattison, after repeated experiments, discovered the insulating properties of asbestos. . . . By the time World War I broke out in 1914, Keasbey & Mattison had become the world's largest manufacturer and supplier of asbestos [textile] products."[2]

The mainly rural Montgomery County towns such as Ambler, Flourtown, Fort Washington, Lower Gwynedd, North Wales, Broad Ax, and Blue Bell were largely populated by German American and Anglo-American families. When the new plants opened in their backyard, these residents, who worked primarily as farmers, farmhands, and artisans, were hesitant to become laborers. As a result, starting in 1883, the company turned to Europe to recruit its proletarian class—an immigrant workforce. Curiously, however, for reasons that I haven't been able to determine, a small segment of the proletarian class that Keasbey & Mattison brought to Ambler was recruited from a community of African American farm laborers in Westmoreland County, in the eastern region of Virginia known as Tidewater. In 1860, the Tidewater counties had a Negro population that contained more free Negroes (59 percent) than enslaved (39 percent). After the Civil War, thousands of Black families among Westmoreland County's formerly free Negro population migrated across the Chesapeake River and headed north to Maryland, Delaware, Pennsylvania, and beyond.[3] Keasbey & Mattison drew a factory labor force from this population from the 1880s into the early decades of the twentieth century–roughly the same period when many African Americans were recruited to work on the farms of Penllyn. "To build the business, as well as the town that would shelter his burgeoning workforce," Quattrone writes, "Mattison hired laborers from France, Germany, Poland, Hungary, and Ireland, *and African Americans from Westmoreland County, Virginia.* Perhaps his greatest contribution to Ambler's long-term life was importing countless Italian stonemasons and builders. . . . At the start of the 20th century, with the help of these workers, Mattison created modern-day Ambler."[4]

Quattrone's evidence regarding Keasbey & Mattison's conscious decision to recruit African Americans for its early labor force has influenced my view of Richard Mattison as a benevolent capitalist owner in an American company town. Such a business decision during the first decade of the twentieth century was not typical of American companies, regardless of their size. After all, racist attitudes toward Black people were widespread in American society in the early 1900s and were held by both upper-middle- and working-class white Americans. Such racist attitudes applied especially to the hiring of laborers in factories, which meant that Black workers were typically at a disadvantage when seeking factory jobs. The creation of the federal Fair Employment Practices Committee under President Franklin Roosevelt in 1941, which required the hiring of Black laborers by companies with federal wartime contracts (e.g., automobile and shipbuilding companies, clothing producers that made armed forces uniforms, food-processing companies that sold to the armed forces), was necessary to change the complexion of the American workforce.[5]

The most noticeable feature of the Mattison family's benevolence was that by 1900, the ownership had built some four hundred homes for its factory laborers. These solid-stone and brick row houses were available to workers at low rent or low mortgage payments. If you visit my hometown today, you'll find most of them still standing—along Church Street in East Ambler, in the old Irish American and Polish American Upper Dublin neighborhood in Northeast Ambler, on Old Ambler Road and Orange Street in Central Ambler, and in working-class neighborhoods in South and West Ambler. Many of my Italian American and African American childhood friends lived in those Mattison-built homes during the 1930s and 1940s.

The Mattisons also funded the early elementary school and contributed to the early public school system's budget; as a result, the elementary school was named after Richard Mattison. Frank Quattrone recognizes other elements of Mattison's philanthropy, pointing out that "he built the streets and Trinity Memorial Episcopal Church [a magnificent edifice constructed in memory of a deceased child], improved the town's water supply and introduced electric streetlights, enhanced culture by building Ambler's first opera house and [public] library and sponsoring plays and other entertainment, and generally took good care of his employees."[6]

From the 1920s through the 1940s, the managerial class at Keasbey & Mattison and others of Ambler's professional class enjoyed attending performances staged by opera companies out of Philadelphia. The monumental three-story Ambler Opera House, however, was not entirely off-limits to poorer folks and staged events mainly for Ambler's working class. I remember quite vividly the events geared toward Ambler's so-called masses. Italian American and African American working-class children looked forward to an event that took place each year during the week before Christmas, a company-funded party that involved a Christmas chorus made up of church choirs, performances by clowns, and especially the distribution of fruit and candy. The other Opera House event I recall well was the annual March of Dimes gathering that Ambler's public schools and churches mobilized Ambler's youth to attend. From my father's church, it was the women's auxiliary that got us there.

The Opera House had the largest and most adorned auditorium most of the town's working-class kids had ever seen, and that was probably true for the middle-class kids, too. The only other sizable auditorium most of us had experienced was the Ambler Movie Theater, the town's only cinema, which was located on the commercial thoroughfare Butler Avenue. It is still standing today, but the Keasbey & Mattison Company factories that covered a mile along the Reading Railway line in South and West Ambler were sold to a plastic company in the early 1960s. To the chagrin of building-preservation advocates in Ambler—including me—the new factory owners were faraway capitalist outsiders with no community ties to Ambler and demolished the magnificent Ambler Opera House in what they claimed was a "sign of progress."

While Richard Mattison's upper-middle-class mindset was largely benevolent, it contained certain deviations that, while not malevolent, hewed more closely to the dictatorial. This was natural, because we human beings will never master the purely benevolent character; that belongs to God alone.

Mattison and his inner circle of upper-middle-class WASP managers believed in a rigid pattern of ethnic and class organization of housing among the social groups living in Ambler. Quattrone describes "the magnificent stone mansions on 'Lindenwold Terrace' . . . for his executives" and "the twin houses [built of stone] along Highland Avenue for his [factory] supervisors."[7] These homes were built solely for executives and middle managers, respectively, all of whom were white.

In her 1992 article "Gay Talese Traces Roots in Ambler," based on interviews with Talese about his memoir *Unto the Sons*,[8] *Philadelphia Inquirer* sociology reporter Wendy Greenberg writes: "Dr. Mattison believed in racial segregation and in establishing a kind of caste system within [Ambler's] residential community. He had selected certain areas of Ambler where housing could be built for black and Italian families—two groups that he saw as having potentially a stable place in his community as employees in Keasbey & Mattison's asbestos factories. . . . While he would not permit blacks and Italians to rent houses on the same blocks, both groups would inhabit the residential area closest to the factories."[9]

This rigid organization of housing by ethnicity, race, and class was emblematic of the pattern that existed during this period in company towns and cities across the country.[10] The middle- and upper-middle-class WASP community (Anglo-Americans, Scots Americans, German Americans, Dutch Americans, and so forth) also lived within their own social enclaves.

Workable Ethnic and Racial Patterns

The quest for workable and fair ethnic and racial patterns in the industrializing phase of American society was a long and difficult one. It started in the 1880s, when white ethnic populations exploded—notably those of the Irish, Jews, Italians, and Poles—as a result of massive waves of immigration from Europe to the United States and lasted through the third-generation period of the mid-1950s and 1960s, by which time Americanization of these groups had become acceptable in the eyes of the WASP groups. Until this "WASP acceptability" became more commonplace, these white immigrant-descended groups remained separated socially and culturally from the established WASP groups, which held them in generally low regard, as has been documented by many sociological studies.[11] Of course it is common knowledge among all kinds of Americans that it has taken much longer for African Americans, who had to gain freedom from slavery before they could get on the "conveyor belt of American equality" and reach the status level of either the established WASP groups or the white ethnic immigrant groups.[12]

The road to workable and fair ethnic and racial patterns in my hometown was paved by the melting-pot–friendly public school system. Another liberal social dynamic that advanced equitable ethnic and racial patterns in Ambler was one I call liberal civic activism. It was a counterweight to a variety of forms of racial bigotry that existed in my hometown.

All working-class Italian Americans and African Americans who grew up in Ambler when I did experienced some form of ethnic and racial bigotry. When my Italian American childhood friends walked or bicycled through Irish American, Polish American, and WASP neighborhoods, they endured the humiliation of ethnic slurs. When they reached their teenage years and thought maybe they could get work as soda jerks, stock boys, or sales clerks at one of the mainstream commercial stores in Ambler such as F. W. Woolworth's, the Brennan & Brady Pharmacy, or the Ambler Trust Company, they experienced discrimination. Such jobs went more regularly to white youth from Irish and WASP backgrounds.

But while African Americans were not the only group to be subject to prejudice, they experienced a unique pattern of bigotry, not only in Ambler but in most American towns and cities outside the South, from the end of the Civil War onward.

This pattern persisted because of the institutional framework of social life in our country, as everyday businesses such as restaurants, hotels, banks, and movie theaters often discriminated against African American citizens. Although this pattern prevailed in Ambler during my youth, it did not do so in the perniciously legalistic way that it was carried out in the former Confederate states. In his classic 1944 study *An American Dilemma: The Negro Problem and Modern Democracy,* the sociologist Gunnar Myrdal summarized the core, vicious character of Southern racism: "It is the custom in the South to permit whites to resort to violence and threats of violence against the life, personal security, property and freedom of movement of Negroes. . . . There is a whole variety of behavior, ranging from mild admonition to murder, which the white man may exercise to control Negroes. . . . Any white man can strike or beat a Negro, steal or destroy his property, cheat him in a transaction and even take his life without much fear of legal reprisal."[13]

Thankfully, Ambler didn't resemble these dark places in the least, but nevertheless, benign racist patterns without a doubt existed in my hometown—if any racist patterns can be called benign. While their lives may not have been physically in danger, this insidious, persistent racism had a lasting impact on Ambler's Black folks, causing them unhappiness, personal and emotional pain, and maybe even a sense of not belonging in or to America.[14]

I remember listening to my mother speaking in the 1930s with Emanuel AUMP Church folks about a painful event that had happened a decade before, when a middle-class African American visitor from Philadelphia was refused a room at the Ambler Hotel, a rather majestic stone edifice in the central part of downtown. Of course, there was nothing that Ambler's Black civic and religious leadership could do about this act of bigotry. By the 1920s, at the state, regional, and national levels, civil rights organizations— among them the NAACP (National Association for the Advancement of Colored People, founded in 1909), the National Urban League (founded in 1910), and the National Council of Negro Women (founded in 1920)— and the several mainstream Black American churches that were developing legal capabilities to oppose segregation and defend Black folks from discriminatory assaults were still in their infancy, too institutionally immature to mobilize challenges in state and federal courts. Indeed, it wasn't until 1929 that the first generation of African American civil rights lawyers had the means to found the NAACP Legal Defense Fund. This important civil rights development was realized by several of the first African American lawyers trained at Harvard Law School: William Hastie, Charles Hamilton Houston, and Raymond Pace Alexander, all of whom earned their degrees in 1923. Several Howard University Law School graduates and faculty also contributed to the development of the fund, including Thurgood Marshall (Howard Law graduate, NAACP legal counsel, and future Supreme Court justice), George Johnson and James Nabrit (Howard Law deans and practicing civil rights lawyers), and Bedford Lawson (Howard Law graduate and Washington, DC, civil rights lawyer). During my years as an academic and as a participant in several such organizations, I was fortunate to meet some of these early leaders of civil rights organizations that challenged the bigotry that was practiced even in a small American factory town such as Ambler, Pennsylvania.

The incident at the Ambler Hotel certainly wasn't the only such instance of bigotry directed at Black folks in my hometown. Because of the broad setting of segregated residential life that the Mattison family supported, virtually no Black family in early twentieth-century Ambler lived on a residential block that was inhabited by white families.

Of course, since many of the businesses in my hometown, such as Ambler Savings and Loan and the First National Bank, had connections with the Mattison family and Keasbey & Mattison Company, only one or two deviated from Richard Mattison's racial prejudices. For example, the Ambler Hotel Restaurant, Niblock Restaurant, and Howard Johnson's denied African Americans dinner service into the 1950s. The most talked-about instance of such bigotry occurred in the early 1940s, when the Howard

Johnson's, where I later worked as a busboy, refused to serve one of Ambler's most prominent Black citizens, Dr. Esquire Hawkins, the town's only African American medical doctor. Gloria Stewart Jones candidly describes the feelings that this nasty instance of racial discrimination engendered in the Ambler-Penllyn Black communities: "Even Dr. Hawkins and his wife suffered the humiliation of being refused service at the Howard Johnson Restaurant that was then located on Bethlehem Pike and Butler Avenue. . . . Niblock's Restaurant on Butler Avenue, in the heart of Ambler, was also off limits to blacks. Segregation was not only a Southern issue. It was a national problem. Ambler was our [Penllyn folks'] closest town, we patronized its . . . shops and businesses; of course we felt these [racial] slights."[15]

Racist Cultural Patterns

Of course, it was only the dozen or so middle-class African American families in my hometown and neighboring Penllyn who could afford fine meals at the three major restaurants and thereby even experience the sting of racial bigotry in that particular setting. For our communities' typical working-class African American citizens, their experience with racial bigotry lay in more pedestrian places, such as Ambler's only movie theater.

When my childhood buddies and I went to see a Saturday movie serial, such as one featuring Tom Mix, Flash Gordon, or the Lone Ranger, the Black folks sat on the right-hand side of a three-aisle seating arrangement. There were no official "Negro seats" as such. Sitting on the right side represented a cultural habit that existed from the 1920s to the 1940s. Again, Gloria Stewart Jones graphically captures this unofficial but ingrained racist behavior that we all lived with:

> Blacks were subtly segregated in the Ambler Theater. There were no signs, but if one sat in a seat other than in the back of the theater on the right side, the usher would come and make you move or try to anyway. My cousin Alicia [Stewart] and I sat wherever we wanted and refused to sit in those segregated seats. Once, after attending a Girl Scout meeting, this writer and a friend stopped at one of the drug store fountains in Ambler [Brennan & Brady Drug Store] and were ignored while the owner waited on other people who came in after us. We had our own sit-in that day and just sat there until he finally came over and sullenly waited on us.[16]

When I read this account, I marveled at the boldness of Jones and her cousin in challenging a white movie theater usher and a shop owner during the early 1940s. Then it occurred to me: Gloria and Alicia were from light-skinned middle-class Black families. Had they been working-class Black youth in the early 1940s, Gloria and Alicia would likely not have been so assertive.

Discrimination manifested itself most cruelly in educational and economic ways. Jones discusses African American students of Ambler High School who studied the commercial curriculum (typing, shorthand, book-keeping) but were rejected when they applied for summer clerical jobs in Ambler's businesses. I experienced this firsthand. I applied for a summer clerical job in a Keasbey & Mattison chemical laboratory in 1946, took and passed an entry test, but was never contacted afterward. Jones reveals that this was a common pattern in our communities: "During the '40s and early '50s, teachers [at Ambler High School] referred students for jobs in the community. White students taking commercial courses at the high school were offered summer and part-time jobs working for companies in the area [Keasbey & Mattison Co., American Chemical Paint Co., First National Bank, J. W. Craft Lumber Co., etc.] but Black students were never given that opportunity. . . . Blacks were not allowed to work [as sales clerks] at Woolworth or clerk in other stores in Ambler."[17]

It was not until the 1960s that our federal government, under Democratic presidents John F. Kennedy and Lyndon B. Johnson, enacted legislation outlawing the kind of discrimination against Black folks that Jones candidly reported on in my hometown. The Civil Rights Act of 1964 rendered illegal most forms of everyday bigotry against African American citizens, including segregated seating on public transportation and the refusal of service at a soda fountain or restaurant, department store, liquor store, bar or pub, or grocery store.

The enactment of the Civil Rights Act was facilitated by a decade of activism by African American civil rights organizations such as the NAACP, the National Urban League, the Congress on Racial Equality (CORE), the National Council of Negro Women, and the Southern Christian Leadership Conference (SCLC), led by the Reverend Dr. Martin Luther King Jr., in conjunction with liberal white groups including the Quaker organization the American Friends Service Committee and such religious organizations as the Presbyterian Church, the Congregational Church, and Reform Jewish synagogues. This activism was resisted violently by both police and white vigilante citizens groups before the ultimate passage of the federal Civil Rights Act.[18]

Enormous credit for that historic, liberal federal legislation goes to President Johnson. Despite being reared in the state of Texas, where racist patterns were the norm, he had a kind of epiphany, a conversion, to democratic decency regarding America's racist patterns. He thereby used the power of his presidential office to help America finally make illegal many of its institutionalized and customary racist practices.[19]

The Power of America's Pastime

In small factory towns in the North, liberal civic activism patterns facilitated the transition away from racial discrimination. These were typically initiatives by a small number of white upper-middle-class individuals who used a variety of local institutions to plant seeds of anti-bigotry, which could advance interracial friendships that might eventually grow into institutional arrangements. These local institutions included liberal white churches and Reform Jewish synagogues, library associations, YMCA and YWCA, local sports groups, and the Boy Scouts and Girl Scouts. In fact, the Scout headquarters in Harrisburg let it be known in 1944 that multiregional jamborees held in Valley Forge could be interracial, involving both Black and white troops.

In the case of my hometown, I don't remember liberal white churches initiating activities to facilitate friendships between African American and white youth. Neither of the Catholic parishes in Ambler (St. Joseph's in South Central Ambler and St. Anthony's in North Ambler) did anything of the sort, nor did the Presbyterian and Lutheran churches. Instead, it was the personal initiative of a liberal-minded, elite white family—the Ledeboers—who worked to nurture these patterns between Black and white youth. John Ledeboer was a vice president at Keasbey & Mattison from the 1920s to the 1950s, and in interviews I conducted with white and Black laborers in the K&M factory, they invariably viewed him as a liberal personality among the company's managerial class.

The Ledeboer family homestead was located on the prestigious Lindenwold Avenue thoroughfare that commenced at downtown's Butler Avenue and ended at the main gate of the Mattison family estate, Lindenwold. A map of Lindenwold Avenue, with its homes belonging exclusively to WASP families, would read like a "Who's Who of Elite Ambler." The King & Betz grocery that catered to the bourgeois class was located on it, as were the well-appointed homes, mansions, and medical offices belonging to some of Ambler's leading citizens. As Lindenwold Avenue crossed Bethlehem Pike it became Lindenwold Terrace, at the mouth of which was the entry gate of the Mattison family's twenty-five-acre estate. Interestingly, these elite white families were liberal-minded enough to accept that only one block away was North Ambler's African American neighborhood, where I grew up. In fact, the backyards of three white families on Lindenwold Avenue abutted the property of an African American family on North Street.

Thanks to their proximity and their principles, the Ledeboer family interacted with two groups in particular: civic-minded and liberal members of Ambler's white elite and African American community leaders who worked at Keasbey & Mattison. The Ledeboers collaborated with the African American K&M community-leader factory workers Albert Newman Sr. and Millard Scott as well as George William Sr., who worked at American Chemical Paint Company, to organize an informal youth sports group that included Black and white kids from North Ambler.[20] During the summers of the wartime years, North Ambler's WPA playground became our baseball field. This informal interaction facilitated John Ledeboer's decision in 1947 to organize in the North Ambler community an interracial sandlot baseball team also made up of Black and white teenagers, including his youngest son, Jack, who was a secondary school student at the elite Germantown Friends School.

When I use the word *informal* to describe the wartime interracial group, I mean exactly that. Our baseball activity depended upon who among the North Ambler youth showed up around ten or eleven o'clock on hot summer mornings. Maybe six would show up on one day, maybe eight on another. Whatever the number, we'd arrange some kind of pickup baseball game and play for several hours until we were exhausted or bored. Each of the guys had his own baseball glove (Jack Kleinfelder always had a left-handed first-base mitt), and Jack Ledeboer always brought several baseballs and bats. Ledeboer also brought along an old catcher's mitt that I used a lot, because I agreed to play catcher when the other guys wouldn't. It's a tough position, after all, and I never shied away from a dare!

Sometimes when the activity wound down, Jack would invite the guys back to his house, where his mother would feed us peanut-butter-and-jelly sandwiches, a glass of milk, and a glass of Kool-Aid. The guys relished Anna Ledeboer's late-afternoon goodies. I also know that my brother Richard and I, as well as the other Black youth sitting in that backyard, knew intuitively that this kind of interracial gathering at the Lindenwold Avenue home of an upper-middle-class white family during the war years was not a normal, everyday happening in the rest of Ambler, Pennsylvania. Of course none of us, Black or white, had an explanation for the interracial camaraderie going on in the Ledeboer family's backyard. But we did know that it was real, authentic, and informed by what today we call a liberal ethos. Before she died, my mother, who attended Ambler's public schools with Mrs. Ledeboer, called her and her husband "good white folks."

There was a large slate patio in the Ledeboers' backyard where the guys in our group gathered. We reached it from the old WPA playground field by trekking through a half acre of community gardens, then climbing over a split-rail fence that marked the border of another half-acre area that was divided between the Ledeboer property and the property of the Knight family, who had an apple orchard in their backyard. These community gardens belonged to three North Street Black families: the Thompsons (father Frank was a gardener by trade), the Browns, and the Newmans. I can recall seeing Andrew Newman and Robert Brown, or his son-in-law Sherman Wright, carrying buckets of water and lugging garden tools across North Street through Frank Thompson's driveway to their garden plots. They'd do this after dinner several days a week, ensuring that their crops would be ready for harvesting by early August.

At some point in the spring or summer of 1946, inspired by their son Jack, Mr. and Mrs. Ledeboer suggested transforming our informal youth sports group into a formal baseball team. One of the African American workers at Keasbey & Mattison, Sherman Wright, was persuaded by Mr. Ledeboer to organize and coach the new team. From there, the Ambler Tigers roared into life in 1947.

The Ambler Tigers

Before he died, I had several conversations with Sherman Wright about the formative phase of the team, but I never uncovered precisely how it got its name. Wright was an ideal person to lead the Tigers. From his early years in Ambler in the late 1920s, when he wed the town's first African American schoolteacher, Evelyn Brown, Sherman Wright played with semiprofessional baseball teams that had been organized in Ambler and its neighboring towns (Lansdale, Flourtown, Doylestown, Norristown). These teams were white or Black, not interracial. Wright, though, had a rather unusual relationship to the white teams. Although he clearly lived in an African American community in North Ambler, he played as a pitcher for one of the white teams. He was a fair-skinned African American, fair enough to pass, as Black folks say, which allowed owners of the white teams to ignore his identity as a Black American. Sherman Wright was born in 1908 in Westmoreland County, Virginia. The Black folks' information grapevine claimed that his father was a white landowner and his mother a Black American. Only his mother was mentioned in the official obituary that was read at Sherman Wright's funeral service at Zion Baptist Church in 1990. My mother's grandfather, Luther Clayton, was also born in Westmoreland County, Virginia, and, like Sherman Wright, was fair-skinned enough to pass.

Sherman Wright's semiprofessional baseball experience provided him top-flight baseball knowledge and savvy, both of which contributed to his perfect fit as a coach for the Ambler Tigers. He was also a gentleman in the old-fashioned meaning of that term, skillful at nurturing and disciplining teenagers. He told me that sometime between the fall of 1946 and spring of 1947, he, John Ledeboer and his son Jack, and the chief sports writer for the *Ambler Gazette* were involved in conversations that spawned the idea of a formal teenage baseball league. Shouldering the primary responsibility of arranging the league, the journalist contacted interested civic groups in nearby towns, and by June 1947, there were enough favorable responses that the league was formalized and launched.

The new Ambler Gazette Baseball League drew kids from Ambler, Fort Washington, Penllyn, Spring House, and Upper Dublin. Fort Washington, Spring House, and Upper Dublin fielded all-white teams; Penllyn's was all Black (Penllyn was still a predominantly Black community at the end of World War II), and Ambler's was interracial. Just two years after World War II, there was no doubt that something fundamentally new characterized my hometown's initiating role in pioneering a small-scale interracial teenage baseball league within a thirty-mile radius of Philadelphia County.

It was a liberal civic ethos that inspired the Ledeboer family to take on basic organizational tasks for the newly launched Tigers. This wasn't one of those Lions Club–type business families that subsidized local youth sports in exchange for having their generosity advertised on the backs of baseball jerseys. The Ledeboer family, instead, acted out of high-level cultural values, values associated with the furtherance of interracial possibilities in our country. Thanks to them, the furtherance of interracial possibilities occurred in my hometown on a small but authentic scale a decade ahead of it happening on the national stage, as the Reverend Dr. Martin Luther King Jr. catapulted the civil rights movement to the fore in the late 1950s.

The Ledeboers committed themselves financially to the Ambler Tigers, bearing the costs for establishing the team and providing uniforms, gloves, bases, and plenty of baseballs, plus an honorarium for umpires and a rental fee for use of the marvelous Lindenwold Field, a community playing field at the southeast corner of Ambler. (This field was one of two provided to Ambler by the Mattison family in the early 1920s.) They also contributed two of several automobiles required to transport the nine of us for our away games to Penllyn, Fort Washington, Upper Dublin, and Spring House.

Both John Ledeboer and Sherman Wright preferred that the team be interracial and that Black *and* white Ambler teenagers be recruited as potential players. Accordingly, a Black youth from West Ambler—Stewart Johnson—became our third baseman. There were three Italian American teenagers from South Ambler on the team: John Catanzaro (pitcher), Joe Minnio (shortstop), and John "Booty" Zollo (pitcher). From North Ambler came a racially integrated group of players. Among the white players were Jack Ledeboer (left field), Norman Wilcox (centerfield), Robert Hinkle (pitcher), and Jack Kleinfelder (first base). Among the Black players from North Ambler were my brother Richard (second base), Lewis Thompson (catcher), and me (right field and sometimes catcher). Albert Newman was the team manager.

Much to our surprise, from the first summer contest of 1947 to the last in 1949, the Tigers won two league championship trophies. Inevitably, it was the heavy hitters (home-run and extra-base hitters)—Jack Ledeboer, Lewis Thompson, Stewart Johnson, and Joe Minnio, who were also recognized as team leaders among the Tigers and among competing teams—who secured our victories. Around 2002, I received a catch-up letter from Jack containing copies of the baseball scorecards for Ambler Tigers games that he had found among his mother's papers. I was delighted that he opted to send them to me instead of discarding them. They were treasures.

Jack read the cards closely and discovered something that both he and I had completely forgotten. They revealed that the Ambler Tigers had several players who might be called steady hitters, and in that category was none other than Martin Kilson! Though I seldom smashed a double or triple, let alone a home run, I could always be counted on to hit the ball to a clear spot and thus gain first base. To my surprise, those old scorecards also revealed that I was the *best* steady hitter. A regular singles hitter was I, with an occasional double thrown in.

Perusing those old scorecards further, I discovered that I had the Ambler Tigers' best overall batting average *and* led the team in RBIS. My old man's soul was pleased no end reading those old cards that Jack Ledeboer's mother had hung onto all those years. I was only a so-so athlete while at Ambler High School, so much so that the junior high football coach advised me to "Go back to your studies, Martin" after my first year trying out. Of the two of us, it was always my younger brother, Richard, who was the athlete, making the varsity team in two high school sports.

But enough about me. After each championship, the Ledeboer family organized a championship dinner for us. Mrs. Ledeboer hosted the catered dinner in their large dining room, the delicious meal topped off by an even more delicious victory cake. Victory was truly sweet. After each dinner, Mrs. Ledeboer took a photograph of the team members, all of us dressed in our best suits and neckties. No open sport shirts for us at those special dinners at the Ledeboer home in the late 1940s—not on your life!

During one of my numerous visits to my hometown from the late 1960s onward, I ran into one of my old Italian American buddies—John "Booty" Zollo—while eating a hamburger and reading a Sunday edition of the *Philadelphia Inquirer* at a McDonald's located just behind the old Ambler railroad station in South Ambler. Booty was politically alert and even kind of radical in a primitive way. We chatted about American politics and world events. We also talked about those "old Ambler Tigers years." At one point Booty confided in me, rather emotionally: "I was never in an upper-class WASP home before those dinners, Martin. Mr. and Mrs. Ledeboer treated me to something very special, and I'll always remember it."

Liberalism

Looking back on the experience of the Ambler Tigers from my vantage point here in the early twenty-first century, I believe an appropriate American-English term for that team is *multicultural*. Players from mixed racial groups (African Americans and white Americans) and mixed ethnic groups (Italian Americans, WASP Americans, Irish Americans, Polish Americans) filled out the team's roster. Before I go on, let me insert here a historical note. It is not usually recognized that African Americans (variously called over the years *Negroes, colored people, American Negroes, Blacks,* and now *African Americans*) are both a racial group (owing to a long history of racist oppression) as well as an ethnic group, just as, for example, Irish Americans, Italian Americans, and Jewish Americans are ethnic groups. That is, African Americans possess a variety of what I'll call generic traditional attributes, among them religion, folklore, cultural traditions (foods, music [e.g., spirituals, blues, work songs]), and language patterns that define their ethnicity.

From conversations I've had since the heyday of the Ambler Tigers, I don't recall any of the former participants mentioning that formal interracial ideas were discussed at the conception of either the team itself or the overall Ambler Gazette Baseball League. Yet in everyday cultural terms, with players on the Tigers representing both Black and white teenagers, that team was an interracial endeavor—no doubt about it!

I do recall, however, that my closest friend among the players, Lewis Thompson, and I chatted now and then about the racial makeup of the team, about how unusual it was in a Pennsylvania town in the post–World War II era—an era slowly emerging from America's prewar, racist-defined past. By the time Lewis and I were tenth graders at Ambler High School, both of us had a small degree of political awareness, owing to our parents' involvement as engaged citizens. Lewis's father, Joshua Thompson, was one of two African Americans on the Montgomery County Republican Party Committee during the 1930s and 1940s, and my father always mobilized church members at Emanuel AUMP to participate in local and national elections during the 1930s.

For Lewis and me, ideas had already lodged themselves in our heads that pointed us toward a degree of positive racial understanding about what the Ambler Tigers represented beyond simply being a regional baseball team. Furthermore, a larger arena of hometown interracial tendencies was afoot during the middle and late 1940s in Ambler, one that involved modernization of a rather humdrum varsity football regime at Ambler High School until the fall term of the 1945–1946 school year. This was another example of racial progress in our town. Owing to a sports-crazed group of Ambler businessmen in the Lions Club and the Rotary Club, the idea surfaced that the high school should have a fully professional varsity football coach, not the usual faculty member who taught social studies and coached sports at the same time, which had been the practice there since the 1920s.

That shift got underway with the hiring of John Meyers in 1945. With private funding provided by local businesses, Meyers's varsity team spent two weeks in the late summer of 1945 at a professional football training camp for high school teams in the Pocono Mountains. The positive results were apparent during the 1946–1947 school year, when Ambler finished first in the Bucks–Montgomery High School Football League.

An important cultural aspect of that championship team could be seen in the ethnic groups represented. Out of forty-five first-team players, there were seventeen Italian Americans, the largest number of a particular group, followed by African Americans, with ten players. The remainder were of Irish American and WASP heritage. This was the first time in the twentieth century that a majority of first-team players on the Ambler High School varsity football team were from mainly working-class, Italian American and African American backgrounds.

In 1946–1947, my junior year, I recall vividly that something akin to a multicultural spirit reigned throughout the school's social life and, within that, a coexisting interracial spirit. One piece of social behavior that was visible the following year was the changing pattern of fraternization among the ten upper-middle-class WASP American female youth who made up the cheerleading squad. By the late 1940s, not one Italian American female had been recruited into this prominent social circle. There was an unwritten rule that the role of cheerleader was a WASP-American preserve, not yet ready to subscribe to the melting-pot–friendly attitude adopted by so much of the Ambler public school system. Yet the multicultural spirit arising from the football team's victorious 1946 season began to influence the social behavior of several cheerleaders. Between 1946 and 1948, the high school grapevine circulated news—gossip, really—that several of the upper-middle-class white cheerleaders had been fraternizing with several Italian American varsity football players. Another rumor went around that one of the cheerleaders was fraternizing with an African American player. There were some handsome youth among the Italian American and African American varsity football players, no doubt about that. While those were certainly juicy items, I don't recall any of the gossips publicly attaching names to the rumors. Discretion ruled, and the gossips respected the private lives of their peers. Finally, by the 1950–1951 school year, two new girls—one Italian American and one African American—were admitted to the revered Ambler High School cheerleading squad.[21]

A rising multicultural spirit was indeed palpable among youth at Ambler High School, and it spilled beyond the high school into the broader Ambler community. As the formation of our teenage sandlot baseball team coincided with the varsity football team's victorious two or three seasons, I believe there was a positive spillover effect between us and the high school. The multicultural spirit at the high school seeped into the Ambler Tigers' bloodstream, and vice versa. There was a great deal of crossover between the Tigers and the high school sports team. Ambler Tiger Norman Willox also played for the 1946 football team, and my friend Booty Zollo, who pitched for the Ambler Tigers, had a brother who was quarterback and captain of that team. Lewis Thompson and my brother Richard, both of whom played for the Ambler Tigers, also played varsity basketball for the high school from 1946 through 1949.

Neighborhood children at WPA Playground, Ambler, Pennsylvania, 1938. Martin Kilson is in the front row on right, with bandaged forehead. To the left of Kilson in the front row are Northern Thompson and his brother Paul; James "Skeeter" Roane and his two sisters; Charles Williams; and several Allen children. Flossie, Anna, and June Hopson are on the right end of the second row, as are Laura Mahoney and Dorothy Turner. The last row includes Erma Williams, Charles's sister.

Ambler Tigers, 1948. Front row (*left to right*): Richard Kilson, Norman Willox, Mustard Mastronmatto, John Zollo, Joe Muinnio, John Catanzaro, Martin Kilson. Back row: Sherman Wright (coach), Lewis Thompson, Jack Kleinfelder, Jack Ledeboer, Robert Hinkle, Albert Newman (manager).

61

Lincoln University freshman
advisers, 1950–1953. Front
row (*left to right*): Julian
King, Martin Kilson. Second
row: Joseph Daniels,
Donald Ukkerd, Ora
Alston. Third row: Samuel
Dismond, Ernest Smith,
Ted Whitney. King became
a lawyer; Daniels, Dismond,
Smith, and Whitney became
medical doctors; Ukkerd
became an engineer;
and Alston became a
schoolteacher. Daniels also
rose to the rank of captain in
the US Army.

Martin and Marion Kilson on their wedding day, 1959

Martin and Marion Kilson with E. Franklin Frazier, 1959

George Bond and Martin Kilson, Oxford University, 1959

Martin Kilson and Marion Kilson with their children and Martin's father, Ambler, Pennsylvania, 1968

The Kilson family, Dublin, New Hampshire, 2008. Front row (*left to right*): Hannah, Martin, Marion, Zuri, Joe, Ciaran. Middle row: Liz, Maya, Caila, Rhiana. Back row: Peter, Jacob, Phillip, Jennifer.

Martin Kilson, 1990s

Martin Kilson, 2008

Martin Kilson Dinner with former students, hosted by Lewis P. Jones, Harvard Club of New York, winter 2009. Front row (*left to right*): Douglas Schoen, Martin Kilson, Ira McGowan, Lewis Jones. Middle row: Cornel West, Richard Lyons, Charles Perkins, Lee Daniels. Back row: Michael Robinson, Henry McGee, Neil Brown.

The Kilson family, Harpers Ferry, West Virginia, 2015. Standing behind Martin Kilson are (*left to right*): Caila, Maya, Joe, Rhiana, Jennifer, Marion, Peter, Hannah, Ciaran, Jacob, Zuri, Phillip.

6

—

Lincoln University, 1949–1953:
Part I

I entered Lincoln University in the fall of 1949, starting college a year later than the rest of my Ambler High School class. I didn't want my mother to sell one of the five houses she had inherited from her father to help finance my college costs, so to raise funds, I took a job as a chef's helper at Ambler's Howard Johnson's restaurant on Bethlehem Pike, which ran between my hometown and the steel-producing city of Bethlehem, Pennsylvania, almost one hundred miles to the north.

I told a white lie to the head chef, Commander William Foster: I said I wanted to be an apprentice under him and rise to a full-chef rank one day. Commander Foster, as the kitchen staff called him, was a liberal-minded white man who had been a top-rank chef in the US Navy during World War II, held the title of commander, and served on Admiral Nimitz's command ship. After a year, I told him that I was quitting in order to attend college. His response was rather sharp: "Young man, you're a preacher's son, and you lied to me about your apprenticeship intentions when you started this job."

I had in fact planned to work for two years before quitting for college, but I was notified in May 1949 that I had been granted a State Senatorial Tuition Scholarship by the commonwealth of Pennsylvania; I had thought it would take longer before my application would be processed. The scholarship was designated for academically eligible high school graduates in Pennsylvania who would attend state-related colleges such as Allegheny, Moravian, Penn State, Susquehanna, Temple, Lincoln, and Cheyney State Teachers College (later Cheyney State University). The application had to be presented to the state government in Harrisburg through a state legislator, and mine was initially submitted by Joshua Thompson, one of two

African Americans on the Montgomery County Republican Committee. Thereafter, I had a deep personal debt to Joshua Thompson, as I often mentioned to him. In 1965, after the *Ambler Gazette* reported that I had been appointed an assistant professor in Harvard University's Department of Government (which most colleges and universities refer to as political science), I returned to Ambler to visit my mother. I also visited Chef Foster at his home on Tennis Avenue, across from Ambler High School. Standing several inches above me at six feet three inches, he hugged me, saying, "You've brought much pride to this small town, Martin. I've long forgotten about that deception you pulled many years ago in order to become my chef's helper."

Soon after, I departed Ambler for Lincoln University. My college years witnessed the birth of my leftist ideological intellectual development, and my graduate school years at Harvard saw its broadening. But what were the roots of my leftist ideological tilt *before* my college years? Alas, there were none.

When I entered college in 1949, my mind was a clean slate, ideologically speaking. However, I did carry with me to Lincoln University a kind of "baggage of attitudinal predilections." The helping-hand ethos that informed social patterns in the communities that shaped me was by no means leftist, but it might be viewed as ideologically liberal, in the sense of being socially beneficent.

I saw examples of this ethos both in families helping their own blood and in community institutions helping others. First, it influenced members of many Black families to harness their hard-earned incomes—as factory workers, launderers, chauffeurs, domestic workers, and the like—to advance their children's social mobility. Second, dinners organized by Black churches during the Depression era generated funds to assist poor families. Third, I witnessed the helping-hand ethos up close, as my clergyman father raised around one hundred Rhode Island Red chickens in the backyard of the Emanuel AUMP Church's parsonage during the Depression, often giving a roasting hen and eggs to poor Black families in our congregation, and occasionally to nonmember families too. I recall my father, responding to requests from several families, going out on a cold winter morning to retrieve hens, placing their necks on a wood block and chopping them with an ax.

Apart from an understanding of how this helping-hand ethos operated in the African American community of my childhood, I can't recall any other mental predisposition I possessed that resembled a political orientation.

However, what I did have stemmed from the insecurity derived from my mother's lower-middle-class status. For instance, she kept me and my brother Richard, one year my junior, in britches longer than our neighborhood peers because, she said at some point, "it's sinful for boys to look like grown men too soon." My brother and I were often warned not to use "swear words," though I'm not sure either of us heeded that demand as faithfully as we should have. In general, Mom reminded us that we were the sons of a preacher—"You're Reverend Kilson's boys"—and as such we were expected to "set a good example." Reinforcing this injunction, my mother often referred to the leadership role of her Civil War veteran grandfather, Jacob Laws, and her housebuilder father, William Laws, in organizing the churches in Ambler-Penllyn during the late nineteenth and early twentieth century.

I now know that my mother's concern for her sons "to stand out" reflected the nervousness about lower-middle-class status that prevailed among such African American families when I was growing up. Indeed, according to tales told at dinner by both my mother and my father, this apprehension was typical even among our free Negro ancestors in nineteenth-century Delaware and Maryland—struggling landowning farmers, artisans, and clergymen who, in the post–Civil War period, also were schoolteachers and caterers. This discomfort found expression in positive teachings and behaviors as well as in anxiety. Our mother implored us to "work hard," "save your money," and "keep your obligations." I believe that my two brothers and I honored her injunctions pretty well.

I entered Lincoln University weighed down with the baggage of those African American lower-middle-class predispositions. My mother also entertained a special regard for the well-to-do elements in African American society in general and for the few examples of those elements in my hometown in particular. In the 1930s, Ambler's Black community had a small handful of well-to-do-families. My mother was impressed by the outward status manifestations of these contractors, medical doctors and dentists, housebuilders, and grocers—a stylish automobile, fashionable clothes, a large home.

Thus, it was my mother's deepest hope that my enrollment at Lincoln University would one day result in my joining the well-to-do ranks of African American society. She wanted me to be a medical doctor. However, for reasons that remain unclear to me to this day, whatever it was about well-to-do African American families that deeply impressed my mother failed to do the same for me. No doubt I had a core respect for the manful and courtly dignity of the grocer Howard Gordon, the housebuilder Robert Brown, the construction contractor General Dickson, the dentist Foster Smith, and the medical doctor Esquire Hawkins, but I don't recall expressing my respect in the same worshipful, idealized terms that my mother did.

Instead, I entertained a certain caution toward what might be called the bourgeois mystique that surrounded the few well-to-do African American families in my hometown. I did so, I think, because of occasional comments I heard my clergyman father make when I was a little boy. Such comments communicated his wariness toward what he perceived as the standoffishness among members of these upper-crust families toward Ambler's "hardworking Negro plain folk." Although both my mother and my father came from a long line of free Negro families, largely artisans and farmers, tales my father told suggested that his ancestors traveled a hardscrabble, grit-under-your-nails route to viability. Accordingly, from conversations I had with my father when he was in his sixties, I detected he was uncomfortable with the bourgeois aura that shrouded well-to-do Black folks—uncomfortable, that is, with that pretense of specialness that the well-to-do sector generally exhibits in American society.

Thus, my father's displeasure with and leeriness toward attitudes he detected among the Black bourgeoisie was a progressive addition to the African American lower-middle-class baggage that I carried upon entering Lincoln University. Put another way, there were two strands to this baggage: an attitude of Black lower-middle-class status nervousness and one of generic respect for hardworking Negro plain folk. Both functioned as a roadmap for my sojourn at Lincoln University.

Liberal Elements

I was one of roughly one hundred African American men entering Lincoln University in the fall of 1949, joining a campus of nearly six hundred students in all. Lincoln was founded just before the Civil War, the first institution to advance the higher education of Negro youth. Concurrent with my matriculation, several other African Americans who would become prominent in their fields were entering Howard University in Washington, DC, an illustrious Negro college (as institutions of higher education for Black youth were called in 1949). Toni Morrison, the daughter of a factory worker from Lorain, Ohio, would go on to become a Pulitzer Prize–winning novelist, the Nobel laureate in literature in 1993, and a professor at

Princeton University. LeRoi Jones, the son of a schoolteacher from Newark, New Jersey, would also distinguish himself in the field of literature and as a Black nationalist intellectual under both his given name and his chosen one, Amiri Baraka. Florence Ladd, a Washington, DC, native and daughter of a Howard University administrator, would become a psychologist, novelist, and director of the Bunting Institute at Radcliffe College of Harvard University.

Indeed, some 95 percent of African American youth who entered college when I did in 1949 enrolled not in white-majority institutions but in Black-majority colleges, among them Howard University, Cheyney State Teachers College, Morgan State College, Fisk University, Hampton Institute, Dillard University, West Virginia State University, Wiley College, Talladega College, Xavier University (the only Catholic college for Blacks), and Wilberforce University. Nearly 120 Negro colleges existed at that time. "Technically" segregated or not, the vast majority of white colleges in the North, whether public or private, would admit barely a thimbleful of Black youth. Penn State admitted about twenty African American students in 1949, and the University of Pennsylvania admitted five. When the prominent novelist John Edgar Wideman entered the University of Pennsylvania a few years later in 1956, he was one of only six Black youth in the freshman class. By contrast, nearly one thousand African Americans enrolled as first-year students at Howard University in that year. In the South, only one white institution of higher education, Berea College in Kentucky, enrolled Black youth (and very few at that).

Upon entering Lincoln University, some students in the freshman class might have understood the sociological character of the administrative leadership and the faculty in the post–World War II era. But I wasn't one of them. I did know that Lincoln was a Negro college, thanks to my brother-in-law, Salathiel Brown, a 1940 graduate, and also courtesy of a brochure that the Registrar's Office sent to new students that contained a brief historical sketch of the institution. I learned that in the fall of 1945, the first African American scholar became president of Lincoln at a time when there were only three African Americans on the faculty. Having been founded in 1854 as America's first institution of higher education for Negro youth, why was it that after nearly a century, the university had such a scant African American presence on its faculty and had for the first time selected an African American president?

Although the upper-middle-class white Presbyterian families who provided the funds to launch Lincoln University several years before the Civil

War were liberal on racial issues (they participated in the antislavery movement, for instance), they nevertheless entertained a paternalistic view of who should administer and teach at a college for Negro youth. This "white folks know best" attitude defined the running of Lincoln University from its founding until 1945, some ninety-one years later!

Not surprisingly, Lincoln was one of several top-level Negro colleges founded by upper-middle-class white religious groups to embrace white paternalism. Fisk University, which was founded in 1866, had only white presidents until the appointment in 1948 of the prominent African American sociologist Charles S. Johnson. Similarly, Talladega College in Alabama didn't appoint its first African American president until the early 1950s, following the retirement of the college's last white president, Buell Gallagher, who initiated the "Afro-Americanization" of the school's administration and faculty during his presidency in the late 1930s and 1940s.

By the time Horace Mann Bond began his presidency at Lincoln University, only one African American professional had been appointed to the university's Board of Trustees, and just three African American scholars had been appointed as faculty: Joseph Newton Hill, a Lincoln graduate appointed in 1932 as a professor in English and dean of college; John Aubrey Davis, a graduate of Williams College appointed an instructor in political science in 1936; and Laurence Foster, a 1926 Lincoln graduate who was the first African American to earn a PhD in anthropology at the University of Pennsylvania and who became an assistant professor in sociology in 1940. Bond himself was a 1923 summa cum laude graduate of Lincoln who earned his PhD in sociology and education at the University of Chicago in 1934.

At the top of Bond's governance agenda for Lincoln University in the fall of 1945 was this pressing issue: how does the first-ever African American president of the oldest college for Black American youth, and among the most prestigious, go about Afro-Americanizing that institution? From conversations I had with Bond before his death in 1972, I learned that Afro-Americanization had been his goal: to intertwine facets of the university's academic milieu with the history, culture, and institutional dynamics of African Americans. During the ninety-one years before his arrival as president, the institution's academic regime differed from that of other Black colleges such as Hampton, Howard, Fisk, Wiley, and Wilberforce, where, as early as the first third of the twentieth century, aspects of the academic program had already been interlaced with the history and culture of Black people. But given the rigid paternalistic mindset that reigned among the white administrators who had previously governed Lincoln University,

Bond had a hefty task to checkmate and reverse that paternalism and its vestiges.

As discussed in Wayne Urban's biography *Black Scholar: Horace Mann Bond, 1904–1972,* during his first year as president, Bond recognized that the main perpetrator of the paternalistic governing ethos among Lincoln's administration was the incumbent dean of faculty whom his administration had inherited. Harold Fetter Grim had come to Lincoln University from the all-white Lafayette College in Pennsylvania to teach biology in the 1930s. Urban writes, "Grim took in the affairs of Lincoln University an almost proprietary interest, one that was intimately related to his long-term efforts as a benefactor of the black race. Grim was not averse to lecturing Lincoln students and alumni on the appropriate ways for them to behave."[1]

During the fall term of 1947, on the eve of the annual Howard-Lincoln football game, which was to be played at the rented Temple University stadium, Dean Grim sent a letter to the Lincoln Alumni Association chapters across the country in which he haughtily addressed them as if they were children, enjoining them to be on good behavior while in Philadelphia. Urban writes that Grim "told [Black Lincoln University alumni] that they, along with their Howard counterparts, would be 'on trial' during the game and their citizenship would be evaluated by [white] officials from the state of Pennsylvania as well as those from Temple University."[2]

The Howard-Lincoln game occupied an iconic status among alumni of both schools and thus was typically a well-attended event. "Provoked," as Bond's biographer described them, the alumni association chapter chairmen around the country reacted angrily to Dean Grim's condescending letter, giving President Bond his first opportunity to publicly challenge the paternalism Grim practiced unapologetically toward Black folks. Bond had experienced more than his fair share of this attitude in the early 1940s among the white state legislators who controlled the annual budget of Fort Valley State Teachers College in Georgia, the Negro college where he held his first presidency. Now, here in the North, Bond stood firm.

According to Urban, much to the surprise of the dean and his circle of friends in the administration, President Bond called Grim to his office and told him to cease and desist from sending public letters as an official spokesman of Lincoln University. President Bond made his reprimand official, first through a letter sent from his presidential office and then through one addressed to all the alumni chapters: "Bond assured the alumni that the dean of the university spoke only for himself and that he had recently been asked to clear all public statements about the university or to the university community with the president."[3] Unfortunately, however, key trustees who held more conservative political views never forgave President Bond for his head-on challenge to Dean Grim.

A decade later, according to Urban, in the summer of 1957, these conservative trustees—only two of whom were African American—voted to ask for Bond's resignation as he was traveling back to the United States from the West African country of Ghana, where he had gone to represent the college at the inauguration of that country's first president, Kwame Nkrumah, himself a 1930s graduate of Lincoln. This strikes me as an unseemly act on the part of the board, and Bond's widow, Julia Washington Bond, told me President Bond viewed his forced resignation as the foul event it was. Before he died, the board sought reconciliation by offering him an honorary degree, but he declined. Who, pray tell, could blame him? At virtually every level of existence on campus during Bond's tenure, a new era had been ushered in. These years witnessed an expansion of the school's Black teaching staff, a modernization of its academic curriculum, and an enhancement of the quality of student life, such as higher-quality meals served at the dining hall. (During his presidency, Bond even appointed a professional, Mrs. Renwick, to manage student meals, while her husband operated a campus barbershop.) That the conservative elements who still controlled the Board of Trustees had remained so intellectually immature as not to recognize the advances that Bond's presidency had fashioned was a downright shame.

In his drive toward the Afro-Americanization of Lincoln University, President Bond encountered a significant initial hurdle that involved a complex attitudinal issue among many Lincoln's students; namely, some of them had doubts themselves about appointing African American scholars as faculty members. This perplexing conservatism—African American students who objected to Bond's Afro-Americanization of the school—is something that I returned to again and again in my quest to understand it.

This level of conservatism was nothing new among Lincoln students. The subject, Bond discovered in doing research for his monumental work *Education for Freedom: A History of Lincoln University, Pennsylvania* (published in 1976, after his death), had been tackled head-on nearly two decades earlier by none other than Langston Hughes, himself a Lincoln student at the time. In 1929, Hughes and two fellow students, Richard Lowery and Frank B. Mitchell, coauthored an undergraduate student seminar report that contained a survey of then-contemporary student attitudes and campus life. The data were equally salient during Bond's tenure.[4] Bond summarized the report's findings regarding students' willingness—or lack thereof—to welcome African American faculty members: "To the astonishment of [Professor] Labaree and Hughes, the survey revealed that nearly two-thirds of Lincoln upper classmen [Juniors & Seniors] were strongly opposed to the appointment of Negroes to the [Lincoln] faculty."[5]

Viewed more fully, of the 129 Lincoln University students Hughes and his colleagues surveyed (out of a total student body of 323), some eighty-one opposed appointing Black scholars to the faculty, while forty-six favored it; three expressed no opinion. Fifty-two students offered the following reasons for their opposition:

Eleven said, "We [Lincoln students] are doing well as we are."
Ten said, "Students would not cooperate with Negro teachers."
Eight said, "Lincoln is [financially] supported by whites."
Seven said, "White faculty provides greater [professional] advantages for students."
Five said, "Mixed faculty would not get along together."
Five said, "Not enough capable Negro teachers available."
Three said, "Have read or know that conditions at colleges with mixed faculties are not good."
Three said, "Just do not like Negroes."[6]

Hughes—who within a decade would emerge as a top-tier African American writer and intellectual figure—is scathing in his reaction to the students' indifference to the historical and cultural experiences of Black folks. Given that the ancestors of these students, through unpaid slave labor, contributed significantly to laying the economic foundation of American society, the experiences of African Americans had deep and influential roots in our nation's history, stretching back to the seventeenth century.

Hughes writes, "The mental processes of the [conservative] hat-in-hand, yes-boss, typical white-worshiping Negro is, to my mind, very strongly shown in the attitude of some of the students here toward an all-white faculty. 63% of the members of the upper classes favor for their college a faculty on which there are no Negro professors. And since I have never heard otherwise, I judge that the faculty of Lincoln University itself supports this attitude."[7]

Hughes is most perturbed by the synergistic collaboration between students and faculty in what he views as a pattern of anti-Negro academic and attitudinal practices:

It seems to me the height of absurdity for an institution designed for the training of Negro leadership to, itself, support and uphold on its own grounds, the unfair and discriminatory practice of the American color line. And the fact that 81 members of the Senior and Junior classes at this college can themselves approve of such a situation, and give reasons for their approval which express open belief in their own inferiority, indicates that the college itself has failed in instilling in these students the very quality of self-reliance and self-respect which any capable American leader should have—and the purpose of this college, let us remember, is to educate "leaders of the colored people."[8]

Hughes's criticism of student attitudes is rivaled by his disdain for the curriculum. He makes two critical observations about the absence of courses on the history and lives of Black Americans. First, he notes, "No courses in Negro literature or writings are listed [in the catalog of courses], yet this is an institution for the education of Negro leaders who should certainly be acquainted with the writings, both past and present, of their own people." Then, Hughes ruminates, "Courses dealing with the problem of the American Negro, or courses applying the general college knowledge to those problems are lacking."[9] Indeed, he goes beyond critical description to prescribing in sharp language how to correct this deficit in Lincoln's curriculum: "For the sake of the racial pride and self-respect of the students we seek to educate [we need] the abolition of the color line on the Lincoln University faculty. For the thorough education of Negro leaders and a greater ability on part of our students to better apply their college education to the problems of their own race [we need] the addition of courses in Negro History, Negro literature and Negro Education to the curriculum."[10]

This is precisely what Horace Mann Bond sought to rectify. Owing to the absence of an Afro-American studies curriculum during Lincoln University's first ninety years, Bond, shortly after assuming its presidency, made changes in governance and academics that eventually facilitated the school's cultural shift toward Afro-Americanization. This meant that the Lincoln University I entered in the fall of 1949 was in the throes of full-fledged liberalization. Bond's first step was to increase the number of Black administrative officials and faculty. This in itself was absolutely revolutionary, like the French Revolution that challenged the rigid aristocratic order in eighteenth-century France.

As shown in table 6.1, President Bond began by appointing an African American to the post of administrative secretary. Grace Jackson Frankowsky

TABLE 6.1 Lincoln University Faculty/Staff, 1949–1953

Faculty

Humanities

Samuel Bradley (English)
*Roscoe Lee Brown (English)
*H. Alfred Farrell (English/Journalism)
Walter Fales (Philosophy)
Armsted Grubb (European Languages)
*Abram Hill (Drama Studies)
*Joseph Newton Hill (English/Dean of College)
Paul Kuehner (German/Registrar)
Francis McCarthy (Art Studies)
*James B. McRae (Education/ Dean of Men)
Andrew Murray (Dean of Theology School)
*Samuel Stevens (Assistant Dean of Theology)
*Orrin Suthern (Music)
David Swift (Religious Studies)
*Walter Waring (French)
*Emery Wimbish (Assistant Librarian)
Donald Yelton (Head Librarian)

Social Sciences

*Jerome Bryant (Sociology)
*Henry G. Cornwell (Psychology)
*Milton P. Crook (Political Science)
*John Aubrey Davis (Political Science)
*Laurence Foster (Sociology)
*Jerome Holland (Sociology)
Thomas M. Jones (European History)
Dwight W. Morrow (American History)
Sayre P. Schatz (Economics)
*Samuel T. Washington (Accounting)

Science

William Cole (Physics)
*James Frankowsky (Mathematics)
*Norman Gaskins (Chemistry)
Harold Fetter Grim (Biology/Dean of Faculty)
*Peter Johnson Hall (Biology)
DeForest Rudd (Chemistry)
*Kenneth Sneed (Biology)

Athletics

*Robert Gardner (Physical Education)
*William Hunter (Physical Education)
*Manuel Rivera (Physical Education)

Staff

*Toye G. Davis (University Physician)
*Grace Frankowsky (University Secretary)
* Julia Renwick (University Dietitian)
*Austin H. Scott (Business Manager)

* African American

was the daughter of a Lincoln alumnus. I once told Mrs. Frankowsky that I hoped she would write her memoirs, because she was present at the birth of the Afro-Americanization of Lincoln University and therefore had a special knowledge of that crucial event, but unfortunately she never did. Bond also appointed James Bonner McRae as the dean of men, Austin H. Scott as treasurer, Toye G. Davis as university physician, and Samuel Stevens as assistant dean of the School of Theology. The remaining top-level governance positions were still held by white Americans: Dean Grim, Paul Kuehner, the registrar, and Andrew E. Murray, the dean of the School of Theology.

With several key administrative positions filled by African American professionals by the 1946–1947 academic year, Bond proceeded to broaden the ranks of two new groups among the university's faculty. One comprised a cadre of liberal-leaning white personalities, who were not the least bit standoffish in their personal interactions with the African American youth they were teaching. Through their behavior they exhibited a core respect for African American realities.

Among the professors whom Bond inspired the trustees to appoint were Thomas Jones in history and David Swift in religious studies. Both were Quakers who, as young men, had been pacifists and antiwar activists. Another white Quaker scholar appointed by Bond was Dwight W. Morrow in history. He was the son of Dwight Whitney Morrow Sr., a US senator from New Jersey and the ambassador to Mexico during that country's revolution in the early 1920s. Bond's presidency also witnessed the appointment of the first Jewish American professor at Lincoln University,

Sayre Schatz, a liberal economist who after several years at Lincoln became a full professor at Temple University, where he evolved as a leading scholar of African economic development and published the first major book on the Nigerian economy.[11] Another white academic appointed during Bond's presidency was DeForest Rudd, who served as chair of the Department of Chemistry. On a biographical note, Rudd was married to an African American woman.

By the time I started at Lincoln, Bond had begun a second wave of hiring African American academics. (Their names appear in table 6.1.) The introduction of these scholars strengthened and broadened curricula across all disciplines. James Frankowsky in mathematics, Norman Gaskins in chemistry, Peter Johnson Hall in biology, and Kenneth Snead in biology brought a new level of expertise to the teaching of the sciences. Milton Crook in political science, Jerome Bryant and Jerome Holland in sociology, and Henry Cornwell in psychology expanded the purview of the social sciences, and H. Alfred Farrell in English and journalism, Roscoe Lee Brown in English, and Orrin Suthern in music had a powerful impact on the humanities. Abram Hill broadened interest in drama studies by bringing top-rank actors, including Ruby Dee, to the university to perform in plays that he directed, while the Music Department developed a first-rate choir that produced brilliant performances of classical music and Negro folk and religious music, especially Negro spirituals. In addition, a group of first-rate creative writers was launched on campus, thanks especially to English faculty such as Dean Hill and Professor Farrell.

Under President Bond, there was also a politicization of liberal discourse, by which I mean growth—albeit slow—of an orientation toward civil rights activism among a small sector of students and professors. This leftward shift was partly evidenced in the top-level intellectual personalities whom Bond invited to the university as convocation speakers.

Shortly before my class entered the university, Paul Robeson, the African American classical singer as noted for his beautiful voice as he was for his leftist politics during the 1940s and 1950s, delivered a convocation address. Another convocation speaker who displayed an outright liberal ideology was Ira Reid, a major African American Quaker pacifist and professor of sociology at Haverford College. But no invitee of Bond's was more illustrious than W. E. B. Du Bois, who spoke at a convocation during my first year. That momentous occasion took place in the university's Mary Dod Brown Memorial Chapel. I sat in the front-row pews, enrapt, eagerly imbibing the words of the great figure speaking at the podium. In the University Archives in the Langston Hughes Memorial Library are photographs of Bond with Robeson during his visit and of Du Bois with Bond and his two children, Jane and Julian. Julian Bond, of course, became a leading figure in the civil rights movement, helping to found the Student Nonviolent Coordinating Committee (SNCC) and serving as chair of the NAACP's national board for more than a decade.

Experiencing the multilayered facets of the university's liberalization had a major intellectual and ideological influence on me. I found especially powerful my experience in Bond's full-year course, The Negro in the Old and New World, in which he discussed the dynamics surrounding the Civil War and especially the postwar federal government policy of Reconstruction, which he had studied in his University of Chicago doctoral dissertation.[12]

Outside the classroom and beyond the confines of the campus, during the 1948–1949 academic year, Bond himself contributed directly to hands-on civil rights activism. He participated in an early example of what later became known as sit-in activism when he joined professors John Aubrey Davis and Laurence Foster and the student NAACP branch, led by senior Jacques Wilmore, to stage a demonstration in the neighboring town of Oxford, Pennsylvania.[13]

The group entered the Oxford Hotel, the town's only hotel, which was located in the center of town, to have lunch and a drink. They were refused service and decided to sit in. After the police were called to remove them, they proceeded to picket the hotel. Of course, civil rights activism back in the late 1940s was both courageous and dangerous in southern Chester County, Pennsylvania. That part of Chester was known to be home to the Ku Klux Klan in the post–World War II years. One branch of the Klan was located in Oxford's neighboring town of Rising Sun, at the boundary between Pennsylvania and Maryland. The picketing event was groundbreaking—an early instance of the sit-in tactic so famously and courageously employed throughout the South in the decade following—and, given the involvement of the Lincoln University president and two of its professors, newsworthy. The event was reported in Negro news organs around the country, including *Jet* and *Ebony* magazines and the weekly newspapers including the *Philadelphia Tribune* and New York City's *Amsterdam News*.

One might have thought that a momentous and unprecedented activist event at a Negro college during the late 1940s would have sparked campus-wide discussion among my enrolling Class of 1953, but this was not the case. Once again, Langston Hughes helps to explain why.

Hedonistic Students

As the 1949–1950 fall semester passed into spring, I learned about the Oxford Hotel incident from the first left-wing Lincoln student I encountered on campus, Roland Jones. Like me, he was one of four first-year students to whom the dean of students, James Bonner McRae, had given a campus job as a dishwasher—a job which provided income for some of my basic first-year costs, such as books, notebooks, toiletries, and even a new article of clothing now and then. Roland Jones was from Philadelphia, the son of a longshoreman on the city's docks who was in the left-wing Longshoreman Workers of America. My other two dishwasher mates were Alfred Kase, also from a working-class family in Philadelphia, and Samuel Woodward of East Orange, New Jersey, who, like me, was from a lower-middle-class family.

Roland Jones was disappointed that the picketing and sit-in at the Oxford Hotel did not generate serious civil rights interest on campus during our first semester. Samuel Woodward and I asked why this was so, and Roland's answer was a real eye-opener for me.

Hailing from the big urban area of Philadelphia, Roland had a keen understanding of the social and cultural mindset of the largest pool of students on Lincoln's campus, who came from similar areas—New York City; Newark–East Orange, New Jersey; Philadelphia; and Baltimore-Washington. He had discovered from big-city students in his dormitory that they embraced a kind of hedonism ethos, their worshipful materialism reinforced by an obsession with status climbing. It was beyond a normal American social-mobility quest. Roland learned that the campus Greek fraternities were the primary propagators of this hedonism, which he described as "a rage among many upperclassmen"—so much so that he concluded there wasn't much appetite among Lincoln students for civil rights activism. I recognized this fact myself in the fall term of my sophomore year, when several student friends and I attended a meeting of the campus NAACP branch, which had about a dozen members.

Thanks to Roland Jones, who became a leading Baptist clergyman and civil rights figure in Philadelphia after graduating from Lincoln, I had my first intellectual introduction to the hedonistic mania for status climbing that reigned on Lincoln's campus during my undergraduate years. I soon discovered that my brother-in-law, Salathiel Brown, who attended Lincoln from 1936 to 1940, had deceived me somewhat when he told me before I enrolled that "you'll encounter lots of academically stimulating students at Lincoln, Martin." I was myself an academically engaged high school student, so much so that two of my favorite teachers insisted that I attend college.

As I became interested in writing about my undergraduate years, I was perplexed by this widespread hedonistic ethos and political conservatism. Turning back to Bond's brilliant historical work on the university, *Education for Freedom*, I discovered that the mind-boggling mindset I encountered among undergraduates had antecedents on Lincoln's campus a whole generation before my class arrived, and those antecedents were perverse in their ideological implications. Langston Hughes had addressed the topic in his seminar report. He and his coauthors were unusual among their peers in that they occupied the progressive side of the political spectrum during the first year of the Great Depression.[14] Their findings on the student body's view toward Black educators dovetailed with the students' lack of interest in activism. It was beyond a lack of interest; it was an obstacle, not only at Lincoln University but at some other Negro colleges during the 1920s.

Some, but certainly not all. At Negro colleges in the South, Black students had begun to press for the appointment of African American professors at their schools. In his study of this early wave of Black student mobilization to expand integrated faculties at Negro colleges, University of Maryland professor Raymond Wolters connects it with the "New Negro Movement," a broader Black intellectual activism that had evolved in several urban areas, including New York City, Chicago, Philadelphia, and Cleveland, during the 1920s.[15]

Yet, for some strange reason, the undergraduates at Lincoln University seemed unaware of the civil rights activism that was rampant at other Negro colleges, and Hughes makes no mention of it in his report. It is interesting, though, that his concluding paragraph on the issue of an integrated faculty refers to several cases of Black academics teaching at other Negro colleges. He begins this paragraph by dismissing outright the various reasons that some Lincoln undergraduates gave in defense of their opposition to having African American faculty members. "Upon careful inspection," he writes, "none of these reasons is found to be a strong one." Hughes continues:

> There is a mixed faculty at Fisk, and certainly the work done there is quite on par with Lincoln. Howard University, with a predominantly Negro faculty, produces graduates no less capable than our own. Both Howard and Fisk are supported, to some extent, by white philanthropy, but their faculties

are not all white. . . . Tuskegee has an all Negro faculty, as have many other schools dependent upon white philanthropy. (But have we forgotten that for 300 years Negro slavery created wealth for whites? Must we need stoop so low as to believe that we are thanking white philanthropy by saying we are not fit to become teachers in our own schools?) And certainly [with] men like [sociologist] Charles S. Johnson, [historian Charles] Wesley, [writer and philosopher Alain] Locke . . . and [biologist Ernest] Just in the teaching fields, besides large numbers of colored graduates every year from the best Northern schools, it is stupid to say that there are no capable Negro teachers available. Not an all Negro faculty—possibly not even a predominantly colored faculty is to be desired, but certainly one of our 11 professors might well belong to the race from which all of the 323 resident students of this institution come.[16]

I searched the report for commentary on the conservative pattern among Lincoln students of the 1920s–1930s that might connect it with the conservatism that my dishwashing circle and I discussed during the spring term of 1950. I found it in a subsection titled "The Students," where Hughes presents basic sociodemographic attributes of the university's 323 students in 1929. "Slightly more than half of them are from the South where both educational and cultural opportunities for the Negro are below the American standard," he writes, adding, "Their ages range from 17 to 32, but by far the larger group falls in the late teens and early twenties."

Hughes fashions a general sociological portrait of Lincoln University students, which makes clear that the vast majority came from working-class homes and therefore entered Lincoln with a narrow range of sociocultural experiences. Many students, he says, had "parents not 'educated' in the college-trained, well-read sense of the word" and "lack[ed] . . . adequate scholastic preparation exemplified in poor Southern schools." He concludes:

Such is the background of the majority of the students at Lincoln University. Certainly very few of them are in any sense rich. Of the 129 students in the two upper classes, only 7 do not work regularly during the summer. And the kinds of work done by our students [in summer] can scarcely be called elevating or worthy of the intellectual capacities of a college man. [For example] 77 or more than three-fourths of these students are [domestic] servants doing menial labor for white people [e.g., waiters, bus boys, Pullman porters, redcaps, cooks, valets]. 5 are unskilled manual workers. Thus, more than four-fifths of the total number are engaged in summer occupations which require no usage of their college training or their mental intelligence.[17]

The only other account of Lincoln University students and their backgrounds in the early years of the twentieth century that I am aware of—an autobiography by William Ashby, who graduated in 1911—presents characterizations similar to those described by Hughes. The son of a seamstress mother who worked hard to accumulate his fifty-dollar college tuition, Ashby might be described as a lower-middle-class student among a sea of students from working-class backgrounds. He grew up in East Orange, New Jersey, and after graduating from Lincoln he went to Yale University's School of Theology, returned to New Jersey, and became the first director of the National Urban League Newark branch.

Ashby describes Lincoln as "remotely located, halfway between Philadelphia and Baltimore. There are no big towns near it. The rural surroundings afforded no avenue whatever for student recreation or pleasure. We had to invent our own fun. Only on the rarest occasions could we expect to get to the city."[18] (Many students of the era came to Lincoln via a railway line from Chester, Pennsylvania, that passed through a village four miles south of the Lincoln campus—originally an Underground Railroad settlement—on its way south to Wilmington, Delaware. By the end of World War II, it transported freight only.) Ashby continues:

> No parents enjoyed the financial affluence to send their boy to Lincoln and pay the entire cost of his education. All of us worked to earn our way through college. There were three occupations open to us. We could be waiters or bellboys at a summer resort hotel at the [Atlantic Ocean] shore or in the [New York] mountains. We could be porters (perhaps waiters if lucky) on a Pullman train. We could be porters, waiters, linen men, or checkroom clerks on the Hudson River boats, plying between New York and Albany, or boats to Fall River, Providence, or Boston.[19]

Writing eighteen years after Ashby's graduation, Langston Hughes saw the working-class background of most Lincoln students as the main explanation for their overwhelmingly conservative orientation. These students, he believed, had grown up in an overall proletarian milieu that did not provide them with a broad understanding of and appreciation for the cultural and institutional achievement of Black folks throughout American history. And, as Hughes knew well, those achievements were realized against the grain of centuries of American slavery and following the failure of postwar Reconstruction policy, leading to decades of white racist restrictions on Black people's participation in American life.

A generation after Hughes's college years, during the post–World War II era of the 1950s, there were still social class patterns among Lincoln students that facilitated a continuation of conservatism—what my dishwashing circle and I viewed as hedonistic orientations. But both the social class patterns and the conservative orientations differed somewhat from those of Hughes's student days.

Specifically, the mainly working-class students who prevailed on the Lincoln campus of Langston Hughes were replaced twenty to thirty years later by a cohort of primarily middle-class students. Some were from lower-middle-class families (carpenters, bricklayers, barbers, clergy, salespersons, postal clerks), others from solid middle-class families (nurses, schoolteachers, businesspersons, school administrators, barbers, caterers, electricians), with a few from upper-middle-class families (lawyers, doctors, dentists, newspaper owners, well-off businesspersons, and administrators).

By the time I was a student at Lincoln, only a minority segment of students were from the working class, meaning that there was not a generic conservatism prevalent on campus like the one that Hughes had described in his 1929 report. Roland, Samuel, Alfred, and I realized that the conservatism that existed among our peers was not deferential to white folks; it was not demeaning or of the "hat-in-hand" sort, as Hughes calls it. Instead, it was what might be called an establishmentarian conservatism orientation. The post–World War II students on the Lincoln campus (and on other postwar Black college campuses such as Atlanta University, Fisk, Howard, and Morgan State) who brought to college a more cynical middle-class consciousness than was found at Lincoln in the 1920s and 1930s had become especially aware of the status boundaries between themselves and the Black working-class and poor masses, whose numbers were expanding in postwar urban communities.

Lincoln University, 1949–1953: Part II

During my four years at Lincoln University, the prominent African American sociologist E. Franklin Frazier, a professor at Howard University, produced his notable book *Black Bourgeoisie: Rise of the New Black Middle Class*. The book had to be published overseas, in Paris, because no major American publisher would touch it, owing to its polemical assault on what Frazier called the Black bourgeoisie's "world of make-believe," what he saw as its exaggerated aping of white middle-class patterns in the postwar years. For Frazier, that mimicry also involved an obsession of the Black middle class with distancing itself from the social patterns of most Black folks, who were still toiling as domestic servants for white families or employed as low-paid agricultural and factory working-class citizens.[1]

Student Liberalism

Faced with many undergraduate peers who exhibited a conservative, worshipful deference toward the Black bourgeoisie, my dishwashing buddies and I began to discuss how to inspire a liberal student consciousness. When we enrolled as freshmen, there was already evidence of a liberal faculty consciousness as far up as President Bond's office, demonstrated particularly by the faculty and student sit-in at the Oxford Hotel the previous year. That liberalness, however, had not yet come close to penetrating the student body.

Why was this so? Unlike Langston Hughes and his two colleagues back in 1929, we didn't conduct an official poll of student attitudes. We did, however, engage in conversations with a number of our peers during the fall term in 1950, and those conversations revealed an important fact: Greek-letter fraternities were what you might call conveyor belts of bourgeois conservatism among Lincoln students.

According to Hughes's seminar report fraternities had an even greater influence in the 1920s and 1930s than in my era. "Over all student activities here at Lincoln like a guiding hand, or shall we say like a dark shadow?— there hovers the fraternity," Hughes writes. "There are four on campus: the Phi Beta Sigma, the Kappa Alpha Psi, the Alpha Phi Alpha, and the Omega Psi Phi. Their total membership numbered 145 students, approximately three fourths of the student body above the Freshmen Class. Of the 129 upper classmen, only 26 do not belong to a fraternity." Hughes describes the enormous impact of fraternities on the lives of undergraduates: "In the Senior Class only four men are non-frat. Of the 28 campus leaders (including club and class presidents, athletic captains, managers, student councilmen, and student instructors) all but one are Fraternity men, and that one has long been pledged. This would indicate that it is highly improbable, if not impossible, for a non-frat-man to hold a position in student activities if said position must be gained by student voting. Fraternity politics control all positions of campus leadership."[2]

During the lead-up to my class's fiftieth reunion, my wife, Marion, and I thought it would be useful to survey the surviving members of the Class of 1953. We asked the Alumni Office to mail a questionnaire we prepared to all living alumni from the class and compiled their responses in a booklet, *A 2003 Portrait of the Lincoln University Class of 1953*.[3]

Table 7.1 shows some basic attributes of the class: home state, academic major, and fraternity membership. The data are based on the graduation yearbook of the Class of 1953, which included the photographs of the seventy-two students who sat for their portraits (thirty class members didn't show up) as well as basic attributes about them. Among the seventy-two graduates, forty-five were fraternity members, which represented two-thirds of the students photographed. The largest fraternity membership was claimed by Alpha Phi Alpha, with twenty members. Kappa Alpha Psi had the second-largest membership, with ten members, followed by Omega Psi Phi with seven, and Beta Sigma Tau and Phi Beta Sigma with four each.

In our booklet, Marion and I included a discussion of the status of campus fraternities while I was a student. We wrote that "we think [60 percent fraternity membership] was a rather high proportion of Lincoln undergraduates linked to fraternities in the 1949–1953 years, and it was also

TABLE 7.1 Attributes of the Lincoln University Graduating Class of 1953

Home State (N = 66)*

Alabama 1
Connecticut 1
Delaware 3
Georgia 2
Illinois 1
Maryland 1
Missouri 2
New Jersey 9
New York 6
Pennsylvania 34
South Carolina 1
Washington, DC 5

Major Academic Fields

Humanities

English 2

Social Sciences

Economics 6
History 6
Political Science 9
Psychology 5
Sociology 6

Math/Sciences

Biology 25
Chemistry 8
Physics 1
Mathematics 2
Physical Education 2

Fraternity Membership (N = 45)

Alpha Phi Alpha 20
Beta Sigma Tau 4
Kappa Alpha Psi 10
Omega Psi Phi 7
Phi Beta Sigma 4

*The Class of 1953 also included 6 students from Nigeria.

Source: Questionnaire Survey and 1953 Lincoln University Yearbook

somewhat unfortunate." Some might have been surprised by this negative observation, but we outlined the reason behind it:

> The undergraduate years of the Class of 1953 coincided with the formative years of the rise of the militant and radical phase of the Negro Civil Rights Movement. . . . Our point here is that the sizable number of undergraduates in the 1949–1953 years who belonged to Greek Letter fraternities, the partying life character and macho-male "hazing" character of activity among Lincoln's fraternities in this era were politically reactionary. The "partying-life" and macho-male "hazing" features of Greek Letter fraternities isolated a large segment of Lincoln students from participation in [and from learning about] those important civil-rights activist trends going on simultaneously among African-Americans. Trends like the NAACP Legal Defense Fund's challenge in federal courts of school segregation. . . . The Fund was directed by a Lincoln alumnus by the way—attorney Thurgood Marshall who in the 1960s became the first African-American U.S. Supreme Court justice.[4]

I joined Lincoln's small NAACP branch during my freshman year. From that point through my senior year, the organization had maybe a dozen members. By this time, my circle of buddies had expanded beyond my dishwashing friends to include, among others, Frank Hutchings, an upper-middle-class student from Georgia whose father and grandfather were morticians and Lincoln graduates; Robert Gregg, a middle-class student from Baltimore whose grandfather graduated from Lincoln during the 1920s; Ernest Smith, a lower-middle-class student from Bethlehem, Pennsylvania; and Joseph Daniels, a working-class student from Linden, New Jersey. Several others were fleeting members of our circle: working-class students Bernard Duncan, from Baltimore, and Thomas "Mingo" Williams, from Atlantic City, New Jersey; and middle-class students Samuel Diamond, from Richmond, Virginia, and Richard Marshall, from Washington, DC.

The lunch-and-dinner conversations among my growing circle at the Refectory, the campus dining hall, located in McCauley Hall, centered on a variety of topics related to African American society in general and to campus life, including the prominence of fraternities and their conservative influence. One aspect of fraternity life that drew particular ire from my friends was their apparent indifference to the budding civil rights activism across the country.

The framework of a new civil rights activism was then evolving, thanks to activist Black clergy in much of the urban South, activist leaders of NAACP branches in both the North and South, and such prominent Black intellectual figures as W. E. B. Du Bois, Paul Robeson, Esther Jackson (founder of the Southern Negro Youth Congress in the 1930s and 1940s), and Charlotta Bass (editor of Los Angeles's African American weekly *California Eagle*), who linked up with left-wing white organizations such as the Progressive Party. The movement was taking place largely in major Black urban communities on the East Coast—in New York, Philadelphia, Baltimore, and Washington, DC—and farther south in such cities as Richmond, Atlanta, and Charlotte. On the national level the NAACP and its Legal Defense Fund functioned as the "coagulating instrument" of those budding Black-activist agencies. By 1954 that activism bore fruit with the landmark civil rights case *Brown v. Board of Education,* in which the US Supreme Court declared segregation in public schools unconstitutional. By 1955, activism would also spark the Montgomery bus boycott in Alabama, catapulting a young Black clergyman named Martin Luther King Jr. to the forefront of the nascent civil rights movement. It would also make a household name out of Rosa Parks, a valorized civil rights activist from a middle-class community in the Deep South.

Thus, by the spring term of my sophomore year in 1951, several of my liberal buddies and I decided to openly criticize the campus fraternities for not using their outsize influence to wake Lincoln undergraduates to the burgeoning civil rights movement. We started with a caucus meeting attended by Roland Jones, Frank Hutchings, Robert Gregg, Alfred Kase, Richard Marshall, Ernest Smith, and me, as well as a couple of other students whom I can't recall. Together, the group composed a letter to the campus weekly newspaper, the *Lincolnian,* in which we took to task our fellow students for their compulsive commitment to the affairs of fraternities while ignoring the growing interest in civil rights off campus, where activists were issuing head-on challenges against the American racist oligarchy that nakedly and violently blocked a majority of the country's Black citizens from equal citizenship rights and full-fledged participation in American society.

Our liberal circle felt that it was morally shameful for Black students to exhibit such glaring indifference to the burgeoning civil rights movement. Because a couple of members of our circle knew that I could type (I had taken a typing course in high school), they asked me to draft a letter. I did so on an old Royal typewriter that was available to students in a meeting room in the basement of Amos Hall, the campus activities building. I placed the letter in the mailbox of the *Lincolnian*, but you could say it went nowhere. To the surprise of all of us, the editors refused to print it, no doubt out of loyalty to their fraternity brothers.

At our next meeting, the majority of our members wanted to drop the matter. I dissented, as did Frank Hutchings—my closest friend in our liberal circle—and I suggested to Frank that if the paper wouldn't print it, we should. Nothing was stopping us from copying the letter on the mimeograph machine located in the basement of Amos Hall and then distributing it among students during lunch and dinner at the Refectory. Frank, however, hesitated to sign the letter with me (his older brother was a Lincoln graduate and a fraternity member whom he didn't want to vex), so I signed it as sole author. Going beyond the Refectory, Hutchings and I asked the head librarian, Professor Donald Yelton, if we could attach the letter to the big oak entry door of the Vail Memorial Library. Our letter stayed on that door into the fall term of our junior year![5]

While attending the 1999 Lincoln University commencement, I was catching up with academic journals in the Langston Hughes Memorial Library and ran into a member of the Class of 1952—a medical doctor from Richmond, Virginia—who asked if I recognized him. I told him that I did indeed remember his face and that he often bought double-egg milkshakes at the student canteen in Amos Hall, where I was the soda jerk during my junior and senior years. He then reminded me of a campus event involving the two of us that I had completely forgotten.

During the fall term of my junior year, the liberal circle I ran with supported my candidacy for the student council with the goal of allowing us to participate in decisions on campus-wide affairs, such as selection of the homecoming queen. The fraternities put up this future doctor as a challenger, ultimately generating enough votes to defeat me and elect him. After failing the first time, I made a second run for the student council in my senior year and won a seat, though the inner-circle fraternity members still controlled enough votes to dictate the choice of homecoming queen.

The gap between this goal and our activist motivations was not as wide as it may first appear. Throughout my undergraduate years, those homecoming queens were always very fair-skinned, middle-class women. Neither brown- nor dark-skinned candidates stood a chance at wearing the crown back then. It took the rise of a nationwide Black-consciousness movement before the color-caste patterns that prevailed at Lincoln and other Black colleges changed. The movement didn't gain steam until the late 1960s, as documented in *Ebony* magazine's annual photography section on homecoming queens at Black colleges.

Varieties of Liberal Students

Commencing with the campus NAACP chapter in my freshman year, and adding activities in subsequent years (the Social Science Club, which I helped to organize; the Philosophy Club, of which I was president my junior year; and the Lincoln debating team, directed by Dean Hill, which I joined as a junior), I became part of a network of liberal-leaning students who functioned as an activist counterweight to the Black bougie campus world that the fraternities inspired and sustained.

The Philosophy Club and the Social Science Club were concerned with the reading and discussion of materials related to our courses, especially of student papers. But in the NAACP branch, broad political issues were discussed, particularly the emergent national civil rights activism among Black folks of the time. Our campus had launched the first-ever NAACP student branch back in 1916, when Archibald Grimké, chair of the NAACP branch of Washington, DC, the most prominent one in the country, traveled to Lincoln to inaugurate it. Grimké was an 1870s graduate of Lincoln and an 1880s Harvard Law School graduate. He was a colleague of W. E. B. Du Bois, supporting the Niagara Movement that Du Bois helped found in 1905 and himself serving as a founding member (along with Du Bois) of the NAACP in 1909.[6]

Students who belonged to the campus NAACP branch represented a sweeping cultural and ideological range. Witold Cohn was a refugee from Soviet-dominated Poland who got to Lincoln University through the Quaker American Friends Service Committee, which helped place refugee students at American colleges. Several students from West African countries gravitated toward our branch, among them Charles Dennis, a Liberian from one of his country's governing elite families, and Nigerians Nwabueze Agbin, Kalu Ezera, and Olufemi Akinrele, who was my roommate during my junior and senior years. The remaining members were African American students, including my dishwashing buddies Alfred Kase and Roland Jones; my closest undergraduate friend, Frank Hutchings; middle-class students Eugene Brockington, from Philadelphia, Richard Marshall, from Washington, and Robert Gregg, from Baltimore;

and working-class students Joseph Daniels, from New Jersey, and Ernest Smith, from Bethlehem, Pennsylvania.

Several of my closest friends were interested in the academically oriented Philosophy Club and Social Science Club but did not participate in the more activist NAACP branch. One was Robert Gregg, who I thought was the most brilliant student on campus. Like me, Gregg majored in political science and minored in history, and also like me, he received As in his courses. But while I usually read required materials for courses twice before I felt I had mastered them, Gregg almost never read them more than once. I tried my best to persuade him to pursue graduate study in political science as another buddy, Kalu Ezera, and I did, or to apply to law school.

I thought he had so much to offer that it would be a shame for him not to go into one of those fields. But Gregg was shy and stubborn. He was motivated by a desire to engage in hands-on service back in his hometown urban Black community, so he became a schoolteacher and eventually an administrator at the Paul Laurence Dunbar High School in Baltimore.

Two other buddies were interested in our liberal circle's academic activities. Joseph Daniels, who majored in biology and chemistry, attended Howard University Medical School, became a medical doctor in the US Army, and was later a professor at New Jersey College of Medicine and Dentistry. Ernest Smith also majored in biology and chemistry. He completed medical school at Howard, specializing in pediatric medicine, and spent more than a decade practicing on a Sioux reservation in South Dakota, after which he directed the pediatric department at a hospital in Los Angeles.

It was through my membership in the African Students Association—founded during my sophomore year by several students from Nigeria—that I encountered the largest number of assertively political-minded students on campus. Their activism was rooted in the expanding nationalism movements on the African continent during the 1950s that sought the transformation of countries ruled by European states into independent governments. American political analysts called such transformation decolonization. Supporters of these nationalist movements during the 1950s and 1960s were typically on the left side of the political spectrum, both in African countries and here at home. American supporters tended to be Black middle-class civil rights activists.

About twenty-five students on the Lincoln campus in the early 1950s hailed from Africa, mainly from the West African countries of Ghana,

Liberia, and Nigeria, but there were also two students from Kenya and one from Southwest Africa (after independence renamed Namibia). The leading political activists in the African Students Association were the Nigerians Kalu Ezera (the head of the association) and Olufemi Akinrele, the Kenyan Mugo Gatheru, and the Namibian Eric Getzen. During my sophomore, junior, and senior years, Frank Hutchings, Eugene Brockington, and I were also members.

While we were juniors, Frank and I suggested to Ezera that the association ask President Bond about organizing a one-day conference on the rise of African nationalist movements and their impact on decolonization developments. Happily, President Bond thought such a conference was feasible, and since he personally knew the first Black American diplomat at the United Nations—Dr. Ralph J. Bunche, who was a member of Lincoln's Board of Trustees and the director of the UN Trusteeship Division—he agreed to contact Bunche's office.

Within two weeks, President Bond learned that Bunche had persuaded two staff members from European states—Britain and Belgium—to participate. The leaders of the African Students Association then enlisted two Lincoln professors with an academic interest in the emerging decolonization movements: Sayre Schatz, an economist who studied economic development in non-Western countries, and Milton Crook, a political scientist who spent two years with the US Army in North Africa during World War II and studied postwar African decolonization movements. President Bond was also a member of the panel, which he asked me to introduce, giving me a small role in the conference. By my junior year, some of my buddies in the liberal circle had dubbed me one of President Bond's favorite students. The *Lion* yearbook for the Class of 1953 carried a photograph of the conference's panel, which shows me standing behind the participants.

The conference, held during the 1951–1952 spring term, critiqued the US State Department's foot-dragging decolonization policies in African countries and inspired an activist impetus in several students. One of them, Mugo Gatheru, was from Kenya's largest tribal group, the Kikuyu, which by the end of World War II had produced a greater number of educated Kenyans (grammar and secondary school) than had other ethnic communities. Several educated Kikuyu individuals traveled overseas in the 1930s for college education, most prominently Jomo Kenyatta and Mbiyu Koinange, who attended the University of London in Britain and Hampton Institute in America, respectively. At the end of World War II, the two led

the group of educated Kikuyu who founded their country's first nationalist organization, the Kenya African National Union (KANU). The British
colonial government in Kenya considered the KANU illegal, so its anticolonial political activity was forced underground. Meanwhile, Gatheru,
then a young Kikuyu grammar school teacher, had joined the KANU, and
through his friendship with Koinange, who knew several Black American
civil rights activists and intellectuals, gained a scholarship to Lincoln University in the fall of 1951.

During the following fall term, Gatheru was notified by the US
Department of State that the British colonial government in Kenya had
requested that his student visa not be renewed on the grounds that he was
an anticolonial radical. Gatheru informed his friends in the African Students Association about his travails. Fortunately, St. Clair Drake, a professor in anthropology at Roosevelt University in Chicago and a noted civil
rights activist and Black intellectual, visited President Bond for a week in
April 1953. Professor Drake had been primarily responsible for facilitating
Gatheru's scholarship in 1951, partly because Mbiyu Koinange had been his
roommate at Hampton Institute in the late 1920s and partly because he had
a long friendship with President Bond. As dean of faculty at Dillard University in New Orleans during the mid-1930s, Bond had hired the young
Drake as an assistant professor of sociology.

After conferring about Gatheru's situation, Drake got the go-ahead
from Bond to mobilize the liberal-circle students and the African Students Association in support of Gatheru's bid to have his visa renewed.
Drake advised the students to send a letter to the immigration office at
the State Department. Meanwhile, Drake wrote to the head of the NAACP,
Roy Wilkins, informing him of Gatheru's situation, and also contacted
James W. Ivy, who had been a friend in college and was now the editor
of the NAACP's monthly journal, the *Crisis*. Ivy agreed to publish an article supporting Gatheru's bid, and Professor Drake asked me and Kalu
Ezera to write it. Ezera, however, was already busy on a political article
for Nigeria's main nationalist organization, the National Convention of
Nigerian Citizens, which had been founded by Nnamdi Azikiwe, a 1930
graduate of Lincoln, who would become the first president of an independent Nigeria in 1960. With Ezera otherwise engaged, I ended up as
the sole author, aided by contributions from Professor Drake. Drake
wrote the accompanying cover letter and mailed the article to Ivy, who
published it in the magazine's June 1953 issue. That was my first published
article.

When World War II ended in the spring of 1945, an array of liberal organizations and interest groups mobilized the US Congress to pass legislation that explicitly compensated the millions of American soldiers who had manned the ranks of the armed forces. Known as the GI Bill of Rights, the legislation provided an array of affirmative action social benefits for World War II veterans, among them federally funded scholarships to attend college. Because in the immediate postwar years the vast majority of white colleges and universities were racially segregated, Black American veterans almost exclusively used their federal scholarships to attend Negro colleges.

Inevitably, the addition of many thousands of veterans at Negro colleges in the fall of 1946 and the following several years placed a strain on dormitory facilities. The enrollment at Lincoln University more than doubled, from 155 in the 1945 fall term to 338 a year later. In the 1947 fall term, enrollment skyrocketed again, to 584 students, before leveling off slightly to 531 by the time my class entered in 1949. In response to the massive new enrollment, Lincoln University built, with federal aid, a network of about ten army-barracks-type buildings on five acres of land on the southwest side of Lincoln's 150-acre campus. In the fall of 1949, I was among about a dozen entering freshmen who were allocated dormitory rooms in the "Vets Village." (An unusual aspect of living there was that the barracks bordered a pasture on a fifty-acre university-owned farm, so when you awoke at six o'clock in the morning to start the day, cows on the other side of barbed-wire fences peered into the bedroom windows. Far more unpleasant were the potent odors wafting through the barracks windows in March and April, when the tenant farmer sprinkled pig dung to supply nutrients to the large pasture. I remember more positively the tastes from the early spring vegetation in the pasture, especially the wild scallions that showed up in the raw milk—nonpasteurized—that Lincoln students drank daily at their meals.)

My roommate that year was a sophomore named Jesse Rines, a 1947 graduate of Ambler High School. The veterans, who constituted about 40 percent of students on the Lincoln campus, were on average five years older than the usual first-year undergraduate and interacted more with other students in their age group, but I got to know several of them fairly well through my courses in political science and sociology.

One student, Harold Brady, was born in Jamaica and came to the United States with his parents when he was an adolescent in the 1930s, so he still spoke with a mild West Indian accent. He was about six feet tall, a brown-skinned chap with a somewhat courtly bearing and an assertive intellect. During frequent bull sessions among the upperclassmen that I occasionally listened to, I thought Brady won the day more often than not.

Campus bull sessions had also been popular in Langston Hughes's day, as he wrote in his 1929 seminar paper: "Among the most prominent of the less organized campus activities, one might mention pinochle, weekend trips to town, and 'bull-sessions' dealing frequently with the comparative speed of trains, the abilities of a big league baseball player, and vagaries of women."[7]

A lot had changed from Hughes's time to mine, and the bull sessions that Jesse and I occasionally listened to during my freshman year had become far more serious in subject matter. Perhaps this was because the veterans who often dominated the sessions had spent several years in the armed forces, and a few had seen battle, so idle or vapid chatter didn't interest them.

Two of the veterans with combat experience were James Young and Jacques Wilmore. They were majors in sociology and became converts to Quaker pacifism during their undergraduate years, probably influenced by two prominent Quaker pacifist and antiwar faculty members, Professor Thomas Jones in European history and Professor David Swift in religious studies. The latter had such an impressive scholarship record that in my senior year he was persuaded by Yale University Theology School to join its faculty. Both Young and Wilmore remained at Lincoln after graduation in 1948 to teach as instructors in the Sociology Department and School of Theology. (Founded in the 1890s, it is one of the oldest theology schools among Negro colleges.) They were teaching assistants in several pacifism-oriented courses that dealt with the three-way interplay among Christian humanitarian thought, Quaker pacifist thought, and civil rights activism discourse. Several senior faculty also taught undergraduate courses in those areas, among them Laurence Foster in sociology and Walter Fales in philosophy, the latter a German Jewish scholar who fled to the United States as a refugee in the 1930s and after time in this country joined the Quaker faith. Two School of Theology professors headed up the several pacifism-oriented courses: Andrew Murray, dean of the School of Theology, and Samuel Stevens, an African American philosophy scholar and assistant dean. Jacques Wilmore later joined the staff of the Pendle Hill Quaker study center that was connected with Haverford College's Department of Sociology. That department's chairman was Ira Reid, a pacifist African American scholar who taught most of his career at Fisk University in Nashville but joined the faculty of Haverford after World War II as chair of its Sociology Department, making him the first Black scholar to teach at the college.

As for my friend Harold Brady, who graduated in June 1950, a mutual acquaintance told me that he migrated to Jamaica after graduation with plans to enter the newly independent world of Jamaican politics. As a freshman I enrolled in two courses taught by the brilliant political scientist John Aubrey Davis, who had launched courses in the subject at Lincoln in 1936, and I recall how impressed I was with the intellectual give-and-take during discussion period—the last fifteen minutes of class—between Brady and Professor Davis in the course on American constitutional law. I also recall thinking at the time that Brady could be a first-class lawyer, and when he returned to his homeland, that is exactly what he became.

Assessing Fraternities

The last sizable group of veterans graduated from Lincoln in June 1950. By the end of the following spring term, my sophomore year, it dawned on me that the Lincoln campus was now inhabited by two generic types of students: frat brothers, who constituted nearly two-thirds of my class, and non-frat students.

In general, it was the campus lifestyle of these two categories that defined each. The frat-joining undergraduates were steeped in rituals and social life revolving largely around events that took place on campus several times a year: the homecoming game in the fall and party weekends in the spring, when middle-class female students from the Baltimore-Washington area and the Philadelphia-Newark-New York City area came to the campus, by Greyhound or Trailways bus, on Friday evening and stayed until Sunday afternoon. For frat brothers, the desire to participate in campus parties was strong indeed, mesmerizing perhaps. The organization regime of Lincoln fraternities involved an endurance hurdle, one requiring that each fraternity pledgee (or pledge)—as students wanting to join a fraternity were called—be tested in regard to tolerating vicious verbal and physical assault from frat brothers, the survival of which represented a ticket of entry.

The substance of that ticket was the frat-hazing ritual. It was a world of mindless authoritarian dominance between full-member frat brothers on the one hand and fraternity pledgees on the other. It amounted to an aura of hegemonic dominance during the pledge period, a dominance that was daily ritualized by full-member frat brothers' verbal assaults (e.g., "dog," "monkey," "frog," and, yes, "nigger") upon pledge members. I'll never forget during the spring term of my freshman year, when I was entering the Refectory for lunch with my dishwashing buddies Roland Jones and Samuel Woodward, seeing two lines of pledging frat brothers queued up along the stairway, bowing in a slave-like manner to full-member frat brothers as they ascended the stairway, the latter spewing vile and vicious insults at them.

Coming from Philadelphia, Roland was savvy about campus life at Lincoln in a way that I, from a small factory town, was not. I remember asking him, "What the hell is that vicious stuff all about, Roland?" He responded, "It's what you do if you want to join a fraternity, Martin," to which I replied, "You don't mean it, Roland! Why would a sane Negro student submit himself to such nastiness just to join a fraternity?" "Well, Martin, some students just want to be on the inside of a fraternity so badly, they want close bonds with friends, that they're willing to endure nasty verbal assaults from their frat brothers. And what's worse, Martin, there's also physical assaults that they endure which take place at fraternity hazing events at night." And I replied quite loudly to Roland, "What?! You mean the frat brothers physically attack pledgees? How, Roland?" He said, "Oh, they kick them, make them crawl on the ground to frat brothers—and on a rainy night, too. They spit on them, drive them several miles from campus on a cold winter's night, and make them walk back to campus. And what's worse, Martin, they physically beat them with rowing paddles. Beat them hard, too."

Roland sat down at the lunch table after getting a tray of food from the servers, muttering, "You'll get used to what the fraternities do, Martin." Of course he was right. I got used to it because I had four years left on the Lincoln campus. But I always despised the fraternities. To me, fraternity hazing on a Negro college campus was a facsimile of a slave dominance ritual that somehow gained legitimacy for many male students at some Negro colleges by the end of World War II.[8]

That hideous ritual practiced by fraternities held no legitimacy whatever for me and my liberal buddies. Robert Gregg, Frank Hutchings, Ernest Smith, and others in our circle viewed those rituals with contempt. For myself, I had ancestral cultural roots that predisposed me against such authoritarian-type displays. After all, I hailed from a long line of free Negro families in Delaware and Maryland in the early 1800s on both my maternal and paternal sides. When the Civil War commenced in 1861, and again when President Abraham Lincoln issued the January 1863 Emancipation Proclamation, it tested the toughness and seriousness of free Negroes outside the South. It gives me enormous pride that my Laws and Kilson ancestors joined the Union Army to fight for the freedom of four million Negro slaves in the South. I've always been proud of their decision to risk their lives and livelihoods to help free millions of enslaved brothers and sisters and children.

Accordingly, when I witnessed those dominance-type practices in the front of the campus dining hall during the spring of my freshman year, a viscerally negative feeling surfaced in me toward the Alphas, Kappas, and Omegas. Some students observing these twisted performances would just laugh at them, perhaps laughing to keep from crying, as that old Negro folk adage put it. That response baffled me.

Even after I became a successful scholar at Harvard and got invitations to join a couple of Black fraternities without enduring any hazing horrors, I replied that I wasn't interested. In retrospect, maybe I should have been more forgiving and magnanimous. The African American fraternity Alpha Phi Alpha and the sorority Alpha Kappa Alpha eventually matured ideologically during the period of the civil rights movement and contributed to it. Nevertheless, I didn't change my negative attitude toward fraternities; it was too deeply ingrained in me from my Lincoln University years. Interestingly, my dishwashing buddy Samuel Woodward transferred to a New Jersey state teachers' college at the end of his sophomore year, and I often wondered if it was because of the shock he experienced at witnessing the stupid barbarity associated with Lincoln's fraternity hazing patterns.

What I saw that day was so disturbing to me in its meanness and ignorance that the thought of joining a campus fraternity never entered my mind. During the summer of my junior year, I spent a weekend with my older brother William, who was a salesman with the Parks Sausage Company in Philadelphia, America's first Black-owned meat-packing company, and he asked me, "What fraternity do you belong to, Martin?" I said, "I don't belong to any of those foolish fraternities," to which he replied, "Well, you ought to belong to one of them, because they're important among middle-class Negroes, and they'll help you in your professional career, man." My brother attended only business courses at Drexel Institute in Philadelphia—now Drexel University—so he didn't know a damn thing about the real world of fraternities at Negro colleges during my years at one of them.

I was one of the non-frat students, as were my liberal-circle buddies Robert Gregg, Frank Hutchings, Ernest Smith, Joseph Daniels, and Thomas "Mingo" Williams, as well as Kalu Ezera and other students from Africa. For the students from Liberia, Kenya, and Nigeria, I guess the verbal and physical harassment carried out by the fraternities was just plain weird!

We didn't share this sanctioned and strange brotherhood, but those of us outside of the fraternity system had one interesting thing in common: most of us showed up regularly at the weekly Saturday night movies. Those films, which were shown in the original campus gymnasium building, had a history extending back to the 1920s, when the YMCA provided them on campus. They were the main on-campus weekend attraction for non-frat member students who didn't mount a Greyhound or Trailways bus to travel to the Baltimore-Washington area or to Philadelphia to attend fraternity-sponsored parties. Instead, many of us non-frat students used Saturdays to study in the library and also in the Science Hall, which was kept open on weekends.

Bernard Duncan was one of the liberal-circle students who spent his weekend nights at those movies. In the graduation yearbook for the Class of 1953, the editors wrote next to his photograph that Dunk "has yet to miss a Saturday evening campus movie. . . ." They could have just as easily written that about Robert Gregg, Ernest Smith, Frank Hutchings, or me. Some of us were jokingly dubbed "Dunk's boys." We were all Saturday night movies guys.

Final Reflections

As table 7.1 shows, the humanities (languages, literature, philosophy) attracted only two majors in the Class of 1953. The social sciences (economics, history, psychology, political science) attracted many more students— thirty-two. The sciences (biology, chemistry, mathematics, physics) attracted the largest number of all—thirty-eight.

It's not difficult to explain why science was the most popular major of students at a leading Negro college in the early 1950s. Medicine and dentistry had a prominent attraction among status-focused working-class and middle-class Black youth entering college in the post–World War II period. Remember that some 90 percent of college-going Black American youth in those years—owing to racial discrimination by white institutions of higher education—entered Negro colleges. So when high-achieving Black youth applied to college in 1949 as I did, they applied to the top-tier Negro colleges. For example, in 1956, the white-majority University of Pennsylvania admitted only six Black students. Harvard College admitted a dozen Black students that same fall. Today, by comparison, only 12 percent of college-going African Americans attend Black-majority institutions of higher education. For Black students seeking medical and dental school entry back in 1953, their options were limited. For the first fifty years of the twentieth century, the Meharry medical college and dental school and the medical and dental schools at Howard University produced the vast majority of the roughly two hundred Black medical doctors and one hundred Black dentists who practiced in any given year. It required the civil rights activism of the late 1950s through the 1960s to spark the court decisions and federal legislation that eventually ended long-standing racial discrimination against Black students seeking entry to mainstream, white-majority medical, dental, and nursing schools.

As one of the twelve top-tier Black institutions of higher education during the first half of the twentieth century—the others were Atlanta, Dillard, Fisk, Hampton, Howard, Morehouse, Morgan State, Spelman, Virginia State, Wilberforce, and Xavier—my alma mater, Lincoln University, was well known for the high quality of its curriculum in the sciences. This meant that for talented African American high school graduates in the northern states (especially New York, New Jersey, Maryland, Ohio, and Pennsylvania) who entertained thoughts of entering the medical fields, Lincoln University was high on their list of colleges.

This was nothing new. In his discussion of academic affairs on Lincoln's campus during the 1920s, Langston Hughes writes:

> Not by any means all of the courses listed in the catalog are being taught this year, but courses under the following headings are now being taught: Bible, Biology, Chemistry, Economics, Education, English, French, German, Spanish, Latin, Greek, Mathematics, Philosophy, Physics, Political Science, Sociology, and Public Speaking. . . . Under Biology, Chemistry, and Physics 20 courses are listed. Since nearly one-half of the [324] students here plan on entering the medical profession the work of [the Science division] is tremendously important. Seemingly it does its work well, students are satisfied with the preparation they receive here, and their records at graduate institutions are good.[9]

The proportion of science students Hughes found was just 10 percent below the number of science majors among my graduating class. Of course, the reason for the high proportion in both eras was the same: Lincoln's first-rate faculty in biology, chemistry, mathematics, and physics.

Twelve of the thirty-eight Class of 1953 students who majored in science fields gained admission to medical, dental, and veterinary schools. Several of them told me that their intellectual interests in the medical fields were reinforced by their interactions with Lincoln's campus physician, Toye Davis, one of President Bond's early appointments of African American faculty and staff. Dr. Davis was a 1930s graduate of Lincoln University with an MS from the University of Pennsylvania, a master's in physiology from Harvard Medical School, and an MD from Howard University School of Medicine. While his official duties were to attend to the medical needs of Lincoln students—some five hundred–plus during my undergraduate years—he also spent time tutoring students about the formal and informal academic regime they should pursue for a successful career in medicine. He was an engaging personality—handsome and dapper—who reached out to students.

Dr. Davis, his wife, and their two children resided in the small Negro community that students dubbed the Village. Originally a pre–Civil War Underground Railroad depot lying several miles east of the campus, it had a small antebellum AME church that was still operating during my Lincoln years. I'm told that Dr. Davis occasionally provided medical care to families in the Village, often free of charge. He was a valuable Lincoln University citizen, and many students from the mid-1940s through the 1970s remembered him affectionately. He retired in the late 1970s and moved to a middle-class neighborhood in the nearby town of Oxford, a very segregated town during my Lincoln years, where I once visited him.

Paradoxically, a sizable segment of undergraduates in my class who were fraternity members proved capable of shedding the frivolous social and cultural attitudes and habits they embraced as frat brothers by the time they graduated in June 1953 or soon thereafter. Their vicious, macho male-bonding attitudes were left behind in a fraternity-culture trash can—like a caterpillar's shedding process from cocoon to butterfly. As those Lincoln graduates tackled rigorous academic curricula in medical and dental schools, they fashioned a genuine professional ethos which enabled them to conquer challenging coursework and advance in their chosen fields.[10]

For example, my classmate John B. Boyd Jr., the son of a Lincoln graduate, followed his studies at Lincoln with dental school at Howard University, earning his DDS there and later attending the Indiana University School of Dentistry, where he earned an MSD. He joined the Howard College of Dentistry faculty in the late 1950s and served as the head of its Department of Clinical Dentistry from 1979 to 1991. I recall him as a sort of honcho-type figure on the Lincoln campus, quite immersed in the macho frivolity central to the fraternities. But upon entering professional school, Boyd shed those attitudes and fashioned a rigorous professional ethos for himself. He would successfully communicate this ethos to his several children, two of whom—daughters—became medical doctors.

Another classmate, Adolph W. Johnson, also entered the dental profession. While at Lincoln, he was a topflight athlete, accruing varsity letters in basketball, baseball, and football. He was also a prominent frat brother, so immersed in that good-time/party-time world that the 1953 graduation yearbook said of him, "Constantly inquiring about the whereabouts of the opposite sex and the [fraternity] parties." Dolph, as his buddies called him, entered Howard University to study dentistry and earned his DDS in 1957, going on to spend three years as a dentist in the US Air Force. He joined the faculty at Howard College of Dentistry in 1961 and taught there until 1967, when he commenced a practice in general dentistry. Like John Boyd, Adolph Johnson communicated his professional ethos to his children, who acquired upper-middle-class status for themselves. One daughter became a lawyer and another an aerospace engineer. One son became a medical doctor, another a mechanical engineer.

A third example is Laval Cothran, a frat brother and member of the varsity track team, whom I knew well because he spent lots of time drinking malt milkshakes at the student canteen that I managed for two years. Like his buddy Adolph Johnson, Cothran was immersed in the world of the fraternities and was described in our graduation yearbook as "Philly's gift to the women." After graduating from Lincoln, Laval Cothran entered veterinary school at Tuskegee Institute in Alabama and received a DVM in 1957. He then served on the veterinary faculty at Howard University, which awarded him a PhD in physiology in 1971. He too communicated the importance of a professional ethos to his children, and two of his daughters entered the medical profession.

In conversations with several former classmates at our fiftieth reunion, I mentioned the importance of communicating a professional ethos to African American middle-class children when they enter their teenage years, and all concurred. I pointed out that a recent study of American social-mobility patterns reported a nearly 40 percent downward-mobility rate among middle-class African Americans as of 2002. That compared with a 16 percent downward-mobility rate among middle-class white youth, which might mean that middle-class African American families have not effectively been getting this message to their children.

All of my classmates with whom I had this discussion had successfully dealt with this issue with their teenagers. I told them that my wife and I had done the same. Our oldest child, Jennifer, graduated from the University of New Hampshire and did graduate studies at the Harvard School of Education, earning a master's in education. She has been an administrator at Regis College in Massachusetts and at Massachusetts College of Art in Boston and a consultant on education programs to increase the graduation rate of minority youth in Boston's public schools. Our middle child, Peter, majored in business at the University of Massachusetts Amherst, earned a master's in education at Boston College, taught literature and math in Boston's schools (mainly Black public schools) for more than a decade, and later became an accountant at State Street Bank in Boston. Our youngest child, Hannah, graduated from Amherst College, earned a law degree at Harvard, worked in legal services on behalf of distressed working-class women, became a legal counsel for the Massachusetts Development Authority, and is a partner in a Boston law firm, where she focuses on affordable housing.

My wife, Marion, and I are now old grandparents of six grandchildren—four granddaughters and two grandsons—and one great-granddaughter. We hope our own children will effectively communicate the salience of a professional ethos to them, as I'm sure they will.

....

My Lincoln years were my "understanding Blackness" years. That term for me encompasses many fundamental things. First, since I attended a top-tier Negro college at a time when our country was still at its sociopolitical worst in relation to African American citizens, this period provided the historical context in which I began to understand the social and cultural boundaries that defined the meaning of Blackness for the broader African American society—an understanding not available to me while growing up in Ambler. Coming from a Black community in a small milltown in eastern Pennsylvania in 1949, I lacked an adequate understanding of how our democratic American republic still delineated the social and political status of Black folks along racist lines, with the segregation of public schools and colleges, public transportation, and public institutions generally (restaurants, movie houses, theaters, concert halls), discrimination in job markets and judicial and police systems (the latter often accompanied by violence), and so forth).

Thanks to Horace Mann Bond's presidency at Lincoln University and the liberal-oriented interracial faculty that he fashioned, I was able to develop a viable intellectual understanding of the racist attributes of our American republic, in an era that was preceded by the contribution of thousands of African American soldiers to the defeat of the German Nazi regime's totalitarian and murderous dominance in Europe. Yet these veterans and all Black Americans would have to wait nearly two generations before our country embarked on a serious process for the full-fledged democratic incorporation of its African American citizens.

Second, I should point out that for me, the term *Blackness* denotes the collective Negro folk ideals that guide Black people's pursuit of human decency in America's white-supremacist civilization. At Lincoln I embarked on a quest to fathom these folk-culture ingredients of Blackness. Many parts come to mind when I think about this whole.

One such ingredient occurred to me through my freshman-year dishwashing buddies Roland Jones, Samuel Woodward, and Alfred Kase, when our many conversations plumbed what we viewed as a galling indifference among Lincoln students toward the budding civil rights activism in the wider nooks and crannies of African American society nationally. I had assumed that among the growing college-educated segment of African Americans, there was a natural nexus with civil rights activism and that such a nexus was no less than a God-given aspect of Blackness. It became clear to me by the fall term of my junior year that this assumption wasn't valid.

A second ingredient of Blackness that I was seeking to understand was my assumption about the natural helping-hand interaction between the well-off segment of the African American community and the weaker segments. This assumption in itself led to a third assumption about a generic civic-uplift ethos as an organic element of Blackness, insofar as it was a core piece of the Negro church modalities that characterized life in the small Black communities of Ambler and Penllyn and shaped my childhood. As an undergraduate, I assumed—naively perhaps—that other incoming Black students in the late 1940s had experienced a similar version of this civic-uplift ethos in the Black communities in which they grew up and thus had also brought this outlook to the Lincoln campus.

By the fall term of my junior year I became aware that this assumption was true for only a small sliver of Lincoln students, those whom I dub the liberal circle. But this assumption was invalid when applied to the majority of students there during my undergraduate years. Why? Because I had witnessed the nasty and ignorant macho-male hazing practices of fraternities, practices that favored slave-type ritual deference sickeningly shown by pledgees to frat brothers. Mind you, the fraternity leaders were usually from upper-middle-class families. In short, evidence of a mindset among Lincoln students informed by a civic-uplift ethos was very limited indeed.

As I closed out my undergraduate years in June 1953, I chalked up some progressive experiences that enriched my understanding of Blackness and strengthened my respect for and commitment to Black folks' honor. But there were also regressive experiences that diminished my understanding and complicated my commitment to Black people's honor. No doubt, new experiences relating to my understanding of Blackness awaited me at Harvard University.

Meanwhile, in my final month at Lincoln, several events buoyed me. In the 1953 yearbook I was selected as our graduating class's "Most Radical Student." I was chosen by the Lincoln faculty and administration as valedictorian, and when delivering the valedictory address, I was able to share the dais with the novelist Pearl Buck, who was the commencement speaker, and with the university's president and my primary intellectual mentor during my undergraduate years, Dr. Horace Mann Bond. Following my years at Lincoln and into my time at Harvard University Graduate School, Dr. Bond and I kept in touch.

A high proportion of the students in my graduating class—about 80 percent—enrolled in professional schools. Most who pursued degrees in the medical sciences enrolled primarily at Black colleges because of blatant discriminatory practices. For those of us who did graduate studies in the social sciences, theology, business, accounting, and journalism, the vast majority entered white-majority institutions. In the fall of 1953, I was one of roughly a dozen Black students who enrolled at Harvard Graduate School, four of whom were African.

I earned my doctorate in political science from Harvard in June 1959. My original thought was to return to my alma mater to teach political science, but unexpected events intervened. Neither I nor several other African American students pursuing PhDs at Harvard University back then *had* to seek academic positions at Black institutions of higher education. We were not restricted to follow the path pursued by the two generations of formidable African American scholars and students at Harvard who had preceded us. The brilliant W. E. B. Du Bois (1895), Carter G. Woodson (1915),

Charles Wesley (1918), Rayford Logan (1923), Ralph Bunche (1934), Robert Weaver (1934), John Hope Franklin (1936), Merze Tate (1944, the first African American woman to receive a PhD from Harvard), Robert Brisbane (1948), and Adelaide Cromwell (1950, the first African American to earn a PhD in sociology from Harvard), among others, held advanced degrees from Harvard but were precluded from teaching at institutions like the one at which they had studied. But for us it was different. Three of us in political science secured academic positions at white-majority institutions; the others were Larry Howard, who worked first at Brandeis University and later at the University of Pittsburgh, and Allen Ballard, who got a position at City College in New York after having been the first African American to earn a doctorate in Russian studies at Harvard. In the 1950s, there was one African American graduate student, Andrew Brimmer, in Harvard's Department of Economics and two, Otey Scruggs and Nathan Huggins, pursuing doctorates in history. Upon completing their studies by the early 1960s, they were also hired at white institutions of higher education. This occurred a decade *before* the flourishing of Black studies programs at white colleges and universities.

I am proud to be one of the trailblazing Black academics holding PhDs from Harvard who were finally allowed on the other side of the desk at white-majority institutions. Fortunately, Lincoln University—a Black university—prepared me well for the task.

Harvard: Graduate School
and Teaching

I attended graduate school at Harvard University from the fall of 1953 until June 1959. Kalu Ezera, who was the salutatorian of our class, was accepted as well, marking the first time more than one Lincoln graduate gained admission to Harvard's graduate school simultaneously. Ezera left Harvard after his second year to study at Oxford University. "A British university degree is more useful for my future political career in Nigeria," he told me.

Ezera would indeed go on to have a distinguished political career among the first-generation cohort of the Nigerian postcolonial political class. Unfortunately, that career ended tragically. As a member of the Igbo ethnic group, Ezera ended up on the wrong side of Nigeria's horrific 1967–1972 civil war. When the federal government forces victoriously exited the defeated Biafra territory in eastern Nigeria in 1972, they viciously assassinated Igbo leaders who had launched the secessionist state. Kalu Ezera was one of them. In the 1980s, after I had become a professor in political science at Harvard, I taught my old classmate's son in my courses on African political systems.

By the time Kalu Ezera left Harvard in the summer of 1955, I had become deeply engaged with a couple of student networks. The main one that captured my interest related to the small community of Black students at Harvard, which was evenly divided between undergraduate and graduate students. After spending three of my four years at Lincoln University with a small cadre of students involved in liberal activism, I carried this behavior with me to my new life in Cambridge, Massachusetts.

I knew virtually nothing about the character of Harvard campus life among Black students when I arrived in the fall of 1953, though I had read a sidebar article in the NAACP journal the *Crisis* that reported on a

Black student named Walter Carrington, who in the 1951–1952 academic year helped to organize a student NAACP branch on campus. Walter graduated in 1952, but I got to know him because he stayed at Harvard as a law student. The report in the *Crisis* gave me my first indication of what I might encounter among Black students at Harvard, and in fact I found several who were devoted to liberal activism.

But by the 1954 spring term, I had moved around the campus enough to learn that those associated with the university's NAACP branch made up a small segment of the total number of Black students, both undergraduate and graduate.

Black Students

In 1953, the total enrollment of Black undergraduates at Harvard College (men's) and Radcliffe College (women's) was about twenty—roughly ten at each institution. Another ten were enrolled in the Graduate School of Arts and Sciences; I was among this group, in the Department of Government. By the time I entered my last year of graduate studies, 1958–1959, the numbers had increased somewhat. There were three Black graduate students in Government (Larry Howard, Allen Ballard, and me); two in the History Department (Nathan Huggins and Otey Scruggs); and five in the Economics Department (the African American student Andrew Brimmer and four African students: Amon Nikoi from Ghana and Olufemi Sanu, H. A. Oluwasami, and Clement Isong from Nigeria). Furthermore, the three professional schools on the Cambridge side of the Charles River that had admitted Black graduate students were the School of Design, which counted two African Americans on its class rolls; Harvard Law School, which included six; and the Divinity School, which enrolled four.

Having attended one of the 120 institutions of higher education that existed for Black Americans in the postwar period, I was aware of the tremendous discrepancy in enrollment between a research university for Black Americans like Howard University, with more than three thousand students by the early 1950s, and a major white research university like Harvard, with fewer than fifty. Numbers were similar at the University of California, Princeton, Yale, the University of Chicago, Columbia, and American, to name a few.

What I wasn't aware of, however, was that the variety of Black students at an elite white university differed in important ways from that found at a Black institution like my alma mater, in particular in the cultural pattern that characterized them. During my undergraduate years at Lincoln, although the Black student cultural pattern was deformed by the frivolous and hedonistic role of fraternities, there was nonetheless a small group of liberal-minded and civil rights–oriented students who challenged this mentality, thereby informing campus life with community-minded ideals.

By contrast, during my first year at Harvard, I discovered that although there was a small group of similarly liberal-minded Black students on the campus, there was also a group who were defined not by their ludicrous adherence to the expectations of fraternities but to a related form of frivolity that I characterize as a status-climber mentality. By minimizing or ignoring outright Black liberal or civil rights activism on a white campus, these Black students believed that their white peers would extend egalitarian friendship to them.

Liberal Activism

After about a month of moving around the Black-student social realm at Harvard, I encountered several students who were associated with the liberal-activism cultural pattern, like-minded individuals who were concerned with the civil rights movement, which, by the 1950s, was a broad-based emergent political force nationally among African Americans. In 1954, the spring term of my first academic year at graduate school, the US Supreme Court had a majority of liberal justices headed by Chief Justice Earl Warren, who, in May, wrote the majority decision in *Brown v. Board of Education*. In addition to knocking down a century of legal segregation in American public schools, the decision galvanized a level of activism that found overt expression among Black students, whether on Black or white college campuses.

Walter Carrington emerged as a leading figure who subscribed to this liberal-activism cultural pattern, but before meeting him, I got to know another Black student of a similar stripe—J. Max Bond Jr., the nephew of the president of my alma mater and a second-year graduate student in Harvard's School of Design. During Lincoln's graduation ceremony, President Bond had mentioned to me that I should seek out his nephew when I arrived at Harvard, and I did so during my first week on campus.

Thanks to Max, I gained entry into the group associated with the liberal-activism cultural pattern. At the time, these students did not exhibit the aggressive or militant-activist style that prevailed among Black Harvard students a decade later. Instead, this small but mighty cohort acted as sentinels on behalf of Black people's honor by demanding respect for them.

In response to the vicious burning of a cross, Ku Klux Klan–style, by a group of white Harvard undergraduates beneath the freshman dormitory window where Max Bond and his Black roommate lived, two African American third-year undergraduates—Walter Carrington and James Harkless—mobilized a half dozen other Black students, including Max Bond, to form a campus NAACP branch during the spring of 1951. In general, those Black Harvard students who were associated with the liberal-activism cultural pattern came from small-enclave Black communities, some in urban areas of the North and Midwest, others in rural or suburban counties in states such as Texas, Virginia, and Pennsylvania. These students were mainly from middle-class families or, like me, lower-middle-class ones.

All of these backgrounds were represented among the founding members of Harvard's NAACP branch, which was popularly called the Harvard Society for Minority Rights, or HSMR. Carrington, the president, was from a small-enclave Black community in Everett, Massachusetts, where his family operated a grocery store. He graduated from Harvard College in 1952, attended Harvard Law School, and became a civil rights lawyer. Harkless was from a working-class family in Detroit, where his father worked in the automobile plants. He attended Harvard Law School and devoted himself to labor and civil rights law.

Another three of the founding members—J. Max Bond, Kenneth Simmons, and Bill Norris—grew up in small-enclave Black communities outside of the North: Bond in Louisville, Kentucky, Simmons in Muskogee, Oklahoma, and Norris in Norfolk, Virginia. After attending the Harvard School of Design, both Bond and Simmons embarked on careers as architects, and Norris became a medical technician. All three came from upper-middle-class families. Bond's father was a sociologist and an agricultural officer concerned with advancing the status of Black farmers as part of the Roosevelt administration's Tennessee Valley Authority, the first federal government bureau since Reconstruction that assisted Black American farmers in their agricultural needs, though not on a plane equal to their white counterparts. Simmons's father was a dentist and an official in the Oklahoma NAACP as well as a member of the association's national board. Norris's father was a medical doctor who served Norfolk's Black community.

From the time I entered Harvard in September 1953, there were other Black students in the activist circle who, like me, came from lower-middle-class backgrounds. I alone was from Ambler, Pennsylvania, but I was by no means alone. Melvin Miller was from Boston. After attending Columbia University Law School, he entered law practice and in 1965 founded a weekly newspaper for Boston's Black community, the *Bay State Banner*, which is still published in print and online. Amon Horne was from a rural Black community in Florida. After earning his law degree from Columbia, he returned to Florida and became a civil rights lawyer. Tom Wilson, who hailed from a small Black community in East Texas, was a rather debonair personality, steeped in the pop music world of the 1950s. Within a decade of his graduation from Harvard, Tom gained national visibility as a top-tier entertainment-industry entrepreneur, becoming famous particularly for discovering the white American rock-soul singer Janis Joplin, whose early career he managed.

Several Black students at Harvard in the mid-1950s chose *not* to associate with HSMR. One was a graduate student in economics, Andrew Brimmer, who became a prominent federal government economist. Nathan Huggins from the Department of History similarly kept the organization at arm's length. I once spoke to Huggins while we sat on the steps of Widener Library, after both of us had completed our PhD qualifying examinations and were preparing to select topics for our doctoral dissertations. I told him that I had decided to study a topic related to the emerging decolonization movements in African countries, and I asked whether he would also study a topic related to Black affairs. His response was rather agitated. He thought that we Black graduate students in the humanities and social sciences "should demonstrate to white academics that we could tackle mainstream American topics."

I disagreed, telling him, "Black people's realities *have been* mainstream American topics since the founding of the American colonies." I noted that two generations of Black graduate students at Harvard had already studied topics related to Black affairs and that they had produced first-class scholarly works, among them Carter G. Woodson's *The Professional Negro Man and the Community* (1934), W. E. B. Du Bois's *Black Reconstruction in America* (1935), and John Hope Franklin's *The Militant South* (1940). My reply neither fazed nor swayed him, and he said he would study a topic related to white American history. I don't recall his exact words, but it was along the lines of "We young Black scholars shouldn't segregate ourselves with our scholarship, Martin."

Huggins's dissertation was a study of late nineteenth-century philanthropy in Massachusetts. Many years later, when both of us were teaching at white universities, we chatted over lunch at an annual conference of the Association for the Study of Negro Life and History. He told me a sad story, related with a bitter undertone. None of his Harvard faculty advisers, he recalled, helped him publish his dissertation; he ultimately had success with a new publisher located in Connecticut called Greenwood Press. Eventually, Huggins would publish in the field of African American history; his 1970 book *The Harlem Renaissance* is well known. He went on to become a professor of history and then the chair of Harvard's Department of Afro-American Studies. Alas, life for African American academics evolves in curious ways.

Status-Oriented Students

Of the Harvard students who were beholden to a status-climber mentality, many were female. In the 1950s, though female students were officially enrolled at Radcliffe College, they pursued their courses on the Harvard campus, several blocks east of Radcliffe's. The status-climbing Black students were identifiable not by a formal organization like HSMR but by their campus friendship patterns.

Just as a dozen or so male Black students were in the liberal-activist segment at Harvard, about the same number of male and female Black students were associated with the status-climber group. From my perspective, they assumed that if they minimized civil rights activism on campus, their white student peers would extend them egalitarian friendship. Underlying this assumption was that a veneer of cultural inclusion existed on white campuses in the North during the 1950s—though there was zero evidence of it.

Most of Harvard's female Black students whom I recall as associated with the status-climber outlook hailed from upper-middle-class Black families. Elizabeth Fitzgerald Howard, who graduated in 1948, shared her perspective on her circle of Black friends in the 1993 book *Blacks at Harvard: A Documentary History of the African American Experience at Harvard and Radcliffe*, edited by the comparative literature scholar Werner Sollors. Although Howard (then Fitzgerald) was at Harvard a few years before I was, her descriptions of this segment of Harvard's Black population were still applicable to the campus I knew in the 1950s. Writing in the third person, she provides a veritable blueprint for the demeanor of the Black status climber on a white campus: "She smiled at everyone and everyone smiled at her. If there were any racially motivated barbs flung her way—and surely there must have been—she just didn't notice. . . . In those days [the late 1940s] black students avoided the appearance of clinging together. The rule [among Black students] was to mix, to try to convince everyone [white students] that you were not any different. Betty Fitzgerald didn't feel any different."[1]

In an *Esquire* magazine article, "The Ivy League Negro," William Melvin Kelley, Class of 1960, lauds life on elite white campuses in a tone both indifferent toward and scornful of "Negro consciousness." In Kelley's blissful view of racial dynamics on postwar white campuses in the North, a Black student experienced something akin to a racial Shangri-La. "An academic community," he writes, "especially one like Harvard, . . . is a place where a Negro can forget almost entirely about his skin, his Negro consciousness."[2] He expands on this rather fantastical view:

> The Negro consciousness is the part of a Negro's mind that functions not for him as an individual human being, but for him as a Negro, for his race. It is the part of his conscience which asks him, before he commits any act, "Is it good for the Negro race?" . . . Furthermore, among Harvard Negroes, race pride, as it would be known in Harlem ("If a Negro does it, it's good"), is something like patriotism, in a flag-waving sense—antiquated, shallow-minded and conformist. Everything at Harvard is geared to make a man think for himself, to formulate his own ideas. . . . At Harvard, and at any other Ivy League school, the Negro . . . loses his Negro consciousness.[3]

Of course, my activist-oriented Black friends at Harvard considered the views of Howard and Kelley that Black students should avoid "clinging together" ridiculous. Forging Black ethnic ties among Harvard students to further Black people's citizenship and human rights in our racist country was politically and culturally legitimate, relative to the norms and rules of a democratic nation. It was akin to Irish Americans uniting to advance their cultural needs against anti-Catholic bigotry, with those patterns then reproduced among Irish American college students starting in the 1930s onward, or to Jewish Americans joining together to advance Jewish cultural needs against anti-Semitism in American society generally as well as on college campuses.

Intellectually, Howard and Kelley's shortsighted advice to Black students—to defer to white people and thus guarantee acceptance by them—was absurd. It was intrinsically demeaning to Black folks and to our long and horrific journey in our American racist civilization. Langston Hughes had a forceful and graphic retort to the Howards and Kelleys of the world: he said that he would never "hide [his] face" as a way of "getting along with White folks." In concert with Langston Hughes, my circle of civil rights–oriented Black friends expressed contempt for the Howard-Kelley blueprint for getting along with white students. Above all, we despised these status climbers' blatant disrespect for the honor of Black people—for the honor of the injured souls of our ancestors.

Interestingly, Howard was the daughter of John MacFarland Fitzgerald, who was among the fewer than ten Black students attending Harvard University during the 1920s. Howard observed that, rather than "try[ing] to convince [white students] that you were not any different," her father and several other Black students—including undergraduate Earl Brown and law students Charles Hamilton Houston, William Hastie, Raymond Pace Alexander, and Benjamin Davis Jr.—organized a civil rights organization called the Nile Club. This group was on the other end of the spectrum from the sort of people Fitzgerald's daughter would describe years later. In 1922 the Nile Club invited Marcus Garvey, the head of the New York–based Universal Negro Improvement Association, to address its members at a Black church in Cambridge. As the leader of what was popularly called the Garvey Movement, Garvey propagated a Black nationalist political message, one that viewed Black mainstream civil rights groups such as the NAACP and the National Urban League as "Uncle Tom–type" organizations. Of course, Howard's circle of Black friends at Harvard would never have invited a Black-nationalist civil rights leader to address them!

Fitzgerald published an account of Garvey's visit to Cambridge in the 1978 issue of the *Journal of Negro History*. His coauthor was his son-in-law Professor Otey Scruggs, who taught American history at Syracuse University and was a graduate student at Harvard in the mid-1950s:

> On a spring evening in 1922, at the height of his power and influence, Marcus Garvey came to a Harvard University which was racially segregated in nearly all respects save the classroom. . . . Following dinner in the Harvard Union [the dining hall for freshmen], the charismatic guest of honor spoke . . . of his program for the worldwide emancipation of the Negro through the development of racial unity and black pride. The meeting lasted well into the evening, a good deal of time being devoted by the dynamic black leader in responding to students' questions. Of especial interest

both to Garvey and the students was the role blacks trained in business, education, and political and military organization might play in the program of black redemption.[4]

Thus, within one African American middle-class family that was fortunate enough to send not one but two generations to Harvard College from the 1920s to the 1940s, an ideological fissure relating to Black ethnic identity occurred. Fitzgerald embraced a proactive view of his Black ethnic identity in the 1920s, whereas his daughter minimized her Black ethnic identity on the same campus in the post–World War II period.

What's more, the difference in Black ethnic identity orientation between Fitzgerald's cohort and Howard's can be grasped by examining the undeniably progressive professional careers that some members of the Nile Club in the 1920s fashioned for themselves. Alexander returned to his hometown of Philadelphia and became a leading Black civil rights lawyer. Houston returned to his hometown of Washington, DC, where he taught at the Howard University Law School and became its dean; under his administration, the school trained the second generation of top-tier African American civil rights lawyers, including Thurgood Marshall and James Nabrit. Houston also founded the NAACP Legal Defense Fund in 1929, which executed major antisegregation litigation in federal courts from the 1930s onward, leading to the 1954 US Supreme Court decision in *Brown v. Board of Education*. (Unfortunately, however, the racist ethos remains quite fierce in American life several decades later, so that here in the twenty-first century, segregation patterns in America's public schools approximate the rates of the late 1950s!)

Benjamin Davis, another Nile Club member, was the son of a wealthy Black professional family in Atlanta, the head of which was that city's leading Republican Black political personality. Upon his graduation from Harvard Law School in 1923, Ben Davis became the central African American figure in New York City's Communist Party, a position he would hold for several decades. Indeed, his charismatic, radical personality was a magnet that attracted talented Black intellectuals to the left-wing side of African American politics, among them the classical singer Paul Robeson, the journalist Willard Motley, the cartoonist Ollie Harrington, and the actor Canada Lee.

As for William Melvin Kelley, the onetime status climber turned to creative writing following his Harvard graduation and joined the literature faculty at Hunter College in New York City. His works, including the novel

A Different Drummer (1962) and the volume of stories *Dancers on the Shore* (1964), deal poignantly with African American themes. As the 1960s progressed, in a series of social and political essays, Kelley exhibited a marked ideological reversal that was far removed from the *Esquire* article in which he debunked "Negro consciousness." In the essay "Black Power," published in the *Partisan Review*, Kelley asked, "Is it still necessary, in 1968, to discuss the differences between two peoples, African and European, who inhabit the United States?" His searching answer took the form of a Baldwinesque meditation:

> I thought everybody accepted those differences. I thought that everybody knew the difference between James Brown and Elvis Presley, or Willie Mays and Mickey Mantle, or the waltz and the guaguanco, or the Temptations and the Beatles, or Leontyne Price and Joan Sutherland, or Duke Ellington and Aaron Copland or even old Nat Turner and M. Jefferson Davis. And so I did not think we had to leaf back to Chapter One. But we do.
>
> Please, sir, we are different, sir.
>
> Our ancestors came from Africa, yours from Europe. Our ancestors did not want to come to the United States, yours did. Once we arrived in the United States, yes, we both worked—but separated from each other. We did not mix. You remained, essentially, a European people. We remained an African people.
>
> We remained African because in Africa we had possessed a complex and highly developed oral tradition. Knowledge—of the past, of the environment, artistic traditions, philosophy, myth, cuisine—was passed from one generation to the next, orally.
>
> In the United States, we improvised. An African, a grown man, taken in battle or kidnapped, marched to the coast in chains, forced onto a ship, carried across the ocean, unloaded, sold and told, finally, that he must pick somebody else's cotton, such a man had better improvise. He did. We all did. We improvised on English. We improvised on Christianity. We improvised on European dress. We improvised on European instruments. We improvised on European games.
>
> An African woman may have learned to cook her owner's dinner the way he liked it, but when she cooked her own food, she added a little pepper, as she had done in Africa. And that's the food she fed her children, or the African children she was feeding. And she taught the girls to cook that way, the old way. And those girls taught their girls. Orally. To our day.

We talked. We improvised. And our ancestors came from Africa. That is why you cannot compare James Brown to Elvis Presley, the Temptations to the Beatles, or Duke Ellington to Aaron Copland, or even the Black Power Movement to the Abolitionists and the Anarchists.

We are different.[5]

Criticism of Black Student Activism

My initial association with African graduate students at Harvard was a carryover from my undergraduate years. My college classmate Kalu Ezera and I enrolled together in the Harvard Graduate School in the fall of 1953, both in the field of political science, and at the Harkness Common Dining Hall, where most graduate students took their meals, he introduced me to several of his African friends: Nigerians Olufemi Sanu and Clement Isong, who had attended Howard; H. A. Oluwasami, who had attended More-house; and Ghanaian Amon Nikoi, who was a graduate of Amherst.[6]

By 1958–1959, around the time that I was completing my PhD studies, several African undergraduate students had entered Harvard College. Hillary Nqueno, who would become a newspaper editor, and Wanjoli Waciuma, a future schoolteacher, were both from Kenya. By 1961–1962—the academic year that I began teaching at Harvard—the first larger cohort of African undergraduates had arrived. Three were from Nigeria—Azinna Nwafor, a future academic; Chris Ohiri; and Chuma Azikiwe, a future financier and son of the first president of Nigeria, Nnamdi Azikiwe. Politically, these undergraduate Africans tended to be rather quiescent; they did not create a formal organization among themselves.

The situation changed measurably by the 1962–1963 academic year. Ayi Kwei Armah, an undergraduate who had entered the previous year and was majoring in comparative literature, was ideologically progressive and personally charismatic. Armah, who would go on to become a novelist, became friends with several Black American undergraduates who were also progressive: Karen Fields, who studied anthropology and became an academic; Jack Butler, who studied political science and economics and became a lawyer; and two political science students, Lowell Johnston and James Hoyte, both of whom became lawyers. All four had friendships with a circle of ideologically progressive white students, a situation that within four years helped to form an interracial network of activist students at Harvard.

Before the 1963–1964 academic year had ended, someone in that circle of African and Black American undergraduates floated the idea of a campus organization to focus on their concerns as Black students at a majority-white institution. By the spring term of that year, a group of about ten announced the formation of the Harvard Association of African and Afro-American Students (HAAAS). Among the founders were Armah, Nwafor, Azikiwe, Nqueno, and Waciuma. Among the Black American student founders were Butler, Fields, Hoyte, and Johnston as well as Charles Lovell, a future medical doctor.[7]

The new organization immediately faced criticism and opposition on campus, not from conservative whites but from Blacks, or, rather, from one conservative Black student, Herbert Denton, the only Black student on the college newspaper, the *Harvard Crimson*. In an editorial, Denton expressed concern that if HAAAS was officially recognized as "a Negro organization on campus" by the office of John Munro, the dean of college and a liberal administrator, Black students who did not join might be labeled "Uncle Toms." Denton put forth a second opposing argument, which anticipated that of conservative Black intellectuals of the 1980s: "Unless one adheres to some notion of a racial consciousness, it would seem that the experience of each individual consists of what happens to him within his own concrete social and cultural situation. The tribulations of his ancestors three hundred years ago [under slavery] become relevant only insofar as he is taught to believe them emotionally important regardless of his own position."[8]

Here Denton reveals his limited historical understanding of ethnic groups that have engaged in political activist behavior in modern nation-state societies. Once again I think of Jewish Europeans and Americans, whose Zionist activism grew out of a response to millennia of anti-Semitism, and of the Irish, whose anti-Anglo activism is a response to four hundred years of English oppression of Ireland and the Irish people. Sometimes ethnocentric activism turns violent and militant, but certainly not always, and Black people's response to the historic assault perpetrated against us, our style of activism from the 1960s onward, has been rather benign and culturally pluralistic, geared toward protecting the honor of Black people of the present and the past. Denton, therefore, was just plain wrong in opposing HAAAS. Nevertheless, he successfully persuaded the Harvard Student Council—which comprised conservative white students—to oppose granting official status to HAAAS, and the council advised the dean of college accordingly.

This decision mobilized me, along with a broad swath of Black students, to get behind the quest by HAAAS for official recognition. One of those who came to the defense of HAAAS was Archie C. Epps III. In an astute essay to the *Crimson*, the Harvard Divinity School student argued that organizing along Black ethnic lines was operationally no different from what Irish American students did via the Newman clubs and other Catholic associations or what Jewish American students did via Hillel associations. As was the case with white students who formed ethnic organizations, Black students fashioning such groups, he argued, was pragmatic, not xenophobic. In support of Epps's essay, I sent the *Crimson* a lengthy column of my own defending HAAAS's quest for official recognition.

In my early days of teaching at Harvard in 1962—I was appointed a lecturer in the Department of Government after I returned from a research trip to West Africa—I set myself the task of assisting Black students in their adaptation to life on campus along pragmatic lines. I could have ignored the issue of Black students' increasing numbers on white campuses in the 1960s, but that just wasn't my character. I couldn't just sit on the fence. After all, I myself had learned the elements of activist Black ethnic awareness at the feet of brilliant Black intellectuals at Lincoln University, scholars such as Horace Mann Bond, John Aubrey Davis, Laurence Foster, Henry Cornwell, Joseph Newton Hill, and St. Clair Drake, and I promised myself upon my graduation from Lincoln to be faithful to the best features of Black ethnic activist awareness. So when events in the 1960s nudged a generation of students toward a new phase of Black awakening on white campuses, I was fully prepared to lend a helping hand.

My participation as a Black faculty member in the formation of HAAAS was the subject of an appraisal—and not a particularly kind one—by Randall Kennedy, a contributor to the new Black conservatism of the 1980s and 1990s. He was a faculty member at the Harvard Law School, and his assessment appeared in the introduction to Werner Sollors's *Blacks at Harvard*. In his one-dimensional view of American interethnic patterns, the very existence of HAAAS was little more than a form of "Black racialism." Therefore, any Black academic who assisted a Black students' association must be chastised for aiding unacceptable, nondemocratic forms of ethnic group mobilization. As Kennedy put it:

> One defender of the new [Harvard Black students' association] was Martin L. Kilson, a lecturer in the Department of Government who subsequently became the first tenured black member of the Harvard Faculty of

Arts & Sciences. Another of the Association's backers was Archie Epps III, a first-year graduate who later became the Dean of Students at Harvard College. . . . From his years as a graduate student in the 1950s, when he helped to found The Harvard Society For Minority Rights, to his years in the 1980s and 1990s as the senior black faculty member within Arts and Sciences, Kilson has been involved in all of the many racial controversies that have surfaced on campus. In "Harvard and the Small-Towner" [my essay in *Blacks at Harvard*], Kilson continues to defend [his] early "bid to give vigorous intellectual formation to students' Black-ethnic awareness," contending that the Association was "Black-skewed" but not "ethnocentrically black-skewed." Kilson gives no hint as to how he justifies his confusion; after all, insofar as the student group at issue did limit its membership on a racial basis, it seems that the group could appropriately be labeled as "ethnocentric." . . . For historians of ideas, the task of the future will be to identify the line separating what Kilson defends as pragmatic "ethnic militancy" on Harvard's campus from what he condemns as "ethnocentrism."[9]

From my analytical perspective, Kennedy's mode of conservative discourse on Black ethnic activism lacks a serious comparativist understanding. For one thing, he fails to grasp that Black folks are not simply a "defensive ethnic group" or a group shaped merely by white supremacist forces. Rather, Black folks are also and especially an "organic ethnic group," just like Jewish Americans, Irish Americans, Italian Americans, and other such white groups.

Thus, from the early 1960s on, my own mode of Black ethnic activism on the Harvard campus was defined along pluralist ideological lines, which is to say that a leftist Black intellectual like me was obligated to be vigilant about facilitating democratizing dimensions of ethnic-bloc mobilization on college campuses. At the same time, I and other leftist academics were obligated to help keep in check parochial extremist facets of Black ethnic-bloc activism. I opposed the parochial and mean-spirited patterns among ethnic-activist Black students, and I advanced their universalist-oriented and democratizing patterns.

One avenue I used was to send columns and letters to the editor of the *Harvard Crimson*. A major focus of these pieces concerned my advice to African American students to enhance pluralist dimensions of their activism and avoid those that were xenophobic. This theme, for example, was the focus of a letter published on October 1, 1975, titled "Ethnic Militancy," in which I critiqued Black students' opposition to the selection of Jack

Greenberg, a liberal white civil rights lawyer and former director of the NAACP Legal Defense Fund, to deliver a lecture series on civil rights at the Harvard Law School. Another focus of my columns and letters to the *Crimson* criticized racist behavior among Harvard's white students, as well as the chauvinist mode of ethnic activism among some white students.

Maturation: Research and Scholarship

My graduate school years closed in June 1959 when I received my doctorate at the Harvard commencement. The next phase in my odyssey was one of intellectual maturation. During this time I learned to teach in the fields of comparative and American politics and to conduct research on new states in West Africa as well as on new political inclusion patterns among African Americans. Finally, during the last two decades following my graduate studies, two major political developments occurred that led to my fashioning a humanistic-leftist worldview for myself. One related to decolonization in Africa and other non-Western areas, which had already engaged my interest during graduate school, and the other was the simultaneous political mobilization of African Americans in the civil rights movement.

In the 1956–1957 academic year, after I passed my qualifying exam to advance to the PhD thesis-writing stage, my graduate adviser, Professor Rupert Emerson, asked if I'd like to write my dissertation on the UN Trusteeship Council. He had offered the topic to earlier graduate students, and while none of them had been interested, I was.[1] Just as I had as a youth, I was willing to take on a dare! Professor Emerson and I chose to study the UN mechanism of visiting missions, which functioned as the UN's police agency vis-à-vis European colonies that had been supervised by the League of Nations between the two world wars. The request to find a graduate student to research the visiting missions had come from Ralph Bunche, the first Black graduate student Emerson helped advise in the 1930s.

Professor Emerson found a little research money for me from Harvard's Center for International Affairs, where he served on the executive board. Robert Weaver, the head of the John Hay Whitney Foundation, also gave me some funding. After arriving in New York City by bus in 1957, I spent the academic year at the United Nations, researching the trusteeship system's records on visiting missions and interviewing technicians—lawyers from European countries, mainly—who worked under Bunche. His office kindly provided me a small cubicle-type work space and access to his trusteeship files. I also had the opportunity to interview Bunche himself. By December 1958 I had a draft of my dissertation ready; I wrote quite easily once I had research materials in hand. Happily for me, Professor Emerson and another adviser, assistant professor Stanley Hoffmann, liked it and told me to proceed with a final draft, which I submitted in April 1959. They handed down an evaluation of "excellent," which became the foundation for my future academic appointments at Harvard. I still have a copy of my dissertation; I look at it every couple of years to see how I started as a young analyst in comparative politics and international studies.

Immediately after I received my degree in June 1959, Professor Emerson told me to apply for a Ford Foundation Foreign Area Research Fellowship for fieldwork research in West Africa. One of Emerson's earlier graduate students, James Smoot Coleman, had received a Ford Fellowship to study political development in Nigeria, so I felt confident about my chances. Within a month I had received a grant of around $12,000 to research the modern political development in Sierra Leone.

Oxford, England

Following receipt of that fellowship, a whole new world opened for me. I married Marion Dusser de Barenne in early August 1959. We were an unusual couple—she was a white American, and I was a Black American. We sailed on a French ocean liner, *La Flandre*, for England. I had never been on a liner before. In fact, when we flew from Boston to catch *La Flandre* in New York City, it was my first time on an airplane. At that period of my life, I was still a small-town guy who hadn't been far from home. Just as the world was becoming bigger for me, we had a small-world experience aboard *La Flandre*. To our surprise and delight, one of our fellow passengers was the esteemed E. Franklin Frazier, and we had our meals with him for eight days! We knew his work, of course, but this was our first time becoming acquainted with him. He was going to a meeting of the International Sociological Association, and during the trip he regaled Marion and me with fascinating tales of his august career as a sociologist, referring often to his teaching years at Howard University. When he died a few years later, his wife telephoned us at our small apartment in Cambridge, Massachusetts, to tell us about the sad event.

I found England to be a cohesive society, not scattershot, as I had come to see America's. While there, we did preliminary research in British colonial documents pertaining to West Africa that were located at Oxford University, where Marion also studied the Mende language, the tongue of Sierra Leone's major tribal community. I was provided an office at Professor Margery Perham's Institute of Commonwealth Studies, where I met Thomas Hodgkin's circle of left-wing Oxford academics working in African studies. Hodgkin, an Arab and African studies scholar whose father had been master of Balliol College, and his wife, Dorothy, who later won the Nobel Prize in chemistry, were very kind to Marion and me. Nearly every weekend from September into December, they invited us to dinner gatherings that were like little intellectual confabs, at which a broad range of the Hodgkins' intellectual and political friends came in and out and talked about current political events in Britain, Europe, and elsewhere.

During the weekends, Marion and I would jump on the iconic British double-decker red bus and travel, occasionally around the Oxfordshire countryside but more often to areas of Oxford itself where the working class lived. Those proletarian areas were so different from the world of Oxford University! The streets were often like alleyways; most houses still lacked running water and had outside toilets. George Bond, a roommate during my Harvard Graduate School days, visited us for a weekend from the University of London, where he was doing his doctorate in cultural anthropology, and he joined us on one of those red-bus excursions. George was the brother of Max Bond, whom I met my first week at Harvard, and the nephew of my mentor Horace Mann Bond. We had a great time with George that weekend.

There were only two African scholars at Oxford University when Marion and I were researching there. One was Ghanaian political scientist Willie Abraham, and the other was Nigerian law scholar T. O. Elias. We got to know Elias well; we had him by our small apartment for dinner, and I ate lunch often with him at a hole-in-the-wall Chinese restaurant on Banbury Road, the main road going through Oxford. Elias was a Yoruba, very smart and scholarly, and he was hoping against hope for a fellowship appointment at All Souls College. Personally, I thought he was too independent-minded for the establishmentarian English academics who controlled these appointments at Oxford, and in the end, he was not appointed. A year later he returned to Nigeria—quite bitter, I thought. He worked in the justice department at a top-tier position and became the chief judicial minister during the civil war. As far as I'm aware, he never got back to being a legal scholar. When a military government was established from 1966 to 1972, Elias was appointed minister of justice and held that important office until he retired. I have often thought it strange that no Nigerian academic has written something on the career of T. O. Elias. The guy was brilliant!

The Making of an African State

Marion and I really loved our five-month research visit to Oxford. We went to movies and the theater, ate out often at good restaurants, and above all were befriended by Thomas Hodgkin. Two weeks before Christmas 1959, Marion and I packed our bags and headed for Liverpool, scheduled to sail to West Africa on board the *Sangara*, which had been sunk by German submarines during World War II and rehabilitated by a resourceful Greek entrepreneur for his cargo fleet. To our dismay, we were just two days at sea when the *Sangara* encountered what were officially described as the worst winter storms ever recorded in the North Atlantic.

The ship had four days ahead of it before reaching Senegal, and those proved to be harrowing days indeed! Being in my twenties, young and very adventurous, without a care in the world, or so it seemed, I'd venture out on deck against Marion's advice, taking photographs of the *Sangara* with an old Voltlander camera (a marvelous instrument which had belonged to Marion's father) as the ship was thrown around the turbulent sea like a palm tree in a hurricane. The hull of the *Sangara* was forced straight downward into the sea and then released upward . . . and then downward . . . and so on, a pattern that continued for a day and a half. When the storm subsided, Marion and I went back on deck for more photos and found that all the steel air vents had been bent and twisted, as if they were crumpled newspaper. We still have photographs of that damaged deck.

When we reached the port of Freetown in Sierra Leone, the sight of poorly clad men waiting on the dock to unload cargo greeted us. We hailed a taxi that drove us to the University of Sierra Leone (then called by its original name, Fourah Bay College), where we lived for a year in a two-room apartment in a complex established for the faculty. It was located on an escarpment standing nearly a thousand feet above Freetown, affording us a commanding view of the city and its vast estuary. Within a week we visited the office of the US consul general (there wasn't yet an American embassy because Sierra Leone was still a British colony), purchased supplies for our apartment, and got to know several Sierra Leonean academics quite well as Marion researched Mende society.

During its independence celebration in October 1960, I visited Nigeria for six weeks. Professor Emerson and his wife, Alla, had also come to witness the festivities, and we went to Yoruba areas together and met the first Nigerian chancellor at Ibadan University, the Igbo historian Kenneth O. Dike. I also met a young Nigerian lecturer, Billy Dudley, who was traveling several hundred miles to northern Nigeria to organize an extramural studies program in Zaria and allowed me to ride along. It was an incredible trip. I stayed in Zaria for three weeks, walking around working-class and peasant areas while staying at a colonial rest house.

I returned to Lagos on a slow train, seated in the "peasants' section," which was all I could afford. The Igbo ticket officer considered me too middle class to ride in that section and hesitated to sell me such a ticket. I collected lots of materials on local government systems in Nigeria during my trip and interviewed Nigerian and British officials on governance in the hope of writing a book about local governance in Nigeria. I never did.

I traveled back from Lagos to Sierra Leone via "mammy wagons" (medium-size rickety trucks with wood seats for passengers). That was some experience. The popular yarn was that the drivers of these vehicles ate kola nuts, which were a form of narcotic, to stave off sleep, but this didn't matter to me, because I couldn't afford any safer mode of transportation. The mammy wagons I traveled on traversed Dahomey and Togoland and crossed the great Volta River on a flimsy ferry into Ghana. A day later I caught a cargo ship at Accra headed for Freetown, the capital of Sierra Leone. During that six-week sojourn to Nigeria's independence event, I really gained a rich understanding of how some agrarian and working-class African masses survive, all of which made the trip well worth it.

Only about a week into our year and a half in Sierra Leone, Marion and I had to buy our own means of transportation, which was a very used, very small British car, a Morris Minor. It looked something like the iconic vw Bug of the 1960s. We traveled all over the country—first to the north, then to the south—with a pet cat along for the ride. I arranged through the US consul and the colonial government that we might stay in government rest houses located in districts and provinces; sometimes these houses were provided by tribal chiefs. We ate sparingly and cooked our meals on a small paraffin burner. Most of the time the "menu" included canned corned beef, canned baked beans, and rice, served with locally made bread that we bought. (I was the main chef.) We often ate fruit straight from trees—bananas, avocados, grapefruit, mangoes. Our used car broke down a couple of times deep in the Sierra Leone hinterland, and there we were, stranded in the middle of nowhere. But luckily we were able to locate local African men who fixed the damn car so we could continue our travels.

We ran into a homespun local musicology researcher in the Mende section of rural Sierra Leone, a Syrian chap born to immigrant commercial businesspeople, and he had a genuine love for local African culture. He had a small shop where he recorded local African music. After we left Sierra Leone in February 1961, I often wondered what happened to him. Did he marry a local Mende woman? Settle into the African society, maybe as a schoolteacher? Some African rural societies are quite pluralistic regarding foreign strangers, some of whom might even be culturally absorbed.

Marion did all the driving during our first research trip in Sierra Leone, because I didn't yet have a license. By the time we got to Ghana for our second research trip in 1964–1965, I had a license and was able to share the driving. On that trip, we had another very used, small British car that broke down a lot. We took our two oldest children during that research and teaching trip and all three children when we returned to Ghana in 1968.

Marion and I were a young interracial American couple in our twenties running around a West African country that was still under British colonial rule. That rule, however, was undergoing a process of "governmental decolonization," a political change whereby a cadre of African (Sierra Leonean) educated professionals were being tutored by British overseers to eventually take control of the country's governance and thus its political affairs. In 1960–1961, interracially married couples were still extremely rare in the United States, compared to our contemporary period in which we are witnessing an expanding group of interracial couples and families in our country. Marion and I were trailblazers in this regard!

We were fortunate not to encounter any explicit racist behavior from the British officials still running political affairs in Sierra Leone when we got there in late December 1959. The young African officials who were running a kind of parallel African government regime, which would eventually take over Sierra Leone's government in 1961 at independence, were very friendly to Marion and me. I've often thought that we were just lucky in this regard. By the early 1960s there was a developed, though small,

African middle-class population (schoolteachers, businesspeople, lawyers, academics, government administrators, and so forth) in Sierra Leone— maybe 10 percent of the population. Nor did we experience any kind of African Black nationalist behavior toward us as foreign researchers in their country. We were invited to dinner at the homes of a couple of lawyers who were emerging political leaders, a leading female political figure, and several Sierra Leone academics.

Marion and I read lots of colonial government records and interviewed British and Sierra Leonean officials regarding the politics of decoloniza- tion. Happily, we received much cooperation from those officials, and we returned to Harvard with good research data from which I produced a half-dozen research articles and a book, *Political Change in a West African State* (1966). Recently I've been thinking about my first research experi- ence in West Africa a half century ago, and it occurred to me that *Political Change* might have been the third major book by an American scholar in political science on the development of an independent African country. I believe there were only two prior to it: David Apter's *Ghana in Transition* (1956) and James Smoot Coleman's *Nigeria: The Rise of Nigerian National- ism* (1958).

My book was also the first on modern African political patterns pro- duced by an African American political scientist. African American scholars who came just after me were C. S. Whitaker, who wrote on politics in northern Nigeria; Willard Johnson on politics in Cameroon; George Bond on Zambia; William Shack on Ethiopia; and Elliott Skin- ner on the Mossi in Upper Volta. Others, who didn't publish their African dissertation research, included my Ambler compatriot and Lincoln Uni- versity alumnus Clement Cottingham, who did a brilliant PhD thesis at the University of California, Berkeley, on Senegal's nation-state develop- ment and went on to have a successful career as a professor of political science at Rutgers.

Four Decades at Harvard

When Marion and I got back home in late February 1961 via another low- cost cargo ship (that was all the money we had for travel), we encoun- tered a blizzard along America's East Coast. Apparently we were destined to encounter inclement weather on our voyages. Once we settled back at

Harvard, Professor Emerson again extended to me a helping hand. He encouraged Professor Robert Bowie to give me a post as a research fellow, which later became a research associate post, at the Harvard Center for International Affairs, then located on Divinity Avenue across the street from the Peabody Museum. As a result, during the next several years, I was able to write *Political Change*, my first book, which the center published as part of a multivolume series with the Harvard University Press. Emerson had also gotten me appointed to the position of lecturer in the Department of Government in 1962 and then assistant professor in 1964, putting me on the tenure track.

Writing *Political Change in a West African State* took me four years; I had envisaged for myself a high-level intellectual and political science analytical standard that I was determined to achieve, and I took all that time to attain it. My second book, *New States in the Modern World* (1975), was a Festschrift which I edited celebrating the career of Rupert Emerson, which made the dear man very happy. (A time-honored tradition, a Festschrift is a volume prepared by one or more colleagues to laud the achievements of an academic on the occasion of a birthday or a retirement.) It sold out at the Harvard University Press. When Emerson died in 1978, I, along with Stanley Hoffmann and Karl Deutsch, another professor in government at Harvard, spoke about his career at a service at Harvard's Memorial Chapel. My introduction to *New States* is a theoretical essay that probes the systemic dynamics of evolving new states in Africa. I reread it recently and said to myself, "That's a damn good essay!" The chapter I contributed to the Festschrift is a conceptual analysis of political cleavages in grassroots political systems in new African states, supported by case-study local politics data from Ghana. I subsequently drafted a two-hundred-page manuscript on the subject during the postindependence period, tentatively titled *Chiefs, Peasants, and Politicians: Grassroots Politics in Ghana*, but I never found time to complete it.

The demands on my time were growing. Harvard's Department of Government asked me to teach the course Politics and Society among Afro-Americans, which started my entry into the field of American politics. Strangely enough, my academic career was following a trajectory similar to that of Ralph Bunche, from African to African American studies. I let Aristide Zolberg, a political scientist at the University of Chicago, include a section from my unpublished manuscript in his book comparing political development in Ivory Coast and Ghana. I also published an earlier essay on grassroots political systems in Sierra Leone in the Oxford University journal *Political Studies*.

In 1970 or 1971, my old colleague at Harvard Graduate School, Nathan Huggins, then a professor at Columbia University, asked me to write a chapter for a book called *Key Issues in the Afro-American Experience*. He also asked me to coedit it. I did a lot of research for that essay, titled "Political Change in the Negro Ghetto, 1900–1940s." Marion also contributed a chapter on West African society and the transatlantic slave trade to this book, published by Harcourt Brace in 1971. Ever since that chapter appeared, I have had my academic feet planted in both fields, African studies and American politics.

Meanwhile, Harvard's Department of Government needed additional courses for undergraduate and graduate students, so by the late 1970s I introduced two new ones: Authoritarian Patterns in African Politics and Politics of African Populism. Both kept me extremely busy. I published several articles on those topics. A favorite, and one of my last to be published on African politics, was for a 1993 special issue of the Tufts University Fletcher School journal *Praxis* on political decay patterns in Africa.

I produced a fifty-page manuscript on the topic of African populism and modern development for a research branch of the World Bank where Dunstan Wai, a former African graduate student of mine from Southern Sudan and Kenya, worked. I researched data on agricultural cooperatives and other agrarian organizations, as well as on urban Pentecostal churches in Nigeria, Ghana, Ivory Coast, and South Africa, all of which displayed a capacity to amass funds in the millions of dollars among their working-class congregations. (Marion and I visited one of those churches in Ghana when researching there in 1964–1965.) The analytical thrust of my report was to suggest to the World Bank that such African populist agencies could be mobilized through their mechanisms for facilitating local infrastructure advancement in African countries, just as the churches in my childhood hometown of Ambler, Pennsylvania, did. I suppose my analysis appeared somewhat sophomoric to World Bank bureaucrats, who probably tossed it onto a shelf to collect dust. Although nothing came of it, Dunstan had his office send me a $3,000 honorarium for my work. I have a copy of that report lying in a research-file box where I place unpublished manuscripts.

Throughout my career, Marion kept up her intellectual interests and scholarship in African ethnography. Her 1967 study of the Ga community in modern Accra, *African Urban Kinsmen,* had started out as her PhD dissertation in social anthropology at Harvard, and her main research on Ga religion, *Kpele Lala: Ga Religious Songs and Symbols,* was published by Harvard University Press in the early 1970s. In 2013 she published *Dancing with the Gods,* a collection of her research articles on religious patterns among the Ga people in Ghana. Most recently she edited the collection of essays *Kings, Priests, and Kinsmen,* the work of a Ga scholar.

I haven't written anything on African states since the mid-1990s, but I have done several talks. Since then, work on African American social and cultural patterns has dominated my academic life. Around 1980, I also ventured into work on political culture among white ethnic groups when Hugh Douglas Price, chair of Harvard's Department of Government, asked me to teach a course titled Ethnic Groups in American Political Culture; I taught it for more than a decade. I figured that by the 1990s, as a progressive African American political science scholar, I had fulfilled my intellectual obligation toward African studies. In the 1987–1988 academic year, dean of faculty Michael Spence named me the Frank G. Thomson Professor of Government, a chair that I held until retiring from my final Harvard faculty position as a research professor of government in 2003.

Another issue nudged me away from African studies and toward full-time work in African American studies. As the political-culture character of African states tilted so massively in full-fledged authoritarian directions (riddled with cynical and massive corruption, vicious interethnic violence, and mean-spirited anti-intellectualism), I lost that early, visceral, pro-African nationalist movement empathy that was communicated to me during my undergraduate years at Lincoln University by my intellectual mentors, among them Horace Mann Bond, John Aubrey Davis, Joseph Newton Hill, and Laurence Foster. I gave a talk at my alma mater in the early 1990s, when I was on the Lincoln Board of Trustees and Niara Sudarkasa was president, in which I critiqued the authoritarian-mediated political decay in new African states. I remarked, "I'm glad that my main Lincoln intellectual mentor, Dr. Bond, who was a strong supporter of African nationalist movements, is now deceased, because he would have been gravely disappointed to witness the horrible authoritarian patterns in independent Africa." I got frowns from two of Sudarkasa's Nigerian staff people (one was her official photographer), but, if I recall correctly, they didn't mention anything substantive to criticize my talk. I would have rebutted them, of course.

Closing Down

I formally retired from teaching in the spring term of 1999, when the Harvard dean of faculty, Jeremy Knowles, appointed me Frank G. Thomson Research Professor Emeritus. I held that position until my official retirement in 2003.

Before formally retiring, however, I commenced researching in a steady fashion the development of the African American professional class, a topic I had been pursuing sporadically for a number of years. I developed an interest in this topic in my junior and senior years at Lincoln University. Adelaide Cromwell, an African American scholar at Boston University, spurred me to produce one of my earliest writings on the African American professional class in 1968, when she asked me to coedit the book *Apropos of Africa: Sentiments of Afro-American Leaders toward Africa* (1969). About the same year, I wrote and published an essay on the ideological orientations of the famous Black novelist Richard Wright for the socialist magazine *Dissent.*

When Horace Mann Bond died a few years later, I decided to write an essay on his intellectual career. It took a couple of years because I researched nearly everything Bond had written, and during this process several related incidents occurred. The University of Alabama Press wanted to publish a reprint edition of Bond's second book, *Negro Education in Alabama: A Study in Cotton and Steel,* which was first published in 1939. Bond's widow would give the press copyright permission only if they asked me to write an afterword. (Another scholar wrote the foreword.) My research for that afterword, published in 1990, took me deeper into Bond's career, and after its completion and publication, I planned a book on twentieth-century African American intellectuals.

I had titled the book *The Making of Black Intellectuals,* and it was meant to contain chapters on major personalities such as Horace Mann Bond, John Aubrey Davis, Ralph Bunche, E. Franklin Frazier, Harold Cruse, and Ira Reid. Chapter titles included "Horace Mann Bond: Black Scholar in the Age of White Supremacy" and "John Aubrey Davis: Political Scientist as Activist and Technocrat." The Davis chapter took a couple of years to get right, because I had to research federal government records on President Franklin Delano Roosevelt's Fair Employment Practices Committee (FEPC), which administered antidiscrimination policies in businesses with government war contracts during World War II. Davis was my Lincoln University political science professor and one of about ten Black American policymakers responsible for running the committee. Also involved were the civil rights lawyers William Hastie and Elmer Henderson, Howard University Law School professor James Nabrit, the economist Robert Weaver, the journalist Clarence Mitchell, and the dean of Howard University Law School, George Johnson.

This was the first time ever that Black American professionals held full-fledged policy-making positions in the US federal government! Professor Davis had some of the official records in his personal files and encouraged me to write about his experiences in the FEPC. I let Professor Wilbur Rich at Wellesley College publish a short version of my essay on Davis's experience in the FEPC during World War II.[2] I believe Professor Henry Louis Gates Jr. of the Du Bois Institute (now the Hutchins Center) for African and African American Research read my chapter in Rich's book before he approached me about presenting in the institute's Du Bois Lectures Series on Black Intellectuals in the 2010 spring term.

That was almost six years ago at the time of this writing, and my physical and intellectual energy weren't what they used to be. But by 2010 I had amassed a lot of research materials on the making of the twentieth-century African American intellectuals, so I accepted the institute's invitation as an opportunity to systematically formulate my ideas about how the African American intelligentsia had developed. Professor Gates liked my topic for the Du Bois Lectures, and after I delivered them in March and April, he told me they were "brilliant." He sent them to the humanities editor at Harvard University Press, who responded with a book contract.

Turning a set of lectures into a book manuscript turned out to be more difficult than I anticipated. It took me nearly three years to produce a satisfactory product. I submitted a finished manuscript to Harvard University Press in February 2013, and with intellectual and technical assistance from Marion (a PC-produced manuscript requires more technical know-how than the old typewriter manuscript did), she and I completed the editing chores on the final galley proofs sent us by the Harvard University Press editors. *The Transformation of the African American Intelligentsia, 1880–2012,* was published in 2014 and won a 2015 American Book Award. It's a cliché to say that hard work pays off, but this time it really did.

Before that, the last book that I had published with Harvard University Press was in 1976. *The African Diaspora: Interpretive Essays,* in which both Marion and I have chapters, was planned as the first volume in a series that I designed for the press and coedited with Robert Rotberg, who was then teaching history at MIT. However, in 1978, a new editor took over at Harvard University Press—Arthur Rosenthal, who came from Basic Books in New York City—and, facing a massive budget deficit, slashed planned projects, one of which was the multivolume project on the African diaspora that I designed. It was a long-run project for which the press's former director, Thomas J. Wilson, a progressive WASP, had allocated a small operational budget. The press had even provided us a special project letterhead; I still have copies of original outlines of the three volumes I had planned on it. My goal was to have many more than these initial three volumes on African American social, cultural, and political patterns from the Emancipation era to the twenty-first century, including patterns related to churches, voluntary associations such as mutual-aid organizations and fraternal agencies, farmers' associations in the South, trade unions, business organizations, intellectuals at Black colleges, professional associations, and political organizations. I had lofty goals, and seeing the evidence of my plans worked out on that letterhead made Rosenthal's scuttling of it all the more painful. That was in 1978—thirty-nine years ago as I write this—which means we might have had some twenty books published in that project by now! I suppose the publication and success of my *Transformation of the African American Intelligentsia* sort of makes up for the collapse of my original African American diaspora project at the old Harvard University Press.

Looking back on my project from today's vantage point, I will explain one of the many reasons it pained me so that it fell through. At the time, I was hopeful that as Black studies and Afro-American studies programs developed at major universities such as Harvard, Yale, Columbia, University of Pennsylvania, Boston University, Michigan, Indiana, UCLA, and Howard, maybe one of those new programs would pick up from where my African diaspora project had left off. But none did. Around 1994, I addressed a memo outlining a similar project to the board of Harvard's Du Bois Institute and suggesting that it initiate something like Du Bois's great Atlanta University Studies of Social Conditions among Negroes from back in the early 1900s, but there were no takers. I remember that when I distributed that memo at a board meeting, Professor Orlando Patterson made a putdown remark: "Oh, Martin, we have graduate students who are producing PhD dissertations on these topics." That, by the way, was not true! Professors Preston Williams (Divinity School), William Julius Wilson (sociology and Kennedy School), and Cornel West (philosophy and African American studies) were at that board meeting—but none of them spoke out in favor of my memo, which saddened me a little.

Also in the 1994 academic year, I designed a conference to commemorate the fiftieth anniversary of Gunnar Myrdal's great book on the overall status of Black Americans as of World War II, *An American Dilemma: The Negro Problem in Modern Democracy* (1944). The Carnegie Corporation financed that monumental research project, and several African American scholars worked on it (Ira Reid, Charles Johnson, E. Franklin Frazier, Doxey Wilkerson, Abram Harris); Ralph Bunche helped organize the project and did much of the field research on the political status of African Americans at the time. I successfully coaxed a small grant out of the MacArthur Foundation to launch the conference, and we held it in Cambridge in the fall term of 1995. I persuaded Professors John Aubrey Davis and Hylan Lewis to address the conference. (I also invited John Hope Franklin, but he couldn't come.) Dedicating the conference to these luminaries, I delivered the introductory address. It was a fine intellectual occasion—my favorite during my forty-plus academic years at Harvard.

The Election of Barack Obama

This book has covered my journey through seventy years of the twentieth century and sixteen years of the twenty-first. When I decided to write about that journey, I chose to concentrate less on the personal aspects of my odyssey and more on the network of social patterns such as those formed by the African American family, social institutions such as the Black American church, civic organizations such as the Boy Scouts, public institutions such as schools (which were racially integrated in my hometown), and higher education institutions such as the Negro colleges, as they were called when I enrolled in one of them in 1949. Those agencies did most of the first-level higher education of African Americans from the late Reconstruction era until the 1970s, because our country's mainline white-majority institutions of higher education wouldn't enroll African Americans.

When tracing my intellectual odyssey, I concluded that the historic election in 2008 of Barack Obama as president of the United States was inarguably the major political-culture event of my lifetime. I consider it to have redefined the generic character of what W. E. B. Du Bois called "the souls of black folk" in our white-supremacist American civilization.

In other words, after President Obama's election to the White House, African Americans no longer occupied a one-dimensional sociocultural valuation in the minds of many of their white compatriots. They would no longer merely be victims of a broadcast white-supremacist cultural order. Rather, African Americans would increasingly acquire a multidimensional sociocultural citizenry valuation. Given this new characterization of the cultural valuation of African Americans, I will conclude this account of my odyssey with an analysis of the special role played by African American citizens in facilitating the election of Barack Obama.

This role involved a multilayered political mobilization of core civic, societal, and institutional agencies in Black society. The political growth of those agencies paralleled my own metamorphosis from my childhood, my college years, and my early and mature professional years.

....

By midnight on Election Day, November 4, 2008, it was clear that American political culture had entered a new era with the electoral victory of the Barack Obama–Joe Biden Democratic ticket over the John McCain–Sarah Palin Republican ticket. Obama-Biden won 53 percent of the popular vote and 365 votes in the Electoral College, clinching a unique victory with the first-ever election of an African American as president of the United States of America. The year 2009 witnessed three momentous national celebratory occasions. The first was the inauguration of the first African American president, the second was the celebration of the two hundredth anniversary of Abraham Lincoln's birth, and the third was the one hundredth anniversary of the founding of the NAACP, an organization devoted to the vanquishing of white supremacist practices in American society, without which the election of Barack Obama would not have been possible. In this epilogue I will focus on the Black electoral attributes that contributed significantly to Obama's victory in both the Democratic primary contests and the presidential election. Those Black electoral attributes emanated from what I will dub the Black voter bloc (BVB).

South Carolina

Owing to the solid commitment of African American voters nationally to Bill Clinton during his two victorious elections for the White House in 1992 and 1996, many political pundits of election dynamics assumed that Hillary Clinton would also gain the BVB's support. The earliest Democratic contests in the Iowa primary (January 3, 2008) and New Hampshire (January 8) did not test this assumption because those states had vastly white majorities. (In 2008, Iowa was about 92 percent white, while New Hampshire was 95 percent white.) These states did, however, demonstrate in the 2008 primaries that an African American candidate could surmount some aspects of the "race issue" and thus be fairly competitive with white candidates. Thus in the Iowa caucus, victory went to Obama with 38 percent of the vote, while John Edwards gained 33 percent, and Clinton took 29 percent. Five days later, Clinton won the New Hampshire primary with 39 percent of the vote, but Obama held her to a 3 percentage point victory margin, gaining 36 percent of the votes and thereby outperforming Edwards.

On January 26, Obama surprised the political pundits by defeating Clinton among African American voters in South Carolina. This outcome occurred despite polls that showed a firm BVB support for Clinton. What had changed?

On the Monday before the January 8 New Hampshire primary, in an interview on Fox News, Clinton proclaimed that "Dr. King's dream began to be realized when President Lyndon Johnson passed the Civil Rights Act of 1964. . . . It took a president to get it done."[1] Ostensibly her purpose in making this comment was to put a pin in candidate Obama's high-flying image among New Hampshire's Democratic voters. Although the comment might have contributed to her small, 3 percentage point victory margin in the New Hampshire primary, it nevertheless had a negative impact among the BVB generally and in South Carolina in particular.

During the weekend after the New Hampshire primary, Obama held a press conference on Sunday, January 13, during which he criticized Clinton's comment. As reported in the *Boston Globe*, Obama said, "Senator Clinton made an unfortunate remark, an ill-advised remark, about King and Lyndon Johnson. She, I think, offended some folks who felt that somehow diminished King's role in bringing about the Civil Rights Act."[2] Obama's press conference took place the same Sunday as Clinton's interview earlier that day on NBC's *Meet the Press*, in which she defended her King comment and charged Obama and his staff with having distorted it in the eyes of millions of African Americans. Obama's remarks, then, were a retort to Clinton's defense of herself.

As the second week following the New Hampshire primary ensued, Clinton's King comment began to take on a life of its own, especially among millions of African American voters who, in that election season, gained much of their understanding of race-related issues via urban Black radio stations and internet sources. Accordingly, the crux of Black voters' interpretation of Clinton's King comment was that it was a muted version of a "Southern strategy" vis-à-vis Barack Obama's primary campaign candidacy. Moreover, by the middle of the second week after the New Hampshire primary, the lead editorial column in the *New York Times* pronounced a similar understanding of Clinton's campaign strategy: "It was clearly her side that initially stoked the race and gender issue. Mrs. Clinton followed up her strange reference to the Rev. Martin Luther King, Jr. and President Lyndon Johnson—and no matter how many times she tried to reframe the quote, the feeling hung in the air that she was denigrating America's most revered leader." Regarding tactics used by the Clinton campaign to defend her, the editorial added this observation: "Her staff and supporters, including the over-the-top former President Bill Clinton, went beyond Mrs. Clinton's maladroit comments and started blaming Mr. Obama for the mess."[3]

Just under two weeks after the *New York Times* editorial, the noxious impact among the BVB of the Clinton campaign's initial race-card tactic became fully known. In the January 26 South Carolina primary, African American voters made it clear that they were not going to tolerate any such maneuvers by Clinton's campaign vis-à-vis Senator Obama. Accordingly, the BVB (which was 40 percent of the voters) gave Obama a solid victory. He received 54 percent of the vote (229,352), while Clinton received 27 percent (114,351) and Edwards a mere 19 percent (79,129). More significantly, perhaps, 85 percent of African American voters supported Obama—even though polling in November and December had placed Clinton ahead of him by a two-to-one margin.

Several additional aspects of South Carolina's 2008 primary warrant attention. Some 75 percent of South Carolina Democratic voters said in an exit poll that they "were ready to elect a black president." When asked whether they thought Americans generally "were ready to elect a black president," 90 percent said yes. There was an important difference between Black and white voters as to whether Clinton or Obama would be the "most electable" Democrat in November 2008. According to exit polls, "two-thirds of blacks say Obama is most electable, while more whites think Clinton is most electable."[4]

From Super Tuesday to Pennsylvania

When viewed in developmental terms, we can say that the first solid evidence of a permanent reversal in the long-standing BVB support for the Clinton machine occurred during the twenty-one Super Tuesday state primaries held on February 5, 2008. The results on Super Tuesday can be viewed as rather miraculous for the Obama campaign, which was an upstart event. It challenged the well-established electoral machine within the Democratic Party in this era, and though losing to Clinton in overall votes, Obama emerged in good condition, solidly standing on his feet. Furthermore, Obama received 7,294,851 votes, which meant Clinton had an advantage over him of only 53,120 votes. At the same time, Obama won in five more states than Clinton, meaning that he was able to tie her in the delegate count category (839 delegates each)—which was, after all, the ultimate category for determining the presidential nominee. Thus, the Super Tuesday results were a kind of tipping point for the Obama campaign, and this dynamic was sustained five days later in the Potomac primaries, which saw Obama winning in Maryland with 60 percent of the votes compared to 37 percent for Clinton and in Virginia with 64 percent of votes compared to Clinton's 35 percent.

That the Super Tuesday and Potomac primaries skewed in favor of Obama was broadly recognized by media outlets. In a commentary on February 13, the conservative editors of the *Wall Street Journal* noticed something that others missed:

> The rise of Barack Obama is a remarkable political event, and to judge by last night [February 12] it is only gaining speed. With three more victories in the 'Potomac primary,' including a crushing rout [of Clinton] in Virginia, the Illinois Senator must now be judged the favorite for the Democratic nomination.
>
> Let that one sink in for a moment. The rookie candidate from Illinois . . . is leading the most successful Democratic machine of the last generation.[5]

How did the *Wall Street Journal* prognosis in February 2008, judging Senator Barack Obama as the favorite for the Democratic nomination, become reality? The answer is that the BVB, commencing with the January 26 South Carolina primary, fashioned a pro-Obama mystique that mesmerized Black voters' imaginations—especially their multilayered civil society agencies. I define these institutions as "a variety of Black people's societal and institution-building mechanisms, such as women's clubs, mutual benefit associations, artisan groups, clergy associations and churches, teachers associations, intellectual associations, fraternal associations, business associations, trade unions, and professional associations."[6]

The media—newspapers and television—paid very little attention to the crucial role of Black civil society mechanisms during the Democratic primaries in states with sizable African American populations, including New York, New Jersey, Pennsylvania, Virginia, Maryland, Alabama, Georgia, and North Carolina. In the April 22 Pennsylvania primary, for example, in which African Americans constituted 15 percent of Democratic Party voters, the voter mobilization activity produced a record-breaking Black turnout. As a result, although Clinton won the Pennsylvania primary, the high

BVB turnout enabled Obama to keep her victory margin to 9.4 percentage points. That margin was achieved through cynical Southern-strategy-type appeals to working- and lower-middle-class white voters, which gained her 62 percent of the Pennsylvania vote compared to 38 percent for Obama. An editorial in the *New York Times* claimed,

> The Pennsylvania [Clinton] campaign . . . was even meaner, more vacuous, more desperate, and more filled with pandering than the mean, vacuous, desperate, pander-filled contests that preceded it [e.g., Ohio on March 4].
>
> . . . It is past time for Senator Hillary Rodham Clinton to acknowledge that the negativity for which she is mostly responsible, does nothing but harm to her, her opponent, her party and the 2008 election.
>
> . . . Mrs. Clinton did not get the big win in Pennsylvania that she needed to challenge the [delegate count] calculus of the Democratic race.[7]

The Pennsylvania primary was an important test of the electoral significance of the BVB and of the capacity of the Obama campaign to compete with the Clinton political machine. Put another way, the BVB in that state enabled Obama to hold on to his advantage in the all-important delegate count. Following Pennsylvania's primary was the delegate-rich May 6 North Carolina primary, and here again, the BVB provided Obama a crucial victory, the significance of which was described by *USA Today*:

> Obama's double-digit win in North Carolina [56 percent to 42 percent] widened his lead among pledged delegates and put him on pace to finish the night within 200 of the 2,025 delegates needed for nomination.
>
> More importantly, his resounding victory in one state [North Carolina] and strong finish [in Indiana, where he lost by just 2 percentage points] could convince party leaders known as superdelegates that he had weathered questions about electability and a controversy over inflammatory comments by his pastor.[8]

Moreover, what contributed to the watershed role of the North Carolina primary in advancing Obama's delegate count edge was what might be called the democratization of Democratic primaries. This feature of democratization revolved around the special role of both the BVB and young voters generally: "In capturing North Carolina, Obama relied on voters such as these—students voting for the first time and African-Americans—for his core support. Blacks, who made up a third of the Democratic electorate in the Tar Heel State, backed Obama 13-to-1. . . . Voters under 30 supported the Illinois Senator 3 to 1."[9]

Black Voters and Political Culture

Data gathered by exit polls following the Super Tuesday primaries confirmed the existence of a pro-Obama African American voter mystique. As *Boston Globe* reporter Susan Milligan wrote, "Early exit polls reflected what the campaigns and pollsters had concluded weeks ago: that Obama would capture an overwhelming majority of the African-American vote." Milligan elaborated, "Obama collected an average of 80 percent of the African-American vote in the Super Tuesday states, according to exit polls, winning Georgia last night with 88 percent of the African-American vote. And while the Illinois senator as expected lost Clinton's home state of New York, his campaign calculated that a strong showing among African-Americans in New York City would peel away some delegates in the Empire State [which in fact it did]."[10]

Furthermore, , the votes cast by African American women were especially significant. As another *Boston Globe* political analyst, Lisa Wangsness, observed, "In every state where exit-polling data were available last night, black women overwhelmingly voted for Obama, and they helped him carry states with a high percentage of black voters, including Alabama and Georgia. Black women chose Obama over Clinton by a 7 to 1 margin in both Georgia and New Jersey. Obama carried Georgia where black women made up 33 percent of the electorate."[11] Important as Black female votes were, it was the aggregate feature of the BVB vote that sustained the Obama campaign's capacity to ultimately defeat Clinton.

The Democratic National Convention

An overview of the interface of the BVB and Senator Barack Obama's 2008 victory can be attained through analysis of the Black Americans who attended the Democratic National Convention in August 2008. Some 24.5 percent of the convention delegates were African Americans. Other minority groups attending were Native Americans (2.5 percent), Hispanics (11.8 percent), and Asians (4.6 percent). By contrast, the *Wall Street Journal* reported,

> Of the more than 2,300 Republican delegates who gathered [at the Republican National Convention in St. Paul, Minnesota], just 36—1.5%—were black, the lowest proportion in 40 years. . . .

That is substantially below the figure in 2004, when a record-breaking 6.8% of Republican delegates were black. The number of black Republican delegates running for federal office also has fallen sharply, to about seven from a high of 24 in 1996.[12]

A multilayered understanding of the variegated interactions between Democratic African American voters and the 2008 national convention was provided by a series of astute reporters for the *New York Times*. In a vivid article on delegates at the national convention on August 28—nomination day—reporter Mark Leibovich drew a fascinating connection between the sizable representation of Black delegates and the upcoming Obama presidential campaign:

> The crowd [at the convention] was multiracial, but with a large African-American presence. Black voters, echoing one another, said they simply could not miss this moment.
>
> Lillian Woods, 50, of Phoenix arrived at 1 p.m., seven hours before Mr. Obama would speak. "I had to be here for the whole thing," she said, passing the time in the hot sun. "It's history in the making." . . .
>
> Audrey Johnson Thornton, a black woman who is 82 and does not walk so well anymore, has been registering voters for months, going into Philadelphia's homeless shelters, nursing homes, even into a minimum-security prison.
>
> She had a wide-brimmed purple hat to go with a purple blouse, and she was beside herself. "You talk about living the dream," she said. "I'm 82 years old, and I never thought I would see this. Never, never, never."[13]

The awesome interplay between African American delegates experiencing the historic nomination of an African American to be president and the upcoming electoral mobilization of Black voters by the Obama campaign was also reflected in a *New York Times* column by Bob Herbert. The columnist experienced this interplay secondhand, via television, at an African American restaurant in Detroit. Through interviews with Black restaurant patrons, Herbert related the incredible impact that Obama's nomination and his acceptance address had on the Black twenty-first-century consciousness. He wrote, "Jennifer West, a 47-year-old insurance executive told me: 'We're all sitting on feelings we don't usually talk about. We're starved for a collective sense of affirmation. Barack is the son, the brother, the uncle, the cousin who made good. Who overcame. God bless him for what he means to us.'"[14]

Herbert connected the almost mystical impact of Obama's nomination address on today's Black voters with the country's oppressive racial legacy. Noting that "the suddenness of Mr. Obama's rise added to the sense of amazement," Herbert wrote:

> "It's so very exciting," said Pearl Reynolds, who is 92 and whose elegant bearing and dress belied her hardscrabble origins in tiny Oak Ridge, La., where she worked as a child in the cotton fields.
>
> "I got married at 14 only because I wanted to get out of there," she said. "I had to. At 14, I was just being promoted from second grade because we could only go to school when we weren't working in the fields."
>
> She became quite emotional during Senator Obama's speech. "Barack Obama is a measure of how far we've come as a country since I was a little girl," she said.[15]

For many Black American delegates, the experience amounted to an awe-inspiring, historic political moment, which amounted to a "New World a' Comin'" African American phenomenon.

Finally, as another New York Times reporter argued, one of the basic infrastructure dynamics that propelled Obama to victory over the McCain campaign was fashioned with significant input by the early twenty-first-century Black professional sector, particularly in the area of fundraising. Reporter Michael Luo wrote, "Mr. Obama's acceptance of his party's nomination on Thursday [August 28] on the 45th anniversary of [the 1963] speech by Rev. Dr. Martin Luther King Jr. during the March on Washington, signifies a powerful moment of arrival for blacks."[16]

Luo particularly focused on Gordon Davis, a Black lawyer and the son of prominent African American social psychologist Allison Davis, who taught at the University of Chicago from the 1940s to the 1970s. Luo pointed out that when Davis, "a top fund-raiser for Senator Barack Obama, made partner at his white-shoe law firm in New York in 1983, it was a vastly different world for aspiring black professionals like him. At the time there were just five black partners at major law firms in New York, Mr. Davis recalled."[17] Davis's position with the Obama campaign represented an historic breakthrough. Joining him in the fundraising role was another African American corporate lawyer, Jeh Johnson, the grandson of the prominent African American sociology scholar Charles S. Johnson, who taught at Fisk University from the 1930s to the mid-1950s. When the Obama administration was organized in early 2009, Jeh Johnson became the first African American to function as chief legal counsel to the secretary of defense. (During Obama's second term, he served as secretary of the Department of Homeland Security.)

By the period following the May 6 Democratic primaries in Indiana and North Carolina, when the Obama campaign was reasonably certain of victory over Hillary Clinton, African American professionals in business, banking, media, and law became a fundraising mechanism of the likely presidential nominee of the Democratic Party. In fact, of the three hundred top-level fundraisers on Obama's national finance committee, some fifty-seven were African Americans. Each committee member was responsible for raising at least $250,000. The task, as Luo observed, was "formidable . . . and typically require[d] deep business networks, something relatively few blacks had until fairly recently." However, there were a handful of black fundraisers that the 2008 Obama campaign could draw upon, Luo said:

> The list of top Obama [African American] bundlers includes John W. Rogers Jr., the founder of Ariel Investments, the country's first black-owned management firm; William E. Kennard, the first black chairman of the Federal Communications Commission [during the Bill Clinton administration]; and Mr. Gordon Davis, who [was] the first black parks commissioner of New York City and the first black president of Lincoln Center.
>
> Mr. Kennard and Mr. Rogers are among a half-dozen black bundlers who have raised more than $500,000 for Mr. Obama, putting them in a select group of just three dozen fund-raisers. . . .
>
> Valerie Jarrett, a close friend of Mr. Obama and one of his most trusted advisers, [is another top-level fundraiser].[18]

Victory

On November 5, 2008, Barack Obama and Joe Biden defeated John McCain and Sarah Palin handily, with 69 million votes (some 53 percent of the total) going to the Democratic ticket as compared to 59 million votes going to the Republicans' (some 46 percent of the total).

Several interesting analytical conclusions are notable regarding the combined role of two important electoral voting blocs: the BVB and the "Liberal White Voter Bloc" (LWVB). First, a combination of a pragmatic liberal appeal and skillful intertwining of BVB and LWVB votes enabled the Democrats to stitch together a 53 percent victory over the Republicans.

In overall terms, a variety of subsets produced two-fifths of white voters—43 percent, in fact—for the Obama-Biden ticket.

Second, a combination of pragmatic liberal electoral appeal and skillful voter mobilization allowed the ticket to overcome the deep electoral fissures among white women voters that erupted following Obama's defeat of Hillary Clinton in the primaries and win their vote on November 4. When combined with a massive 95 percent vote among African American women on Election Day, 58 percent of women overall voted for the Obama-Biden ticket.

Third, although throughout the Democratic primaries the Hispanic vote consistently favored Clinton over Obama, it was again a combination of pragmatic liberal electoral appeal and skillful electoral mobilization that enabled the Obama-Biden ticket to win over two-thirds of the Hispanic vote. Obama's election, however, was not just any political victory. It was interlaced with multilayered meanings whose roots were deep in American civilization's awful racial legacy. Its significance was specific to a very particular American political figure and notable because of it.

Barack Obama's leadership persona was deeply intertwined with the civil rights activist African American leadership tradition, which extends back in time to abolitionist figures such as Frederick Douglass and William Cooper Nell, Emancipation-era leaders such as AME bishop Henry McNeal Turner, early twentieth-century civil rights leaders such as W. E. B. Du Bois and James Weldon Johnson, and late twentieth-century leadership organizations such as CORE, the Southern Christian Leadership Conference, and the Rainbow Coalition. Viewed from this perspective, *the impact of the BVB on Obama's election as president was enormous.* Obama was idolized by the BVB as representing African Americans' long and brutal struggle for equalitarian citizenship status in American society. This explains the extraordinary phenomenon of a major American ethnic voting bloc—the BVB—mobilizing and delivering throughout the 2008 Democratic primaries a consistent vote of more than 80 percent for an ethnic candidate.

Furthermore, Obama's quest wouldn't have been ensured but for his unique historical nexus with the Black American civil rights activist leadership tradition. This legacy partly explains the electoral phenomenon of the BVB's 95 percent support for the Obama-Biden ticket in 2008. When the media reported on exit polls showing this phenomenal level of support for Obama, I wondered, "Who were the 5 percent of African Americans who favored the McCain-Palin ticket?"

Although we may never know the answer to this query, research on African American voting patterns in 2008 by David Bositis of the Joint Center for Political and Economic Studies in Washington, DC, gives us partial understanding. According to Bositis's *Blacks and the 2008 Election*, "The total share of the national vote represented by black voters between 2004 and 2008 increased from 11 percent to 13 percent—and the black share of the vote in many individual states increased substantially. In addition to record-setting turnout, President-elect Obama received 95 percent of the black vote, bettering President Lyndon B. Johnson's 94 percent in 1964, the previous high."[19]

Furthermore, the Bositis volume reported that Black women made up a clear majority (58 percent) of the BVB in the 2008 presidential election. However, Black women and men delivered nearly the same proportion of votes to the Obama-Biden ticket (96 percent for women and 95 percent men). Moreover, when other Black voter categories are considered, they, too, delivered a similar share of their votes to the Obama-Biden ticket. The BVB also produced an unprecedented share of overall turnout for Black votes, a record-breaking level in fact. In Bositis's words, "With 16.6 million votes cast, the 2008 black turnout would be 66.8 percent—smashing the previous record of 58.5 percent in 1964; the post Voting Rights Act turnout high was 57.6 percent in 1968."

Finally, another way of characterizing the unique importance of the BVB to the Obama-Biden victory is to note that the McCain-Palin ticket received the support of both an overall majority of white voters on Election Day (53 percent to 49 percent) and a majority in the key battleground states. But it was above all the maximally mobilized BVB turnout that ensured the Obama victory.

A similar characterization of the BVB's crucial and decisive role in the 2008 presidential election was made by Ronald Walters, a University of Maryland political analyst. In an article for the online magazine *Black Commentator*, he observed, "Without the Black vote, there would be no Barack Obama in the White House. Take away the states where the Black vote influenced an Obama victory . . . and John McCain would have won the election. Our claim on policy fairness [from the Obama administration stimulus bill] is strong."[20]

Notes on Professor Martin Luther Kilson's Work

STEFANO HARNEY AND FRED MOTEN

At Harvard in the early 1980s, to be in Professor Martin Luther Kilson's class was to be on the front line of a war of apposition. We were in movement, and movement meant that every week he would come into the classroom with copies of articles from major newspapers, academic journals, and a wide range of magazines. He would distribute them, ask about the ones from last week, and usually launch into an analysis of why it was important that a certain author got space to write something challenging white supremacy, or that a certain enemy was able to perpetuate another sham argument. There was constant attention to international politics and what used to be called "national affairs." His lessons didn't end in the classroom. If you stopped by his office, you were likely to be walked around the room or directed to go pick up more articles and books. We liked going to his office because he'd commandeered a large common table where he worked on a typewriter at one end while having laid out all these materials across the table. His office was really a situation room. And more often than not, a session in the situation room ended with an invitation for dinner at the house Professor Kilson shared with his partner, the anthropologist Professor Marion Kilson. Class would then recommence on the ride to their home and continue through the preparation and eating of our meal and end with coffee in a study that felt more like the situation room's deep archive. And you would leave—of course, with more articles and already annotated copies of his working manuscripts—full from Martin's cooking and happy from Marion's manhattans.

At our last dinner with Professor Kilson, he playfully, but seriously, accused us of having no stomach for incrementalism. We made the mistake of dropping an offhanded insult of Barack Obama, and he gave us our comeuppance after about forty-five minutes of letting us think we'd gotten away with it. And his critique brought back a question we had long posed ourselves: What did Professor Kilson's constant vigilance around electoral politics and the state teach us, we who think of ourselves as beyond, and needing to go further beyond, such politics? How do we negotiate the space between the politics that we refuse and the people—held and constantly at the work of unholding within those politics—that we love?

Professor Kilson inhabited that space while also critically refusing it. That's how he lived and worked and walked. In that sojourn, in that struggle, where the war of position demands a constant and principled refusal of position, Professor Kilson would call himself by different names, a "flat-footed lefty" and a "pragmatic progressive," to name two of his favorites. It would be easy to mistake his attention to *Ebony* or *Dissent* for a politics of liberalism or reform or uplift, but that would be to forget that more than anything else Professor Kilson was a Du Boisian. At base that meant he saw and felt the world not as the opposing positions of liberalism, but in a constantly redoubling, rigorously dialectical vision that could not allow for the stable focus of opposites or choices or identities. This double vision fell at its most concentrated onto the color line, whose fundamental antagonism was constantly differentiated in and by that double vision.

So how could we understand his accusation? Perhaps rather than Gramsci's war of position, it would be better to understand Kilson's situation room as a correction, which is to say an incompletion and misdirection, of Lenin's fundamental political problem, the problem of dual power. Lenin was concerned with the relationship between the state and soviets. He saw the necessity of taking state power and the danger of doing so for the soviets and for revolution. The historic (post-Lenin) absorption of the soviets by the state would eventually shape debates around the sad fate of Euro-communism. Responding to those debates in the 1970s, Nicos Poulantzas insisted that the state was "a terrain of struggle" and that rather than imagining that it could be seized wholesale or destroyed from without, communists should battle on that terrain for gains in modes of parapolitical activity Mario Tronti describes as within and against the state. Of course, Poulantzas was sensitive to being accused of reformism for viewing the state as shot through with social conflict and therefore worthy of everyday battles in electoral and bureaucratic struggle, and he emphasized the need to continue to build the other power, the Communist Party and its associations in his case. But the fundamental problem of dual power is not in the end its duality, but its power. Professor Kilson used to say, "I'm afraid of power," referring to offers made to him of positions of power. But his phrase took on an existential tone over many repetitions. The dual power strategy yokes whatever is emerging outside the state not to the state but to the concept of power underlying the state. This reaches its absurd reduction in Frederic Jameson's call for a universal army to be the counterpower to the state, as if politics could be overwhelmed with another version of its ground and essence, which we must fear and fight. But what happens when we see dual power with the double vision that the color line requires and allows and that, in turn, makes the color line visible? What happens when we see that the split between these powers actually is the color line? That's how we began to learn to see things in Professor Kilson's situation room.

A double consciousness of the state finds the state doubled onto civil society and its basis in power as an organizing principle manifest most ferociously in the white supremacy that operates as an extrastate state power. To makes copies, underline paragraphs, and annotate texts—and to continually give all this to us not only as content but also as practice—was his way of teaching us to recognize and antagonize the organizing principle of power being exercised imminently and inextricably in every statement and position. In tracking these statements and positions—in tending to and extending the care with which Black radical insurgency laid down, and retraced, and dug up, and recovered, and covered up those tracks in complexities of movement of which Pulantzas hadn't and couldn't dream— Professor Kilson helped and still helps us to learn to pose the organizational alternative with and against dual power itself. What emerges, then, is not a fundamental antagonism between state and soviets, since both are shot through with power, but, instead and within and against them, something like nonpower, nonpolitics, sociality—exemplified or maybe amplified especially by what Laura Harris calls Black aesthetic sociality—on the other side of the color line, a line which in turn runs through the state and through today's soviets, that is, today's movements in the squares and streets and across the seas and borders. That line ran through Professor Kilson's teaching, too, snaking and surging with the urgent, insurgent militancy of Black incrementalism.

....

When we met Professor Kilson he was deep in battle with Black neoconservative scholars and commentators. In letters he regularly—almost daily—wrote to the newspapers that gave these Black neocons space, such as the *New York Times* and the *Washington Post,* and to his trusted friends and colleagues, such as Julian Bond, Clyde Ferguson, and Jerry Watts, Professor Kilson pointed out the dangers and errors of this neoconservative turn. The style of these letters, the way their references ranged through the history of Black studies in order to sharply rebut Black neoconservatism, formed a particular body of work that was like a genre of writing, and of study, all its own. And while we could usually understand his arguments, we can also admit that far less often did we understand the urgency and the persistence with which he pursued these neocons or what erroneously appeared to us as his commitment to the public sphere.

It took the publication of the first of his main late-career works, *The Transformation of the African American Intelligentsia,* to help us see the true stakes he was fighting for in Black studies, which is to say the true stakes in the ongoing critique of Western civilization—especially as this civilization found its settlement in the broken rhetoric and mangled thought of official intellectual life in the United States. In that book, Professor Kilson teaches us in painstaking historical detail that, somehow, in ways that were simultaneously a function and a refusal of segregation's genocidal force, the Black community, all but alone among all the nonindigenous peoples in the Americas, resisted division into a class of exploiters and exploited. He tracks the struggle over the looming threat of such division from the 1890s to the present, specifically among the Black intelligentsia. We saw many versions of the chapters of this book over the years, and far more chapters than eventually were published. This sharing and this revision were integral to how Professor Kilson practiced Black studies, and we will come back to that. Now, we want to linger with how it was only the full force of the book's complete argument that allowed us to see with him the threat Black neoconservatism, in the full range of its modalities, poses to this experience.

That is to say that it was not, finally, the willingness of this or that Black neoconservative to suck up to the representatives of white supremacy in policy and academic circles that motivated Professor Kilson. Rather, it is that he was mobilized by the threat he saw to what another great scholar of the Black radical tradition, Cedric Robinson, called the "preservation of the ontological totality." What Professor Kilson perceived so acutely in Black social life and in the best of Black studies (and the two are inseparable and at a certain point indistinguishable) is a stubborn, painful, joyful connectedness among Black people that could not be accounted for or fully regulated by the vicious innovations of "one-drop" racism and the chauvinism of liberal, neoliberal, antiabolitionist and anticommon American culture. Even the necessary exceptions to this resistance to exception enact and imply seemingly impossible solidarities, and it is the antimetaphysical physics of that social force, the laws and rhythms of its conservation, that professors Kilson and Robinson, in their different Du Boisian ways, sought to study and extend. In the end, despite its use in Jewish, Italian, Polish, and other ethnic studies contexts, and despite Professor Kilson's hope that this would be otherwise, the phrase "the ghetto wall has two sides" applies *only* to Black people in the Americas. For all other "peoples," a look inside the ghetto reveals, as Mao said, how the one becomes two, foreshadowing what happens once the ghetto is left behind and the full arsenal of America's expropriating and exploiting weapons are enjoyed. What Professor Kilson teaches us is that there was an internal dynamic of what Denise Ferreira Da Silva calls "difference without separability" at work in Black social life. Inside the ghetto and out, Black people refused the separability that race requires; he teaches us, therefore, that Black people are, in a sense, the only people who are not a race, since race requires the division of the posited same.

To put this another way, and in a way Professor Kilson would have also put it, echoing one of the great Du Boisian scholars of our time, Nahum Chandler, Professor Kilson turned the color line, in his own thinking and in ours, from the problem to the threat of the last century, and of this one. If we had or wanted access to an enlightenment language, so we could let it fertilize the ground that we turn over, we would say, in debt to Sylvia Wynter, that the problem of political life in dehumanization, when and where (the) man overrepresents himself, is always also the threat of social life without dehumanization in that subtemporal, superlocative refusal of representation in which the human takes and gives its place.

....

Today, the (subject) reaction Professor Kilson identifies in the neoconservatism of Black studies has not gone away. The shadow of the separate and unequal conformity that is a symptom of individuation, property, and sovereignty—which Hortense Spillers warns us against under the common term of personality—is what we operate both under and within. We detect its presence not only in straightforward attempts to appease and please the forces of brutality but also in righteous claims to freedom and decolonization. Often, it moves in subtle, nuanced, finely calibrated demands for recognition and claims of ownership, all of which are sanctioned by terrible histories of misrecognition and theft. Professor Kilson insistently urges us to consider that sanction is not justification.

Through the strength and depth of his urgency, we can also better participate in other aspects, extensions, and inventions in Professor Kilson's thought and in how he conducted himself in and with that thought. Professor Kilson was a staunch internationalist. This did not come, as one may suppose, from the two years Harvard gave him to transform himself from a scientist of American politics into an Africanist; nor did it come from his fieldwork in Ghana. If the internationalist impulse came through these experiences it is because it had come through his attending Lincoln University long before. At a time when Harvard could only imagine importing German and English scholars and, when the history of empire which it celebrated and fostered made it unavoidable, a few European Jews, Lincoln University, like other historically Black colleges, boasted faculty from Africa, the Caribbean, South America, and Asia. These scholars were quick to highlight the borders that had crossed Black people in the Americas and beyond and to warn against the dangers of not seeing that those Black lines were actually white. To be in Professor Kilson's classroom was also to be in the workshop of Black internationalism, and the articles, updates, repeated stories he shared, and, most importantly, his sharing of them were expressions of international, antinational solidarity.

Professor Kilson might have described his work on Africa as incremental. He spoke of the basic need to form stable political systems that included all African peoples on the continent out of a social, patient pan-Africanism that could easily be mistaken—and was by us—for caution or even gradualism, and his emphasis on rampant kleptocracy and his pessimistic assessment of postcolonial regimes certainly put off some of our more Afro-capitalist, nation-branded fellow students. But there were two things none of us then quite understood. The first was something he said he'd once heard during his own field research. "I heard it, I knew it was there undermining the whole social system, and then I heard it. During an argument, I heard someone say to his friend, 'I'll sell you! I'll sell you to the white people!'" In that anecdote Professor Kilson was teaching us to abide with and in the catastrophic immensity of African slavery and the transatlantic slave trade far more than had been customary in African studies, either among Western or African and Afro-diasporic scholars (with the notable earlier exceptions of Walter Rodney, Samir Amin, and Basil Davidson, who, along with Professor Kilson, set the stage for pathbreaking work by Babacar M'baye and Jemima Pierre, among many others). The tragic reason for his patience and his clear-eyed look at contemporary Africa was the depth of his understanding of the profound damage to African society that was brought about by internally generated and externally imposed slavery, by colonialism, and by the racial humanism of white supremacist "world" culture. That understanding was further deepened and acutely sharpened by the way he felt the pull of that broken, breaking connectedness in Black social life, which gave him the strength to endure the long duration of African and Afro-diasporic (under)development.

If Professor Kilson's incrementalism is manifest in his patience with institutions, it is also spray-painted with the most profound and profane portraits of the characters who thrive in these institutions by feeding others to power. This took particular shape in his commitment to Barack Obama. Yet, neither we nor our elder brother in Professor Kilson's extended family of study, Cornel West, could muster any criticism of Obama's policies or of his commitment to policy that was underived from Professor Kilson's knowledge and example. If he was less reckless than us in our ability to be against something so many Black folks were for, he was also more prescient than us in his understanding of the horror that ensues when Black folks sell themselves and other Black folk. This is why his criticism, even when its intensity was directed toward individuals who had sold themselves and others, and even when that intensity was muted in ways that we didn't understand, was always, in the last instance, directed toward the common and impersonal danger of Black neoconservatism's viciously separatist, individuating power. Professor Kilson's aim was always to preserve, and it was pursued by way of the relentless and lovingly generative force of his criticism. This is to say that he constantly generated those differences in collaborative Black study that keep it alive. In Professor Kilson's work, which is Black thought at its most fundamental, Black thought refuses to fall into equilibrium in the way that it falls apart together in a dialectic of commonness where the duress of the incremental is resisted in everyday practices. Professor Kilson's patience is, in this regard, a method for the careful cultivation of upheaval.

....

In further elaboration of his incrementalism, Professor Kilson coined and frequently used the term *coping strata* to describe a part of the Black community in the United States. It's not so much that this part comprised families that lived paycheck to paycheck, in a zone of contact in which each family's capacity to so live was dependent upon every other family's capacity to so live. It is rather that this part of the US Black community, in ways that cut across all the various boundaries internal and external to the nation, shared wealth that was not just inextricable from but given in the sharing of its needs in a way that Marx approaches but can't quite get to in *Grundrisse*. But *part* is not the right word and not the right idea. The word *strata* leads us to imagine a part within a stratified whole, but we would be missing something if we left it there, as a modification or even an anticipation of stratification theory.

The coping strata is a class formation that defies simple understandings of class not only as a pure mathematical concept but also as a concept for political economy. When Professor Kilson used that term, he meant its grammatical plurality to refer to something collective, a set of overlapping sets linked by a range of styles, each with their own attitude toward a general understanding of style, of dealing with absolute duress in and with an imperative to survive. That duress was given in all the ways racial capitalism constitutes a field of imposed accidents, the general scattershot rain of real and metaphorical bullets that befalls Black flesh and can hit any Black body, thereby ensuring its fatal individuation. The overwhelming structure of intention and decision that is racial capitalism operates randomly so that a sneeze or a broken taillight or an unset alarm clock or a between-meal hunger pang can all lead to common, uncontained disaster. The coping strata lives in and with that field of actual and potential catastrophe and always in proximity to those who no longer can live with it, having undergone or undertaken a variety of separations: death incarceration debilitating types of immiseration that strain sociality to the breaking point and the various modes of upwardly mobile integration that paradoxically maintain the segregationist structures and practices of newly "inclusive" institutions. The coping strata is sustained even in and against these forms of separation, even when it is scored, striated, and contained by them. It is the shifting ensemble, which preserves the ontological totality and the internal differences of its practices, that points also to the specific and strikingly accurate way that Professor Kilson used a more familiar term, *multiculturalism*, when he noted that Black sociality constitutes an unprecedented and uneclipsed multiculturalism in American life, not only because of the differences internal to it that, in Professor Kilson's wake, we carefully refer to by way of the term *class*, but also, and more importantly, because of its constant and constantly refreshed transnationality, because of the vexed but irreducible force of sexual difference and the ways that what Hortense Spillers calls ungendering reflected and resisted internally and externally imposed norms, and because of its openness—again, as a matter of external imposition and internal predisposition—to non-Black cultural forms and influence, all of which Professor Kilson precisely describes in recounting his youth in Ambler, Pennsylvania. If the coping strata has style(s), or a general attitude toward style that implies and assures this openness and multiplicity, perhaps it is given in the assumption of the beauty, richness, and complexity of the practice of Black social life. Every bit of Professor Kilson's work, against the grain of temporary orthodoxies, follows from this assumption.

So that if, in the context of Harvard in the 1980s, stratification theory in the sociology and government departments denoted a pluralist perspective, Professor Kilson's notion of the coping strata was both deeper and further out. In that era, Talcott Parsons's functionalism and Erik Olin Wright's stratification were taught as two sides of the same coin—depending on whether one believes the talents and rewards of the "recognized" or the "elite" or the "conscious" would be used simply to delineate and entrench social strata or to advocate a more humane (di)vision of society in general. Naturally, since it was Harvard, students were to act on Parsons while agreeing with Wright, thereby uplifting the nation. If Marx was taught at all, much less considered in research, it was as a "conflict theorist." Of course, for Professor Kilson, as always, something else was going on in his relationship to social and political science. The first hint was his constant contact with his touchstones in Du Bois and the Atlanta University conferences and in Staughton Lynd's study of small-town American life, where all was not well and where, at the same time, coping occurred in common study.

Coping is neither the same as striving nor the same as working. *Striving* suggests reform at best, and *working*, in its precariousness, which accrues both to the ones who have jobs and to the jobless, reminds us of the rigid moral reduction that is supposed in the declension from proletariat to lumpen, which everyone from Du Bois to Huey P. Newton cautions against. *Cope* comes from *coup* and bears the sense of a blow that is struck, even as it also implies endurance, holding on, living with. *Coping* bears the sense of putting something in place until something else happens or comes into effect, a something else that is not just more of anything and certainly not just more of the same, which is often more of the same absence that is given in the symbolic registers of income or citizenship or property, especially for the ones who are denied entry into those registers so that they can be kept delusionally open, with real and brutal effect, for the earners, the citizens, and the owners. Coping is combat planning, the burdened, ecstatic enactment of what C. L. R. James calls "the future in the present." It moves by way of a double refusal of stratification, when upward mobility is strictly regulated, where horizontal mobility is urgently exercised.

The coping strata is a Kilsonian idea that tends to unfix people, since the people to whom it refers are not only doing what they are doing but also doing something in lieu of that, in place of that, in the displacement of that, in preparation and in practice of something else. Coping is what Wilson Harris calls an "infinite rehearsal." Workers work, and strivers strive, but copers stick and move. Whatever they do, they're always doing something else, all but always for something else that's somewhere else, before and after. This is to say that the coping strata shares with the lumpen of Newton and with Du Bois's global color line a certain unreliability with regard to layers of stratification, models of society, targets of policy, and reliability of order(s). It is to say, moreover, that the idea of the coping strata perhaps shares something with Robinson's argument in *Black Movements in America*. Just as there have been two ideas of freedom in Black movements which sometimes mix and sometimes compete—one about the realization of freedom in this world and the other about freedom from this world—so, too, there may there be mixed and competing ideas of and in the practice of coping. Yes, it's about holding on, but it's also about moving on; yes, it's about getting by, but it's also about getting through. Such blurring of lines is in the interest of an absolute clarity. This lesson, which Professor Kilson taught us at Harvard, was something he'd begun to learn long before his time there, or in Africa, or at Lincoln. His knowledge of Black movement in America can be traced to Ambler, and his particular path of study was deeply concerned with how that knowledge had gotten there. The reason *From a Pennsylvania Milltown* so memorably begins not with where Professor Kilson comes from but with where the people of his hometown came from, and were coming from, is because what's at stake, finally, is movement, not origin. Professor Kilson taught us that movement is militant preservation in transformation. He taught us that to move is to cope, as we burst the increment.

....

And so we return to what it is to have been taught by him and to be able, now, to see where all that we receive from him, and through him, came from. On the one hand, the privilege of studying with him was a profound experience of being immersed in the waters of Black studies. We both had precedent for this immersion, albeit to different degrees and in different forms by way of different people. Bob Harney was a historian of immigration who said regularly that all immigrants are economic migrants for political reasons. Professor Kilson recognized in this oft-repeated statement a rejection—on both sides of the Atlantic—of the standard Western categories of peoplehood or nationhood and the insistence on seeing the wound that would not heal in the infected hands of these categories. B. Jenkins was an educator and advocate who celebrated with burdened, joyful solemnity the long Black history of the lost and found in constant and social study of its sound and its flavor, its image and its meaning, its movement and its feel. In ways that were reminiscent of our earliest teachers, Professor Kilson linked the analysis of genocidal political economy with the recitational practice of the kitchen table conservatory. For him, teaching was being in touch with all this, and the study we undertook and the study we neglected all got mixed by this feeling of being in touch. His analytic was driven and punctuated by the way he called the names of Black scholars past and present and in how he repeated himself, and commented on himself, naming and renaming himself and us in dozens of ways so that all of it, and all of us, could then be named again. He described his teachers and colleagues by their looks, styles, and mannerisms as well as very exactly by their theories and relationships to their field site, ethnic origins, and sites of birth. Biography and theory stirred without settling. Again, now we can see that the buoyancy and play, and also the most profound condemnation, came from the same source—this refusal of Black social life to cohere and adhere to the prerogatives of the last five hundred years of the primitive accumulation of populations, classes, and races, and what Professor Silva calls "the lethal deployment of identity." The price of this preservation of incoherence is untold, which is why Professor Kilson kept telling it all the time, necessarily at coherence's blurred edge, where every single injury done to every single Black person is an injury to all, in Blackness.

If to be in Professor Kilson's class—and to be in the Kilsons' home—was to be in the life of Black study, it is because that life was already fully lived in a Pennsylvania milltown. In his memoir, Professor Kilson shows that it was lived not with the compulsion of modern specialization and professionalization, but with a looseness, a sense that one could never remember or hold on to everything, but everything was holding you anyway. We have the sense now that the kind of work he was trying to do, the work of preservation that he could do only by constantly risking what is preserved in the differentiating collection, the striated gathering, of his own language, was fostered and exemplified in the classroom of his hometown and all of its variously situated and interacting refugees, especially the racialized Black people whose shared Blackness, whose sharing of Blackness, defied racialization. Having been supplied by them, Professor Kilson offered his students something more than the career of the individual, for which Ivy league education is an elaborate, pampered, carceral support system. How is it that as he grew older he became more radical? This is not just a matter of comparison with those in Black studies whose desire to voice an opinion on Palestine or start a study group in the neighborhood is glamorized by the oscillation between recognition and insult that generates the institutional atmosphere wherein career and personality are supposed to thrive. We see now that he learned to follow Black study with such a deviant and dogged love that he kept finding it, because it got through to him, because his career and personality and individuality were never fully formed and rendered complete in the amazing set of differences that were all him and all his, and more than him and more than his, all of which he so generously shared. How could we have been so lucky?

SELECTED LIST OF
MARTIN KILSON'S WRITINGS

Books

(coedited with Robert Rotberg) *The African Diaspora: Interpretive Essays*. Cambridge, MA: Harvard University Press, 1976.

(coedited with Wilfred Cartey) *Africa Reader*. 2 vols. New York: Random House, 1970.

(coedited with Adelaide Hill) *Apropos of Africa: Sentiments of American Negro Leaders on Africa, 1800s–1950s*. London: Cass, 1969.

(coedited with Nathan Huggins and Daniel Fox) *Key Issues in the Afro-American Experience*. New York: Harcourt Brace Jovanovich, 1971.

(edited) *New States in the Modern World*. Cambridge, MA: Harvard University Press, 1975.

(coedited with Rupert Emerson) *Political Awakening of Africa*. New York: Prentice-Hall, 1965.

Political Change in a West African State. Cambridge, MA: Harvard University Press, 1966.

The Transformation of the African American Intelligentsia, 1880–2012. Cambridge, MA: Harvard University Press, 2014. Winner of 2015 American Book Award.

Articles and Book Chapters

"Adam Clayton Powell, Jr.: The Militant as Politician." In *Black Leaders of the Twentieth Century*, edited by John Hope Franklin and August Meier, 259–275. Urbana: University of Illinois Press, 1982.

"African Political Change and the Modernization Process." *Journal of Modern African Studies* 1, no. 4 (1963): 264–294.

"Afterword: Black Scholar in a White Supremacist Era: Horace Mann Bond's Odyssey." In Horace Mann Bond, *Negro Education in Alabama*, 349–371. Tuscaloosa: University of Alabama Press, 1994.

"Analysis of Black American Voters in Barack Obama's Victory." In *The Obama Phenomenon: Toward a Multiracial Democracy*, edited by Charles P. Henry, Robert L. Allen, and Robert Chrisman, 34–59. Urbana: University of Illinois Press, 2011.

"Anatomy of African Class Consciousness: Agrarian Populism in Ghana." In *Studies in Power and Class in Africa*, edited by Irving Markovitz, 50–66. New York: Oxford University Press, 1986.

"Anatomy of Black Conservatism." *Transition* 59 (1993): 4–19.

"Autocracy, Civil Society and Democratization in African States." *Praxis: Fletcher School Journal of Development Studies* 10, no. 1 (Spring 1993): 9–18.

"Black Politics—A New Power." *Dissent*, July–August 1971. Reprinted in *The Seventies: Problems and Prospects*, edited by Irving Howe and Michael Harrington, 297–317. New York: Harper and Row, 1972.

"Black Social Classes and Intergenerational Poverty." *Public Interest*, Summer 1981, 58–78.

"Blacks and Neo-Ethnicity in American Political Life." In *Ethnicity: Theory and Experience*, edited by Nathan Glazer and Daniel P. Moynihan, 236–266. Cambridge, MA: Harvard University Press, 1976.

"Cleavage Management in African Politics: The Ghana Case." In *New States in the Modern World*, edited by Martin Kilson, 75–88. Cambridge, MA: Harvard University Press, 1975.

"Critique of Orlando Patterson's Blaming the Victim Rituals: Review of *Rituals of Blood*." *Souls* 3, no. 1 (Winter 2001): 81–106.

"E. Franklin Frazier's *Black Bourgeoisie Reconsidered: Frazier's Analytical Perspective*." In *E. Franklin Frazier and Black Bourgeoisie*, edited by James E. Teele, 118–136. Columbia: University of Missouri Press, 2002.

"The Elusive Contours of Postwar Race Relations." *Civil Liberties Review*, May–June 1978, 36–43.

"Emergent Elites of Black Africa, 1900–1962." In *Colonialism in Africa, 1870–1960*, edited by Lewis Gann and Peter Duignan, 2:351–398. Cambridge, UK: Cambridge University Press, 1970.

"From the Birth to a Mature Afro-American Studies at Harvard, 1969–2002." In *A Companion to African American Studies*, edited by Louis R. Gordon and Jane Anna Gordon, 59–75. Oxford: Blackwell, 2006.

"Grass-Roots Politics in Ghana." In *Ivory Coast and Ghana: Perspectives on Modernization*, edited by Philip Foster and Aristide Zolberg, 103–123. Chicago: University of Chicago Press, 1971.

"Land and the Kikuyu: A Study of the Relationship between Land and Kikuyu Political Movements." *Journal of Negro History* 40, no. 2 (April 1955): 103–153.

"Mugo-Son-of-Gatheru." *The Crisis*, March 1953, 140–144.

"Political Change in the Urban Ghetto, 1900–1940s." In *Key Issues in the Afro-American Experience*, edited by Nathan Huggins, Martin Kilson, and Daniel Fox, 167–192. New York: Harcourt Brace and Jovanovich, 1971.

"Political Scientists and the Activist-Technocrat Dichotomy: The Case of John Aubrey Davis." In *African American Perspectives on Political Science*, edited by Wilber Rich, 169–192. Philadelphia: University of Pennsylvania Press, 2007.

"Politics of Affirmative Action: Race and Public Policy in America." In *Minorities: Community and Identity*, edited by Charles Fried, 365–373. Berlin: Springer, 1983.

"Ralph Bunche's African Perspective." In *Ralph Bunche: The Man and His Times*, edited by Benjamin Rivlin, 83–95. New York: Holmes and Meier, 1990.

"The Rise of Nationalist Organizations and Parties in British West Africa." In *Africa from the Point of View of American Negroes*, edited by John Aubrey Davis, 35–69. Paris: Présence Africaine, 1958.

"Sierra Leone Political Parties." In *Political Parties and National Integration in Tropical Africa*, edited by James S. Coleman and Carl Rosberg, 90–131. Berkeley: University of California Press, 1964.

"Thinking about Obligations and Responsibilities of Black Intellectuals." *AME Church Review*, January–March 2005, 40–63.

"Thinking about Robert Putnam's Analysis of Diversity." *Du Bois Review* 6, no. 2 (2009): 293–308.

"Thinking about the Black Elite Roles, Yesterday and Today." In *The State of Black America 2005: Prescription for Change*, edited by Lee A. Daniels, 85–106. New York: National Urban League, 2005.

"Twentieth Century Black Political Development." In *The African Diaspora: Interpretive Essays*, edited by Martin Kilson and Robert Rotberg, 459–484. Cambridge, MA: Harvard University Press, 1976.

"Whither Integration." *American Scholar* 45, no. 3 (Summer 1976): 360–373.

NOTES

Chapter 1. Growing Up in a Northern Black Community, 1930s–1940s

1. For a comprehensive history of the range of the Underground Railroad in Pennsylvania, see Bordewich, *Round to Canaan*.

2. One of Penllyn's native daughters, Gloria Stewart Jones, has written an excellent historical account of how the Black community arose in the village. See Jones, *Penllyn Village*.

3. Excellent resources on these Black denominations formed during the antebellum years are Nash, *Forging Freedom*, and Baldwin, *Mark of a Man*. See also Dickerson, *Liberated Past*.

4. In 1885, Mary P. H. Hough wrote the first published history of Ambler. Hough, an upper-middle-class Quaker and one of the earliest female graduates of the University of Pennsylvania Medical School, was Ambler's first female medical doctor. See Hough, *Early History*.

5. The only Negro burial ground I have found in the area that is older is in Bucks County. Located along an eight-hundred-foot escarpment surrounding a lovely one-story fieldstone AME church in Buckingham Village, with the date *1834* etched at the top of the entrance, the cemetery is in an exquisite location, overlooking a valley of woodland and farmland. Today, the church and its burial ground are preserved by the Bucks County Historical Society in Doylestown.

6. An official count of African American veterans buried at Rose Valley Cemetery was arranged by cemetery committee officials Alice Johnson and Jane Williams Flowers and conducted by Ambler residents Jimmy Flowers and Eddie Curtis. The count culminated in a booklet I produced in 2006, "List of African American War Veterans Buried at Rose Valley Cemetery—Ambler, PA."

7. See Quarles, *Negro in the American Revolution*.

8. The main sections of Ambler's upper-middle-class neighborhoods were located along Bethlehem Pike, Lindenwold Avenue, Euclid Avenue, Mattison Avenue, Highland Avenue, Church Street, upper Rosemary Avenue, and the south section of North Street. For striking images of the Mattison family mansion, Lindenwold, and some of the other homes in the surrounding neighborhoods, see Quattrone, *Images of America*.

9. Johnson, *Growing Up*, 150.

10. Jones, *Penllyn Village*, 12–16.

11. Jones, *Penllyn Village*, 52.

12. *Bethlehem Baptist Church*, 12.

13. Jones, *Penllyn Village*, 46–47.

Chapter 2. A Helping-Hand Ethos and Black Social Life, 1920s–1960s

1. I recall several families being noted for their generosity, among them the Lanes, the New-mans, the Rusts, the Williamses, the Perrys, and the Shaffers. My own family and the family of the assistant pastor, Leon Hill, were also frequent contributors.

2. Jones, *Penllyn Village*, 57–58.

3. For a list of post–high school professional career patterns among mainly upper-middle-class white youth who attended Ambler High School up to 1934, see Ambler High School Yearbook 1934, 554–556.

4. Among those enrolled in the college-prep curriculum were Perry Selheimer and Jack Betts, whose fathers were both stockbrokers, and Daniel Shoemaker, whose father was a factory administrator. The students in the general arts curriculum included working-class Italian Americans Fred Fedele, Mustard Mastromotto, and John Zollo and African Americans Jimmy Dean, George Nelson, and Joe Queenan, all of whom were the sons of factory workers.

5. Jones, *Penllyn Village*, 53–54. During this era, it was customary for segregated parks to open up to African Americans on specific days. Emphasis added.

6. Jones, *Penllyn Village*, 54.

7. Jones, *Penllyn Village*, 54.

Chapter 3. Melting-Pot-Friendly Schools in My Hometown, 1920s–1960s

1. Among these more progressive-thinking families were the Mattisons (the head of the family was an industry owner), the Foulkes (lawyer), the Shelleys (doctor), the Knights (lawyer/real estate), the Houghs (doctor/lawyer), the Fausts (tannery owner/banker), the Webers (banker), the Norrises (painting contractor), the Diners (lawyer), and the Lede-boers (industry manager).

2. Jones, *Penllyn Village*, 70–71.

3. Jones, *Penllyn Village*, 72.

4. Jones, *Penllyn Village*, 73–74.

5. Ambler High School Yearbook 1956, 6. The Newman name is a familiar one in these pages. Born to a family in North Ambler's North Street–Woodland Avenue neighborhood, Rob-ert was the son of Albert Newman, a chauffeur and factory driver at Keasbey & Mattison Company, and Gladys Green Newman, who operated a successful home-based laundry business. His maternal grandfather, Anderson Green, was a carpenter and a deacon at Pen-llyn's Bethlehem Baptist Church.

6. Ambler High School Yearbook 1935.

7. Among the faculty during the 1940s—my high school period—into the 1950s, teachers of German American background included Bork (English), Eichorn (biology), Geary (music), Hunsicker (mechanical drawing), Kistler (English literature), Kulp (business accounting), Kunsman (woodworking), Meyers (mathematics), Oschlager (English), Potteiger (Art), Schleeger (business education), and Volp (Geography). By the way, Ambler High School had only one Jewish American teacher—Abrahams (home economics)—from the early 1930s through 1950s. From the 1930s until 1948, there was also only one Italian American teacher—Menna (mathematics); the second Italian American teacher, Botello (English and mathematics), began to teach at Ambler in the fall of 1948, after I had graduated. In later years, I had conversations with several of the notably liberal high school teachers who were among the longest-tenured faculty, reaching back to the 1930s. Raymond Duncan (social studies/history) and Clifford Geary (music) reinforced the catalytic role that supervising principal J. M. Fisher played in tilting the faculty members' cultural attitudes along a liberal trajectory.

8. Jones, *Penllyn Village*, 70.

9. The Civarellis achieved success in subsequent generations as well. Anthony's son and grandson went on to launch Ambler's first Italian American–owned funeral home, still a prominent business in Ambler today.

10. See the population estimates for Ambler's Italian American community provided in journalist and author Gay Talese's discussion of that community in his memoir, *Unto the Sons*, 222–224, 232–233.

Chapter 4. Black Youth and Social Mobility, 1920s–1960s

1. See Putney, *When the Nation*. Putney, a Howard University professor and historian and herself a lieutenant in the WACS, grew up in the African American community in Norristown, Pennsylvania, the county seat for Montgomery County, which is, of course, home to the borough of Ambler.

2. At the upper end of Forest Avenue was the St. Anthony Parish Elementary School, which the Philadelphia Catholic Diocese built in 1900 for Ambler's middle-class German American and Irish American Catholic communities. It would be nearly thirty years before they built another elementary school, this one across the street from Keasbey & Mattison Company's factories at the southern end of town, for Ambler's largest Catholic community, Italian Americans. The school was called St. Joseph Elementary School. Several of my Italian American high school buddies mentioned that their parents felt bitter about the lengthy time span between the establishment of the St. Anthony's and St. Joseph's.

3. Jane Williams Flowers died in 2018, when she was in her nineties.

4. Robinson, *Disintegration*. Robinson's book is an important one for understanding the tragic spread of the underclass segment of the urban African American society from the 1980s into the twenty-first century.

Chapter 5. Ambler: A Twentieth-Century Company Town

1. For an example of autocratic or boss-rule city governance, see Gosnell, *Machine Politics*. See also Zink, *Twenty Municipal Bosses*.

2. Quattrone, *Images of America*, 38–39.

3. See Brewer, *Confederate Negro*. Professor Brewer was the editor of the *Journal of Negro History* and taught at the Black college North Carolina Central University when his book was published in 1969.

4. Quattrone, *Images of America*, 8. Italics added.

5. See Kilson, "John Aubrey Davis."

6. Quattrone, *Images of America*, 8.

7. Quattrone, *Images of America*, 8.

8. Talese's book has two chapters that trace the history of Ambler's Italian American community. See Talese, *Unto the Sons*. Talese's grandfather and his brother migrated to New Jersey in the 1880s, but his grandfather's brother later moved to Pennsylvania to live with a cousin in Ambler. When writing his memoirs, Talese—a reporter for the *New York Times* in the 1990s—visited his cousins in Ambler and studied the history of their Italian American community.

9. Wendy Greenberg, "Gay Talese Traces Roots in Ambler," *Philadelphia Inquirer Neighbors Magazine*, March 5, 1992, 4.

10. There are many excellent sociology books that detail the ethnic/racial/class patterning of cities and factory towns in late nineteenth- and early twentieth-century America for both working-class Blacks and whites and for WASPs. Among books that deal only with Chicago, I recommend: on Jewish Americans, Wirth, *Ghetto*; on Italian Americans, Nelli, *Italians*; on African Americans, Drake and Cayton, *Black Metropolis*. To delve further into living patterns among WASPs, I suggest Lynd and Lynd, *Middletown*; Hollingshead, *Elmtown's Youth*; Mills, *White Collar*; Baltzell, *Protestant Establishment*.

11. Some particularly enlightening books on this subject are Gordon, *Assimilation*; Higham, *Strangers*; Lipset, *First New Nation*.

12. Perhaps the best book overall on the story of African Americans' difficult road to fair and equal social status in our country is Franklin, *From Slavery*. But there are two other complementary books that must be read: Kluger, *Simple Justice*, and Branch, *Parting*.

13. Myrdal, *American Dilemma*, 558–559.

14. Since my college years at Lincoln University, I have believed that candor with regard to racism in American history and society is the best way to correct it. The Black folks of my generation who grew up in Ambler must be candid about their childhood and their youthful interaction with racism, not quiet about it.

15. Jones, *Penllyn Village*, 62.

16. Jones, *Penllyn Village*, 62.

17. Jones, *Penllyn Village*, 62.

18. There are many excellent sources by a range of historians detailing the story of this reactionary white resistance, including Kluger, *Simple Justice*; Branch, *Parting*; and Arsenault, *Freedom Riders*.

19. For the story of President Lyndon B. Johnson's heroic leadership role in the enactment of the Civil Rights Act of 1964, see Caro, *Passage*.

20. Among the white kids who played in the informal league were Jack Ledeboer, Robert Hinkle, Jack Kleinfelder, Perry and Chuck Selheimer, and Danny Shoemaker; among the Black kids were Bobby Adams, my brother Richard and me, Albert Newman Jr., Lewis Thompson, and Charles Williams.

21. Despite the move toward multiculturalism at Ambler High School during the late 1940s, the school still banned interracial dancing (see chapter 2).

Chapter 6. Lincoln University, 1949–1953: Part I

1. Urban, *Black Scholar*, 125.

2. Urban, *Black Scholar*, 125.

3. Urban, *Black Scholar*, 125–126.

4. See Hughes, Lowery, and Mitchell, "Survey." Copies of the report were reprinted by Lincoln University's president's office in 1950, with an introduction by Horace Mann Bond, and filed in the archives of the university's Langston Hughes Memorial Library.

5. Bond, *Education*.

6. Hughes, Lowery, and Mitchell, "Survey," 2.

7. Hughes, Lowery, and Mitchell, "Survey," 2.

8. Hughes, Lowery, and Mitchell, "Survey," 2.

9. Hughes, Lowery, and Mitchell, "Survey," 7.

10. Hughes, Lowery, and Mitchell, "Survey," 13.

11. See Schatz, *Nigerian Economy*.

12. See Bond, *Negro Education*.

13. Jacques Wilmore graduated in June 1948 and later became a Quaker pacifist and an antiwar activist. During the 1960s he migrated to the new African state of Tanzania, where he taught the philosophy of pacifist antiwar activism for more than a decade. His older brother Gayraud Wilmore graduated a year before Jacques and earned his doctoral degree at Lincoln University's School of Theology, later becoming a civil rights movement adviser to the Southern Christian Leadership Conference in the 1960s.

14. On Hughes's political orientation during the late 1920s and the 1930s, see Trotman, *Langston Hughes*.

15. Wolters, *New Negro*.

16. Hughes, Lowery, and Mitchell, "Survey," 2–3.

17. Hughes, Lowery, and Mitchell, "Survey," 1. In the preface of Hughes's report is a table showing the specific summer jobs that one hundred Lincoln juniors and seniors held. Only ten of those jobs (10 percent) could be classified as middle-class jobs: five clerks, one pastor, one projectionist, one barber, and two postal clerks.

18. Ashby, *Tales*, 36.

19. Ashby, *Tales*, 38. I thank Walter Chambers, Lincoln Class of 1952 and emeritus member of Lincoln's Board of Trustees, for alerting me to and providing me a copy of Ashby's autobiography, which Chambers helped to get published by the Newark Preservation and Landmarks Commission.

Chapter 7. Lincoln University, 1949–1953: Part II

1. See Frazier, *Black Bourgeoisie*.

2. Hughes, Lowery, and Mitchell, "Survey," 9.

3. See Kilson and Kilson, *Portrait*, Lincoln University Archives, Langston Hughes Memorial Library.

4. Kilson and Kilson, *Portrait*, 6–7.

5. Lincoln University's Vail Memorial Library was one of maybe a dozen libraries that the steel magnate Andrew Carnegie funded on Negro college campuses in the late nineteenth century. Along with the Mary Dod Memorial Chapel, which Dod's family built in her honor in the 1890s, the Vail Memorial Library was my favorite building on Lincoln's campus. In the early 1980s the university built the new Langston Hughes Memorial Library, and the old Vail Memorial Library was transformed into the office of Lincoln's president and the office of the university's board of trustees.

6. On Archibald Grimké's fascinating leadership career, see Bruce, *Archibald Grimké*.

7. Hughes, Lowery, and Mitchell, "Survey," 10.

8. I learned during my graduate school years at Harvard University that white-majority public and private colleges had their own nasty fraternity hazing practices. Harvard College, however, outlawed fraternities in the 1930s and replaced them with so-called final clubs, which functioned mainly as dining clubs. Princeton University did the same thing. Though such dining clubs were elitist status arrangements on upper-middle-class campuses such as Harvard and Princeton, they did at least reverse the authoritarian-type fraternity hazing rituals that continued to reign on many white college campuses in the post–World War II era.

9. Hughes, Lowery, and Mitchell, "Survey," 6.

10. From conversations I've had with graduates of other Negro colleges who are in my age cohort, the fraternity macho-male hazing culture that I witnessed on Lincoln's campus had its counterpart at Howard University, Fisk University, Talladega College, Morehouse College, and other institutions. Being an all-male institution might have made Lincoln's fraternity macho-male hazing culture even nastier. Lincoln University became a coed campus in 1964, and the presence of female students had a civilizing impact on the fraternities' hazing practices. I am not aware, however, that here in the early twenty-first century, the Lincoln University governing bodies (president, board of trustees, and faculty) have outlawed hazing practices, as I believe they should.

Chapter 8. Harvard: Graduate School and Teaching

1. Howard, "Three Generations," 306.

2. Kelley, "Ivy League Negro," 55.

3. Kelley, "Ivy League Negro," 56.

4. Fitzgerald and Scruggs, "Note on Marcus Garvey."

5. Kelley, "Black Power."

6. Olufemi Sanu studied economics, and after completing his PhD, he was employed by the Nigerian foreign service. H. A. Oluwasami studied economics and joined the faculty of Nigeria's first university, the University of Ibadan, after he earned his PhD; he went on to become chancellor of Nigeria's third university, the University of Ife. Clement Isong also studied economics, and after earning his PhD became a top-tier economist at Nigeria's central bank, the Bank of Nigeria. Finally, Amon Nikoi became a top-tier foreign policy official in the Ghanaian department of foreign affairs. Sadly, by the time I commenced writing this memoir in the second decade of the twenty-first century, all of my African peers had died.

7. It has often saddened me that I've never been able to stay abreast of the careers of most of the African students I knew both as a graduate student and faculty member at Harvard. I do know, however, that with the failure of democratic practices in the vast majority of African states from the early 1970s onward, authoritarian regimes made them treacherous places for African graduates of Harvard to live.

8. Herbert Denton, "Afro-Americans," *Harvard Crimson*, May 14, 1963.

9. Kennedy, "Introduction," xiv, xxxi.

Chapter 9. Maturation

1. Larry Howard, the only other African American graduate student in political science at the time, was a year ahead of me and did a broad-ranging dissertation on US foreign policy toward the evolving independence movements of African colonies. Allen Ballard,

another Black student who arrived sometime after Larry and me, did his dissertation in Soviet studies under Professor Merle Fainsod, a close friend of Emerson. Ballard's dissertation was a fieldwork study of Soviet agriculture tractor stations. He was the first African American student to earn a doctorate in Russian studies in the United States.

2. See Kilson, "John Aubrey Davis."

Epilogue

1. Quoted in Patrick Healy and Jeff Zeleny, "Clinton and Obama Spar over Remark about Dr. King," *New York Times,* January 13, 2008.

2. Michael Kranish, "Clinton, Obama Spar over Her Comments on Civil Rights Battle," *Boston Globe,* January 14, 2008.

3. "Race and Politics," *New York Times,* January 17, 2008.

4. Associated Press, "Economy, Change Were Key Issues for Most Voters, Polls Show," *Boston Globe,* January 27, 2008.

5. "The Phenom," *Wall Street Journal,* February 13, 2008.

6. Kilson, "Black Civil Society's 21st Century Leadership Burden."

7. "The Low Road to Victory," *New York Times,* April 23, 2008.

8. Susan Page, "Obama Urges End to 'Bruised Feelings,'" *USA Today,* May 7, 2008.

9. Fredreka Schouten, "First-Timers, Blacks Help Give Obama a Victory," *USA Today,* May 7, 2008.

10. Susan Milligan, "Black, Latino Voters Show Clout, Boost Clinton," *Boston Globe,* February 6, 2008.

11. Lisa Wangsness, "Female Voters Torn between Voting for Obama, Clinton," *Boston Globe,* February 6, 2008.

12. Jonathan Kaufman, "Republicans Falter in Outreach to Blacks, Hispanics," *Wall Street Journal,* September 5, 2008.

13. Mark Leibovich, "Politics, Spectacle and History under Open Sky," *New York Times,* August 28, 2008.

14. Bob Herbert, "Champagne and Tears," *New York Times,* August 30, 2008.

15. Bob Herbert, "Champagne and Tears," *New York Times,* August 30, 2008.

16. Michael Luo, "Top Black Donors See Obama's Rise as Their Own," *New York Times,* August 28, 2008.

17. Michael Luo, "Top Black Donors See Obama's Rise as Their Own," *New York Times,* August 28, 2008.

18. Michael Luo, "Top Black Donors See Obama's Rise as Their Own," *New York Times,* August 28, 2008.

19. Bositis, *Blacks and the 2008 Election*, 1.

20. Ronald Walters, "From Stimulus to Recovery: Follow the Money: African American Leadership," *Black Commentator*, no. 312, February 19, 2009, https://blackcommentator .com/312/312_cover_aal_stimulus_follow_money.html.

BIBLIOGRAPHY

Arsenault, Richard. *Freedom Riders: 1961 and the Struggle for Racial Justice.* New York: Oxford University Press, 2006.

Ashby, William M. *Tales without Hate.* Newark: New Jersey Historical Commission, 1996.

Baldwin, Lewis. *The Mark of a Man: Peter Spencer and the African Union Methodist Tradition.* Lanham, MD: University Press of America, 1987.

Baltzell, E. Digby. *The Protestant Establishment.* New York: Oxford University Press, 1982.

Bethlehem Baptist Church: A Century of Service, 1888–1988. Penllyn, PA: n.p., 1988.

Bond, Horace Mann. *Education for Freedom: A History of Lincoln University, Pennsylvania.* Princeton, NJ: Princeton University Press, 1976.

Bond, Horace Mann. *Negro Education in Alabama: A Study in Cotton and Steel.* Washington, DC: Associated Publishers, 1939.

Bordewich, Fergus M. *Round to Canaan: The Epic Story of the Underground Railroad: America's First Civil Rights Movement.* New York: Amistad-HarperCollins, 2005.

Bositis, David A. *Blacks and the 2008 Election: A Preliminary Analysis.* Washington, DC: Joint Center for Political and Economic Studies, 2008.

Branch, Taylor. *Parting the Waters: America in the King Years, 1954–63.* New York: Simon and Schuster, 1988.

Brewer, James H. *The Confederate Negro: Virginia's Craftsmen and Military Laborers, 1861–1865.* Tuscaloosa: University of Alabama Press, 1969.

Bruce, Dickson D., Jr. *Archibald Grimké: Portrait of a Black Independent.* Baton Rouge: Louisiana State University Press, 1993.

Caro, Robert. *The Passage of Power.* New York: Knopf, 2012.

Dickerson, Dennis C. *A Liberated Past: Explorations in A.M.E. Church History.* Nashville, TN: Sunday School Union, 2003.

Drake, St. Clair, and Horace B. Cayton. *Black Metropolis: A Study of a Northern Negro Community.* New York: Harcourt Brace, 1940.

Fitzgerald, John M., and Otey M. Scruggs. "A Note on Marcus Garvey at Harvard, 1922: A Recollection of John M. Fitzgerald." *Journal of Negro History* 63, no. 2 (1978): 157–160.

Franklin, John Hope. *From Slavery to Freedom.* New York: Oxford University Press, 1947.

Frazier, E. Franklin. *Black Bourgeoisie: Rise of the New Black Middle Class.* Glencoe, IL: Free Press, 1957.

Gordon, Milton. *Assimilation in American Life: The Role of Race, Religion, and National Origin.* New York: Oxford University Press, 1964.

Gosnell, Harold Foote. *Machine Politics: Chicago Model*. Chicago: University of Chicago Press, 1935.

Higham, John. *Strangers in the Land*. New Brunswick, NJ: Rutgers University Press, 1955.

Hollingshead, August B. *Elmtown's Youth*. New York: Wiley, 1949.

Hough, Mary P. H. *Early History of Ambler 1682–1888*. Ambler, PA: Kelly, 1936.

Howard, Elizabeth Fitzgerald. "Three Generations of a Black Harvard and Radcliffe Family." In *Blacks at Harvard: A Documentary History of African-American Experience at Harvard and Radcliffe*, edited by Werner Sollors, Caldwell Titcomb, and Thomas A. Underwood, 304–309. New York: New York University Press, 1993.

Hughes, Langston, Richard Lowery, and Frank B. Mitchell. "A Survey of the College of Lincoln University by Three Members of Professor Labaree's Class in Sociology." Unpublished student paper, March 1929.

Johnson, Charles S. *Growing Up in the Black Belt: Negro Youth in the Rural South*. Washington, DC: American Council on Education, 1940.

Jones, Gloria Stewart. *Penllyn Village: A History and Personal Memories of a Black Settlement in Lower Gwynedd Township in Montgomery County, Pennsylvania*. Philadelphia: Xlibris, 2008.

Kelley, William Melvin. "Black Power." *Partisan Review* 35 (Spring 1968): 216–217.

Kelley, William Melvin. "The Ivy League Negro." *Esquire*, August 1, 1963.

Kennedy, Randall. "Introduction: Blacks and the Race Question at Harvard." In *Blacks at Harvard: A Documentary History of African-American Experience at Harvard and Radcliffe*, edited by Werner Sollors, Caldwell Titcomb, and Thomas A. Underwood, xvii–xxxiv. New York: New York University Press, 1993.

Kilson, Martin. "Analysis of Black American Voters in Barack Obama's Victory." In *The Obama Phenomenon: Toward a Multiracial Democracy*, edited by Charles P. Henry, Robert L. Allen, and Robert Chrisman, 34–59. Urbana: University of Illinois Press, 2011.

Kilson, Martin. "Black Civil Society's 21st Century Leadership Burden," AME *Church Review*, October–December 2005, 19–23.

Kilson, Martin. "John Aubrey Davis: Black Intellectual as Activist and Technocrat." In *African American Perspectives in Political Science*, edited by Wilbur C. Rich, 169–192. Philadelphia: Temple University Press, 2007.

Kilson, Martin, and Marion Kilson. *A Portrait of the Lincoln University Class of 1953*. Oxford, PA: Lincoln University, 2003.

Kluger, Richard. *Simple Justice*. New York: Vintage, 1975.

Lipset, Seymour Martin. *The First New Nation: The United States in Historical Perspective*. New York: Norton, 1979.

Lynd, Robert, and Helen Lynd. *Middletown: A Study in Contemporary American Culture*. New York: Harcourt Brace, 1929.

Mills, C. Wright. *White Collar: The American Middle Classes*. New York: Oxford University Press, 1951.

Myrdal, Gunnar. *An American Dilemma: The Negro Problem and American Democracy*. Vol. 1. New York: Harcourt Brace, 1944.

Nash, Gary. *Forging Freedom: The Formation of Philadelphia's Black Community, 1720s–1840s*. Cambridge, MA: Harvard University Press, 1988.

Nelli, Humbert. *Italians in Chicago, 1880–1930: A Study of Ethnic Mobility*. New York: Oxford University Press, 1970.

Putney, Martha S. *When the Nation Was in Need: Blacks in the Women's Army Corps during World War II*. Lanham, MD: Scarecrow, 1992.

Quarles, Benjamin. *The Negro in the American Revolution*. Chapel Hill: University of North Carolina Press for the Institute of Early American History and Culture, 1961.

Quattrone, Frank. *Images of America: Ambler*. Portsmouth, NH: Arcadia, 2004.

Rich, Wilbur C. *African American Perspectives in Political Science*. Philadelphia: Temple University Press, 2007.

Robinson, Eugene. *Disintegration: The Splintering of African Americans*. New York: Doubleday, 2010.

Schatz, Sayre B. *The Nigerian Economy*. Berkeley: University of California Press, 1970.

Talese, Gay. *Unto the Sons*. New York: Knopf, 1992.

Trotman, C. James, ed. *Langston Hughes: The Man, His Art, and His Continuing Influence*. New York: Garland, 1995.

Urban, Wayne. *Black Scholar: Horace Mann Bond, 1904–1972*. Athens: University of Georgia Press, 1992.

Wirth, Louis. *The Ghetto*. Chicago: University of Chicago Press, 1928.

Wolters, Raymond. *The New Negro on Campus: Black College Rebellion of the 1920s*. Princeton, NJ: Princeton University Press, 1975.

Zink, Harold. *Twenty Municipal Bosses*. Athens: Ohio University Press, 1938.

INDEX